The Provisional IRA

Tommy McKearney in 1975 (*left*) and in 2010 (*right*) (both © the author).

THE PROVISIONAL IRA

From Insurrection to Parliament

Tommy McKearney

www.plutobooks.com

First published 2011 by Pluto Press
345 Archway Road, London N6 5AA

www.plutobooks.com

Distributed in the United States of America exclusively by
Palgrave Macmillan, a division of St. Martin's Press LLC,
175 Fifth Avenue, New York, NY 10010

Distributed in the Republic of Ireland and Northern Ireland by
Gill & Macmillan Distribution, Hume Avenue, Park West, Dublin 12, Ireland.
Phone +353 1 500 9500. Fax +353 1 500 9599. E-Mail: sales@gillmacmillan.ie

British Library Cataloguing in Publication Data
A catalogue record for this book is available from the British Library

ISBN   978 0 7453 3075 4   Hardback
ISBN   978 0 7453 3074 7   Paperback

Library of Congress Cataloging in Publication Data applied for

This book is printed on paper suitable for recycling and made from fully managed
and sustained forest sources. Logging, pulping and manufacturing processes are
expected to conform to the environmental standards of the country of origin.

10   9   8   7   6   5   4   3   2   1

Designed and produced for Pluto Press by Chase Publishing Services Ltd
Typeset from disk by Stanford DTP Services, Northampton, England
Simultaneously printed digitally by CPI Antony Rowe, Chippenham, UK and
Edwards Bros in the United States of America

For
Padraig, Sean, Kevin and John McKearney

Contents

Figures

Preface

He of whom they have never stopped saying that the only language he understands is that of force decides to give utterance by force. In fact, as always, the settler has shown him the way he should take if he is to become free. The argument the [colonized] chooses has been furnished by the settler, and by an ironic turning of the tables, it is the [colonized] who now affirms that the colonialist understands nothing but force.

Frantz Fanon, *The Wretched of the Earth*[1]

And if that is how it began in Ireland as in other colonial environments, it is not how it will easily end. The Provisional IRA was formed in late 1969 after Republican ranks split in Belfast. Differences had arisen as a result of dramatic and bloody events in August of that year when the Northern Ireland state had used widespread lethal force in an attempt to quell demands for democratic reforms. Thanks in no small part to the reactionary nature of Northern Irish Unionism, coupled with the duplicitous behaviour of the sovereign power in London, the Provisional IRA grew rapidly over the following three years to become a significant threat to the British state. Forty years after its formation, the old Orange state was definitively buried; the Provisional IRA had decommissioned its arsenal and abjured insurrection but was part of a devolved administration in Northern Ireland.* However, while the sectarian Orange state had been destroyed, a new sectarian state would evolve out of its remains.

This book analyses the underlying reasons behind the formation of the Provisional IRA, its development and where that current might now go (if anywhere). The book also demolishes a misconception that the Provisional IRA was only or even wholly about ending Partition and bringing about a united Ireland. The author argues that while ending the Union and establishing a 32-county republic was always a core and headline demand of the organisation, a major dynamic for the armed campaign was the all too pervasive presence and nature of the Orange state – a state that was not just present as an administrative entity but also as a dysfunctional society.

Although it examines the Provisional IRA in its historical context, this book is not a history of that movement nor does it attempt to disclose the organisation's secrets or identify its personnel. We explore the makeup of the Provisional IRA and its strategy. While taking the view that circumstances and conditions made the resort to arms unavoidable and therefore justified, we are not uncritical of the tactics and strategy of the Provisional IRA. Options available to the movement at different periods in its history are also explored and the argument is made that its inability to develop a clear socialist programme and practice has rendered the movement a defender of the status quo in Southern Ireland and incapable of expanding beyond the Catholic community in Northern Ireland.

In the conclusion, the argument is made that radical, democratic Republicanism has a place in modern Ireland but for it to remain relevant, it must develop a fresh dynamic. For this to happen, Republicanism requires a renewed programme that would treat Republican principles as much more than simple anti-Partitionism and in which armed struggle is never again fetishised and given prominence over wider political, social and economic struggles. In essence, Republicans can no longer see socialist practice as an optional extra.

* NB

- Throughout this book, the author often uses the term 'Northern Ireland' when referring to the six north-eastern counties of Ireland. He does so in the belief that if a majority of the Irish population has voted to endorse the existent constitutional arrangement, that the official title for the Six Counties, which he also uses, is justified.
- It is often difficult to find agreement about definitions and titles for people in Northern Ireland. In this book, the author has decided, in most instances, to use the generic term 'Catholic' instead of 'Nationalist' or 'Republican' unless when denoting a precise political position. As with the term 'Jewish', which is often used to denote membership of a community rather than religious belief, Catholic is often used in Northern Ireland to include people (such as the author) who are atheist or agnostic. The term 'Catholic' in the context of this book denotes a section of the Northern Irish community and thus avoids attributing a political view such as 'Nationalist' or 'Republican' to some who do not share that outlook or position.

- Throughout this book, the terms 'IRA' and 'Provisional IRA' are used interchangeably for the years after 1969. When referring to the Official IRA, that term is used. Since there was only one IRA prior to 1969, there is no need to draw any distinctions when referring to the period before the 1969 split.

Acknowledgement

Without the assistance, advice and constant encouragement of my friend and comrade Paul Stewart, this book would not have been written. He gave freely and generously of his time throughout the entire work as I wrestled with ideas, mulled over the interpretation of past events and discussed concepts. Together we unravelled, and then put order on, the compelling story of the movement from insurrection to Parliament.

Tommy McKearney

Introduction: From Orange State to Sectarian State

Paul Stewart

> ... on Vinegar Hill, the fatal conclave.
> Terraced thousands died, shaking scythes at cannon
> The hillside blushed, soaked in our broken wave.
> They buried us without a shroud or coffin
> And in August the barley grew up out of the grave.
>
> (from Seamus Heaney, 'Requiem for the Croppies')[1]

Early in 1920 Lloyd George approved the reorganisation of the UVF[2] as the Ulster Special Constabulary. Later that year the Government of Ireland Act partitioned the country and gave Six Counties of Ulster their own provincial parliament. The 'Specials' immediately assumed a crucial paramilitary role. So widespread was the arming of 'loyalists' and the swearing-in of 'Specials' that official reports indicate that the strength of the police from 1921 to 1926 'cannot be stated'. (A and B Specials were properly accounted for, but the part-time reserve of C Specials was of unknown numbers. The C men were never formally disbanded but just allowed to 'fade' away. Where their weapons faded to is a matter for speculation.) The Specials were permitted to carry arms even when off-duty and in plain clothes, a privilege which lasted until their transformation into the Ulster Defence Regiment in 1969. For 50 years they played the role of Unionism's private army. (David Boulton, *The UVF, 1966–73: An Anatomy of Loyalist Rebellion*)[3]

At the heart of the insurgency in the north of Ireland, beginning in 1969, was the undemocratic nature of Northern Ireland: this acted as the chief contributory factor in the eruption of peaceful protests into armed street fighting that spread rapidly to rural communities in the North. One of the considerations of this book is the key role of the movement for civil rights and how Unionist supporters of the Northern Ireland state blocked it. To a significant degree, the conflict was not initially about a physical confrontation with the state, since the main motive was to wrestle very basic bourgeois democratic reforms – one man one vote, fair access to employment and fair housing for all. By contrast, many accounts now prefer the

1

view that the insurgency was somehow misguided or that, as with the strategy of the reformist Unionist Prime Minister of Northern Ireland, Captain (Rtd) Terence O'Neill, the civil rights movement went too fast without allowing Unionists any chance to change.

A commonly held view today is that reform was possible had it not been for the intransigence on all sides. One variant of the failure of reform strategy is the influential argument made nearly twenty years ago by Bob Purdy. There is something to commend in Purdy's conviction that the path of radical reform was desirable despite the ossification of Unionist politics at the time.[4] However, we need to give careful consideration to his wish for a more genial way of settling the problems of social and economic repression. Indeed, peaceful reform would have been a great achievement. Purdy recognised that the inability of the Northern Ireland Civil Rights Association (NICRA) to restrain the dynamic of peaceful opposition to the Unionists, which quickly evolved into the armed struggle, was in a number of important respects a result of the Unionist establishment in all its fissiparous forms. These ranged from Orange man to B Special man: it was unfortunately a historically determined route of repression of opposition. We take issue with his assumption that reform and repression were somehow separate and that, by the late 1960s, the state might have been capable either of change or could have addressed the fundamental grievances without creating mass disaffection in its own base.

The element of wishful thinking in this view is all the odder because of the careful account of the structural discrimination inherent in the Northern Ireland state. He found wanting the link that was, and sometimes still is, made to the black civil rights movement in the United States. For Purdy it was, and still is, a largely overwrought parallel which, interestingly for him, seems to fall due to the inability of leaders within the Catholic community at the time to offer secular and cross-sectarian, reforming and non-violent, leadership of the sort offered by Martin Luther King in the United States. But if this were the case, we would surely have to leave aside the fact that instead of King, the early struggle in the North actually had a range of grassroots leaders, prominent among them the Protestant Ivan Cooper, Paddy 'Bogside' Doherty and soon afterwards the socialist, Bernadette Devlin. The problem with his analysis is that it assumes that at any stage from the mid-1960s until the infamous RUC assault on the 5 October 1968 NICRA demonstration that reform might have been possible,[5] and that, by contrast with discrimination against blacks in the United States,

Catholic repression was less 'intense and blatant'.[6] The argument, in effect, is that reform should have been possible had Britain intervened much earlier, had the liberals in the North been able to win a constitutional option for reform of the Northern Ireland state and had NICRA managed to sustain its initial hegemony within the movement for change.

This book will argue that too much of this kind of approach can only rely on forgetting what we already know about the origins of opposition and later, armed resistance, to repression. The problem for the Unionists, NICRA and the reformist option is that while we fundamentally recognise the integral role of 'leaders', the substance of the conflict was not about leaders, at least not in the sense implied by a top-down history of the insurgency. It was the Catholic community that broke the assault by the RUC and the B Specials on their communities between 1969 and 1970. Indeed, and regrettably, Purdy's view is even less uncommon today now that the benefit of hindsight has allowed many to forget the distorted view of democracy that was Northern Ireland: the slum housing, the state apparatus set up to keep the 'Taigs' in their place through gerrymandering,[7] and the common patois of cultural and physical violence against Catholics. It is true: Catholics were not routinely lynched or shot dead in the heat of a Mississippi night.[8] Then again, when they challenged the status quo with mass civil disobedience in 1969, Catholics were driven from their homes by petrol bombs, they were shot down in broad daylight and by the government and its local armed forces. From our perspective, the Northern Ireland state (and for other reasons the government in London) could not simply concede to the civil rights demands in spite of the fact that they were indeed, by the standards on any contemporary 'normal' bourgeois democratic government, straightforward. Yet, founded upon Partition, which was in reality more a partition of the population and society in Northern Ireland than a geographic division of the island, the northern state could not deliver the usual passivity of most liberal democratic states in the post-war (let alone post-1920s) period. The state was overtly repressive and so too was the dominant Unionist society in Northern Ireland, which is why armed struggle became unavoidable and in the eyes of many – including the author – a justifiable and proper response at the time. This is a view that is pertinent today in the context of current British government policy in relation to other areas where it is encountering insurgency.

THE CHARACTER OF THE NORTHERN IRELAND STATE

To get a longer perspective on this, let us go back to the formation of the state in Northern Ireland in 1920. This is important because, while the military struggles for the formation of the fledgling 26-county Irish state are central to most narratives on the rise of the Northern Ireland state, the intrinsically militarised nature of the Northern Ireland state and civil society is often overlooked.

Northern Ireland became a militarised society, albeit one with an indelibly liberal democratic hue. It was militarised opposition to Irish Home Rule both within and without the British establishment from the turn of the twentieth century which created many of the key institutions of the Northern Ireland state in 1920. As was recognised at the time, the Unionists achieved both more and less than they wanted. The formation of the Six-County statelet effectively severed all relations with the remaining Unionists in the rest of Ireland, who had been organising against Home Rule under the auspices of the Irish Unionist Alliance. The creation of the Northern Ireland state established a separate entity, which had been far from the original aim of Edward Carson's movement against Irish Home Rule.[9] Although built upon the militarised mobilisations that characterised the signing of the Solemn League and Covenant in 1912, Carson's anti-Home Rule movement was driven by a commitment to armed opposition. If the Ulster Volunteer Force was symbolic of the zeitgeist at the heart of the narrative of those 'brave men who died for Britain' in the 1914–18 war, resurrection was to be found in the transformation of the UVF into the armed force of the new state formed by Partition.

Thus, the Northern Ireland state was necessarily a militarised state from its inception not simply because of a perceived ever-present external threat, although this would be a persistent element in the cultural repertoire of Ulster Unionism. After all, it was the threat from Britain – that is, Britain's legislation on Home Rule – that led to the formation of an army of loyalty to the Crown but against Britain. The irony here is important. The supposed 'external threat' was founded on two aspects to some degree of the Ulster Unionists' own creation. One was a southern Irish entity created by the very division of the island driven forward by Carson's agenda. The somewhat more nebulous threat bolstered the ideological myth of northern democracy – the rise and institutional development of the Catholic Church in the South. And of course, there was another irony which was central to the myth creation and which we have not yet considered and this was that the prorogation[10] (suspension) of Stormont in 1972 was delivered by perhaps the most important 'enemy' of the Ulster Unionists' own creation: precisely that British establishment against which Carson's people had had to define themselves from the early part of the twentieth century. We return to this in our conclusion on the trajectory of the contemporary sectarian state in Northern Ireland.

In one respect, what tied together state ideological and repressive structures was the continuity that Ulster Unionism established between external and internal dangers. If this danger could be easily described, it would be Irish Nationalism and the Catholic Church (on occasion, communism could be included in this 'evil matrix'): the enemy within and the enemy without were one and the same beast. Ulster Unionism had to create this through clear and obvious spatial and cultural makers of difference, but it also had to achieve this in a discriminatory way that depended upon Catholic economic and political exclusion and subordination. It is in that sense that one could argue perhaps that the consummate role of Stormont was to sustain Orange rule, which was not the same as sectarian rule, though it would be a vital ingredient of it. If the Orange state could be associated with domination in this way, the sectarian state, which has arisen from the ashes of the 40-year insurgency and the defeat of the Orange state, can be characterised in a quite different fashion. This is that we are now in a situation of supposed social and economic win-win outcomes whereby sectarian social relations are not only seen as an acceptable form of what is termed 'conflict resolution', but are in fact given government (and European Community grants) to sustain the fiction that Northern Ireland is now a normal and healthy (or at any rate, recovering) society.[11]

So what now of the pre-history of the current sectarian state? We know that the pattern of sectarian development and under-development constituted social and economic relationships in Ireland from an early period. We have often forgotten, though, that Partition not only created new institutional frameworks within the boundaries of the new society but that it also cemented and recodified a range of pre-existing ones. In many respects, early-period social and economic sectarianism was more open in its character and form. Thus, in pre-Partition Ireland, it was not unusual to find, and we witness this in archival evidence, employment practices which openly and legally favoured Protestants over Catholics in recruitment for certain occupations. It seems paradoxical but with Partition in 1920 it nevertheless made a certain kind of sense, knowing one lived in a state defined as a 'Protestant Parliament and Protestant State'.[12] This allowed for a sectarianism that was more 'silently' transmitted and especially so since this marked a political and cultural security where the defeated Catholic minority no longer posed a persistent, quotidian threat.

That the latter would be seen as simply an abstract threat is not entirely the most helpful way to understand the character of the state's repressive apparatuses, for this would assume somehow that the RUC and the institutional and often unspoken sectarianism in labour markets and housing, never mind political society, were separate. For certainly they were not. It is true, of course, that the institutional matrix that was Orangeism eventually collapsed, in chaotic shambles, as a result of the social insurgency and the Provisional IRA campaign, but the fact that sectarian social relations have been re-created since the peace process began in 1998, highlights the profoundly persistent extent of their sectarianism. Moreover, in keeping the Croppies down, the state, whether in its more lethargic or occasionally egregious moments, was sustaining the perfidious enemy of its own creation: the always treacherous Catholic minority and perfidious Albion. How did this repressive state-civil society work?

O'Dowd, Rolston and Tomlinson (1980) once pointed out that the Northern Ireland state, in what we might term its 'early modern' period, was to be distinguished from other bourgeois liberal states in that it was characterised by an incipient repressive statism in philosophy and practice.[13] That is to say, the separation of the state's repressive forces (the RUC, including its various auxiliary units – the A, B and C Specials) from civil and political society was structurally, and necessarily, incomplete. This is an interesting argument that has often been forgotten with the rise of late 1990s revisionism: the thesis tells us much about the genesis of the insurgency in the late 1960s. Writing about sectarian housing policies during the period of the Stormont regime, they argued that:

> Most liberal and social democratic states attain some degree of legitimacy, in the short run at least, by 'Partitioning' the apparatuses of repression – the army, police and judiciary – from other state institutions. Furthermore ... the institutions of coercion tend to be separated from the economically dominant classes – placing the practice of coercion above sectional interests and equating it with the 'public interest'. Once the existence of the repressive apparatus is depoliticised in this way, 'legitimate'

political struggle can occur in other areas. A 'reformist' politics can then emerge to forge an ideological consensus supportive of the state.[14]

O'Dowd, Rolston and Tomlinson argued that the Unionist Party was the critical political-institutional form ensuring, through the reproduction of sectarian social and economic relationships, the absence of the 'compartmentalisation' of reform and repression typical of most other liberal states. In other words (and as they point out), this is what is meant when one argues that the police force (and the very existence of the Special police units underscored this) was under the control of the Unionist Party and the implications ran more profoundly than this might suggest. Neither community accepted the division between reform and repression. In other words, the Protestant community was content with the clientalist state apparatus in which the repressive wing (the police) and parliament were mutually supportive of the maintenance of a 'Protestant state'. The Catholic community recognised this, but was unable to do much about it until the rise of the civil rights movement in the late 1960s. The consequence was starkly revealing of a pathological polity. It became impossible to reform the repressive apparatuses of the state. Precisely due to the ossification of dominant political and ideological relationships within the Protestant community, any attempt to dig into the exclusionary and anti-democratic aspect of civil society was seen as an existential threat: 'The reformist demands of the civil rights movement were immediately defined as a threat to the Unionist state [and the rest of Protestant society].'[15]

And the Unionist establishment had reason to fear a response from the Catholic minority below, for there was much about the sectarian society that had lain structurally unchallenged for five decades. We write 'fear' because it is only when one realises that if a state considers fair access to decent housing and 'one man one vote' as posing a revolutionary challenge to itself and 'its' society, then arguably that society is beyond reform. Let us just consider the especially flagrant and notorious examples of 'the taken-for-grantedness', the everyday acceptance, of Orange sectarianism.

Historic social exclusion was a process dependent upon a particular complex of civil and political relations and institutions, including housing and an assemblage of local representative practices.[16] These included the organisation of, and arrangements for, the allocation of votes in local government elections, which in turn were linked to the spatial organisation of sectarian social boundaries. Clearly, while it is important to see the process in terms of outcomes, it was the reaffirmation (and gerrymandering) of sectarian boundaries of social and economic repression that characterised Northern Ireland and add to the historical explanation for the insurgency beginning in 1969. These had to be continually remade not only when the opportunity arose, but on a systematic basis. In some respects, the shape of discrimination in housing and politics could look after itself since the gerrymandered electoral boundaries could simply be held in place. Thus where Catholics outnumbered Protestants within electoral boundaries, the divisions were maintained by gerrymandering. Who cared about votes when the Unionists could simply recarve their majority position? And anyway, they ultimately ran the state and always, and without shame, explicitly so.

However, what about housing and housing policy – the how, where and what of the basis of daily life? It was through the reproduction of sectarian housing policy, housing allocation together with the actual fabric of the housing people lived in, upon which the other institutions of sectarianism depended for their reproduction. The 'how' – who got new housing and on what basis? The 'what' – the standard of housing? And of course, the 'where'. It was upon these factors that Northern Ireland's sectarianism, held together and 'secured' by the Orange state, was consciously reproduced. It was no surprise then that it was here that the civil rights movement began. Upon all else did this specific field of discrimination depend: the jobs to live, the places to enjoy one's life and the likely destination of one's children – all depended upon where one lived. This was the fundamental basis of the contradiction at the heart of the continual reproduction of sectarian exclusion and social and political repression. What about the demand for housing? What did this look like? What shape did it take? It was here, in other words, more usually than in the causal actions of the state's obvious repressive apparatuses that one must understand the peculiar character of repression.

Repression was typically characterised, and especially in Catholic urban working-class districts, as a quotidian drip, drip, of inadequate housing both in terms of standards and availability. Moreover, this was important for local (council) and wider (Stormont) state sectarianism, since it was geared towards confining Catholics to specific urban (and other) locales and obviously as a means of reproducing political and economic exclusion. And of course, social and economic exclusions are now more readily understood as manifestations of social and economic repression that in turn depend upon political repression. It is in this way that one must begin to unravel what at first glance seems incomprehensible, not only to any outside observer at the time, but even to those today who might wish to forget the profound significance of this past. One might wonder not only how this state of repression could have been constructed, but how it might, in its obviously absurd form of blatant exclusion, have been allowed to persist by Britain until the conflagration of 1968:

> We are satisfied that … the Unionist councils have used their powers to make appointments in a way which will benefit Protestants … Only 30% of Londonderry's administrative, clerical and technical employees were Catholic. Out of the ten best-paid posts only one was held by a Catholic … In [County Fermanagh] among about seventy-five drivers of school buses at most seven were Catholic. This would appear to be a very clear case of sectarian political discrimination.[17]

Let us be reminded of some of the other absurdities. We can consider just two districts in the North of Ireland where the response to local and wider state repression received initially greatest attention. In 1970, John Carron, Nationalist MP for Fermanagh, prepared a report on discrimination in housing and employment in County Fermanagh and presented it to then British Prime Minister James Callaghan.[18] The data of systemic sectarian discrimination was so compelling that Callaghan introduced a new housing executive for Northern Ireland.

In County Fermanagh, according to the 1961 census, out of a population of 51,531, Nationalists had a majority of 3,313. However, as a result of the gerrymandering of electoral boundaries, Unionists enjoyed 'majorities' in public-sector bodies, despite being in a minority of the population. In what at the time was a newly amalgamated County Council, there were 40 Unionist and only 16 Nationalist representatives. Furthermore, as Carron's report went on to point out, 'All senior public appointments are held by Unionists and almost all minor ones.' These included the county Inspector of the RUC and his assistants – all were Unionists. Carron records it thus:

> The Secretary to the County Council; the County Accountant; the County Surveyor: all were Unionists. Out of all the solicitors, clerical officers, rate collectors, county coroners and county

Agricultural Officers, only 2 (one clerical officer and one rate collector) were not Unionists. On the county education committee the following posts were all held by Unionists: clerk to the Committee, assistant clerk, chief architect, accountant, meals supervisor, transport officer, and all clerical staff. The County health committee: the same story. This included the clerk to the committee, the assistant clerk, the chief dental officer, the county analyst and the chief nursing officer: all Unionists. The County Welfare committee? The same story yet again. In the Rural Districts Councils of Enniskillen, Lisnaskea and Irvinstown, all but one professional post was occupied by Unionists.[19]

So much for local government but what of the Northern Ireland state proper? In 1969, the Campaign for Social Justice in Northern Ireland (CSJNI) produced detailed evidence of the extent of discrimination in civil service employment. The report indicated the sectarian distribution of the full range of professional and technical grades in government.[20]

Table I.1   Technical and professional staff employment in the Northern Irish government, 1969

	Total	Catholics
Cabinet Officers	5	0
Houses of Parliament	6	0
Ministry of Finance	62	3
Ministry of Agriculture	29	1
Ministry of Commerce	9	2
Ministry of Development	32	2
Ministry for Education	7	0
Ministry of Health and Social Services	35	3
Ministry of Home Affairs	8	0
Exchequer and Audit Dept	10	2
Parliamentary Draftsman Dept	6	0
Total	209	13

Source: Campaign for Social Justice in Northern Ireland (CSJNI), *The Plain Truth*, Northern Ireland, 15 June 1969.

In the area of the judiciary, considering High Court and County Court judges, none was Catholic. Only three out of twelve resident magistrates were Catholic. There were no Catholic members of the Lands Tribunal, Commission for National Insurance and Clerks of Crown and Peace. Since the 1930s, no Catholic had held a position as Regional Director of Postal Services in Northern Ireland (there were eight in total).

It was of course, through the immediacy of the television reporting of political repression of the civil rights demonstrations in Derry and elsewhere that the wider world began to learn something of the peculiarities of Northern Ireland's democracy. To ensure adherence to the latter and especially in times of duress, the government had a remedy for backsliders. It was known as the Special Powers Act and so extraordinary were its measures that it was famously coveted by the South African Minister of Justice, who regarded it as preferable to his own repressive powers. The most egregious elements of the Special Powers Act, in operation since 1922, allowed the following:

- Arrest without warrant.
- Imprisonment without charge or trial and without recourse to habeas corpus or a court of law.
- Enter and search homes without warrant, and with force, at any hour of day or night.
- Declare a curfew and prohibit meetings, assemblies.
- Permit punishment by flogging.
- Deny claim to a trial by jury.
- Arrest persons it desires to examine as witnesses, forcibly detain them and compel them to answer, under penalties, even if answers may incriminate them.
- Such a person is guilty of an offence if he refuses to be sworn or answer a question.
- Do any act involving interference with the rights of private property.
- Prevent access of relatives or legal advisers to a person imprisoned without trial.
- Prohibit the holding of an inquest after a prisoner's death.
- Arrest a person who 'by word of mouth' spreads false reports or makes false statements.
- Prohibit the possession of any film or gramophone record.

Derry was to be the place where the full panoply of the Special Powers Act would be unleashed.

THE SITUATION IN DERRY

Let us take a look at Derry's housing and electoral divisions, the city where something of the sordid story of this society's political culture first came to the world's attention. (This story, of course was repeated throughout the North, as was well chronicled in the CSJNI report, in other towns throughout Northern Ireland, *inter alia*, Omagh, Dungannon, Lurgan, Fivemiletown, Armagh.)

Derry provided perhaps the most glaring example of the North's sectarian habitation and spatial apartheid. The city was divided into three wards. In two of these (both Unionist), the electorate was sparsely distributed: 'In the two smaller Unionist wards the electors are thinly spread and allocated the same number of councillors per ward as the anti-Unionists who are crammed into the third ward, and given the same number of councillors.'[21]

Figure I.1 below from the CSJNI provides us with a graphic illustration of what this apartheid system looked liked.

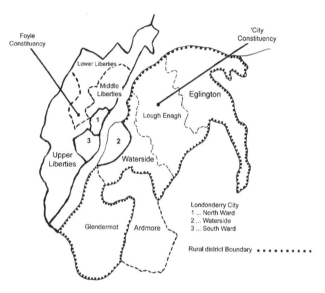

Figure I.1 Parliamentary constituencies in Derry, pre-1969 (from an original document published by Campaign for Social Justice in Northern Ireland, June 1969).

Derry, the capital of the north-west, with its Catholic majority, had since Partition been systematically neglected in terms of economic development. The eastern counties, with their large (or majority) Protestant populations were consistently favoured over the western counties with their large (or majority) Catholic populations, as was highlighted by official figures regarding state-sponsored industrial development: Counties Antrim, Armagh, Down and Belfast city obtained 59 so-called 'advance factories' to encourage industrial

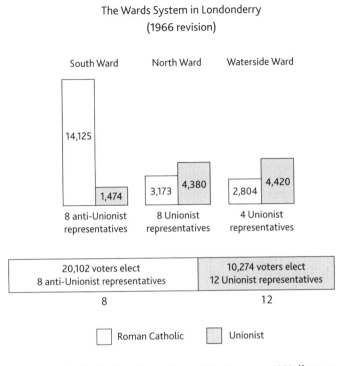

The Wards System in Londonderry
(1966 revision)

South Ward   North Ward   Waterside Ward

14,125

1,474   3,173   4,380   2,804   4,420

8 anti-Unionist   8 Unionist   4 Unionist
representatives   representatives   representatives

20,102 voters elect 8 anti-Unionist representatives	10,274 voters elect 12 Unionist representatives
8	12

☐ Roman Catholic   ☐ Unionist

Figure I.2 The distribution of seats in wards in Derry, pre-1969 (from an original document published by Campaign for Social Justice in Northern Ireland, June 1969).

placement while Counties Derry, Tyrone and Fermanagh in the west obtained a grand total of 15! The same tale of neglect and what we might ironically term 'assisted decline' was a feature across all aspects of development from public transport (the severing of the railway link between Derry and the west) to the illogical (except in the sectarian mindset of Ulster Unionism) decision not to build a new university in Derry. And yet, while Stormont's own Lockwood Report rejected Derry as the site of a new university,[22] some of its own appointed technocrats believed this to be erroneous; specifically, Geoffrey Copcutt, one of its key designers, resigned just over a year later indicating his disillusionment 'with the Stormont scene'.[23] While the technocratic impulse was alive in the north of Ireland even then, tradition, structure, impulse, call it what one will, always triumphed, bolstered by state-driven social and economic repression. This was a comfort zone that Ulster Unionism relied upon because Unionists knew that behind this lay the British state. Fear and loathing in equal measure summed up the Catholic population's view of Northern Ireland, as so graphically portrayed by Seamus Heaney:

> Ulster was British, but with no rights on
> The English Lyric: all around us, though
> We hadn't named it, the ministry of fear.[24]

HOW TO UNDERSTAND THE ORIGINS OF THE PROVISIONAL REPUBLICAN MOVEMENT

Most narratives on the Provisional IRA insurgency which began in 1969 start with the assumption that it arose because of an overwhelming desire to end Partition. From this perspective, the sole Provisional IRA objective was to create a united Ireland. While this was certainly part of a Republican narrative, it was always an overly simplistic view, since the question of Partition was far from being a singularly Republican obsession, as many might believe. Indeed, not only was Partition seen as a problem for many beyond the Republican movement, including many conventional politicians, it was not initially the only, or sole motivation, for the thousands of young men and women who committed to the struggle, first against Stormont and subsequently, against the British state.

This may not be a widely appreciated view. The difficulty is that in developing what we might term the 'other history', it must be remembered what has either been forgotten, or is in the process of being revised. As we saw with the now 'official' history, as articulated in the vapid account by a BBC correspondent on the occasion of the fortieth anniversary of the dispatch of British troops to Belfast and Derry in August 1969, the 'Troubles' began as a result of a Catholic 'belief' they were second-class citizens. A belief like this would surely only be held by sufferers from some kind of chronic delusion. So Catholics at the time simply misunderstood the reasons behind the burning of their homes in Bombay Street by equally misled Protestants, including the UVF, police auxiliaries? In this we-are-all-equally-to-blame type of history, even the Orange state and its social and political base in the Protestant community simply believed Catholics were out of (their) order; out of their place. The burning of Catholic streets and the police riots, intimidation and murder of bystanders in the Bogside in Derry and Belfast in 1969, not to mention to full state assault on peaceful demonstrations throughout the North, were really just attributable to the Protestants' sense that Catholics were over-reaching themselves. But by now, Catholics were indeed beginning to get out of order.

Over thirty to forty years of armed struggle to reach the point where both sides could be viewed in the same way by the British establishment, hoping that the mad Taigs and Prods would realise that all things are the same, equivalences in the pathways of normal societies. This would all be well and good except for the truths, which even the British government came to accept, even if their strategic interests did not match their liberal democratic rhetoric.[25] This could never be simply a conflict between two equally well-intentioned, if misled, interest groups. But the notion of equivalence, which was always the preferred default media perspective during the insurgency, is a powerful view and it is quickly becoming the dominant account of the reasons behind an insurgency that began in 1969.

In many respects, what we are highlighting is the problem of a buried history and why it was important and perhaps, just as significantly, why it is vital for some that it should remain so. Our initial point of departure takes us back to the origins and the trajectory of the Northern Ireland state because only here can some sense be made of the full-to-bursting reservoir of both resentment and despair that underlay the explosion of community sentiment in response to the repression of the demand for civil rights in the late 1960s. As even the Scarman tribunal (1969) recognised at the time,[26] the response by the non-Unionist community to the Royal Ulster Constabulary (RUC) and the auxiliary B Specials (USC) was overwhelmingly spontaneous. While the IRA was indeed present, it was trapped both by tradition and suspicion of mass social participation. Indeed, it was precisely due to their relative marginalisation within the local community in the initial period of response to the state and its auxiliaries that the Republican movement split.

Catholic communities and anti-Unionists desperately needed defence against what Scarman described as 'incursions' by the RUC and 'special constables misbehaving themselves ... by participating in an exchange of petrol bombs and missiles with a Catholic crowd' occasionally aided by Protestant mobs.[27] The absence of either well-organised Republican or other progressive movements to support them in the face of this mobilisation by state and para-state mobs saw communities across the North organising their own self-defence committees. (Amongst others, notable self-defence committees were the Ardoyne Citizens' Action Committee and the

Derry Citizens' Action Committee.) While he was agnostic on the genesis of other defence committees, what Scarman reported to be the situation on the Falls was typical of developments elsewhere: 'we are satisfied that the disturbances produced the committees rather than the committees the disturbances.'[28] And moreover, Scarman was emphatic the IRA did not plan the riots:[29] 'in 1969 there was no organised campaign of armed insurrection ... .'[30]

The assumptions, the social and political mindset of the defenders of the Orange state, were now laid bare. The British recognition of this would not preclude their empathy with Unionist views, as the rebellion intensified and the armed insurgency took hold. But it was a mindset recognised by Scarman when he wrote that 'In fact the police appreciation that they had on their hands an armed uprising led by the IRA was incorrect. Direct IRA participation was slight; and there is no credible evidence that the IRA planned or organised the disturbances.'[31] Forty years later, the old Orange state is no longer, but in its place are a divided society and a sectarian state. If the old Orange sectarian state was built upon pan-Catholic subordination, offering employment and relatively higher growth to all within its (the Protestant) community, the new sectarian state has been dependent upon state and para-state sponsorship of everyone prepared to play the divided communities card.

Having looked at the events leading up to the mass insurgency in 1969 which laid bare the nature of the Orange state to the outside world, we now turn to the sectarian state arising from its ashes. The best critical assessment of this new sectarian state is provided by Peter Shirlow and Brendan Murtagh, in their book *Belfast: Segregation, Violence and the City*.[32]

Shirlow and Murtagh describe the patterns of the sectarian-specific organisation of living and employment relations, though the reasons for these and the conclusions may be contentious. While an excellent description of the sectarian pattern of spatial and employment boundaries which have developed, though based upon obvious historical precedence, we would contest some measure of their explanation for these and the conclusions they draw. That the new sectarian state has perversely, though logically, been a success for some is not in question and it has not only allowed the pathologies of the pre-existing sectarian boundaries to flourish. The settlement underlying the state is a matrix of British state and EU aid and sponsorship driven by a 'post-troubles' entrepreneurial political class in both communities (again based upon pre-existing social and political affinities of local brokerage and patronage).

While previously this political class was, according to sectarian affiliation, locked in armed conflict, those who now constitute it are locked together in a form of boosterism dependent upon a shared interest in perpetuating a discourse of victimhood.[33] While arguably they are victims mostly for themselves, the deeper roots of the poverty of their respective communities is obscured by the demands of these new political entrepreneurs who reinforce already existing understandings which were borne out of real enough truths about the sectarian repressions and exclusions of the old Orange state. For Shirlow and Murtagh, these will not take the 'new' post-Good Friday Agreement society forward. But if the political entrepreneurs will not, what, or who, can?

Depressingly, they highlight that the only cross-sectarian associations on the radar are those identified through middle-class consumption patterns, which at best do no more than 'moderate attitudes, values and behaviour but fundamental ethno-sectarian subcultures dominate socio-spatial relations'.[34] This runs parallel to a sectarian socio-spatial world in which the sectarian divisions they meticulously compile between Protestant and Catholic workers are deeper than ever for the reason that it is the working class, in general, who have been relatively excluded from the benefits of the Belfast Agreement: the dubious good as witnessed in the proliferation of community centres, sports halls and other cultural apparel in tandem, must be weighed against that other proliferation of 'peace walls', increased poverty and rising levels of sporadic sectarian violence set against that other pathology of rising unemployment. Thus the unity that was sold and the peaceful noises we heard after 1998 were in many respects also quite limited. Sectarian social relations, preserved in aspic by neo-liberal 'expansion', are now in crisis as a result of the shock to the growth model of public and private debt such that even middle-class quietude may become less quiet.

In the Orange state, Protestant workers would benefit relative to Catholic workers and others in the Catholic community so long as a mass production industrial economy (shipyards, engineering and aircraft) with its cross-class Protestant institutional social relationships could prosper and in the context of the rise of the Keynesian welfare state. The new sectarian state, entrenched and extended by the Good Friday Agreement, has been based upon limited cross-sectarian social relations deriving their character and power from an alliance between cross-sectarian political entrepreneurs, a new cross-sectarian middle class, civil service, and bureaucratic elite.

Moreover, this has been given meaning by institutional imperatives created by the British and Irish states. Undeniably, the new sectarian state has been both product and purveyor of this situation of stasis in which the changes sold by the media and the state, in alliance with the political entrepreneurs themselves, is no real change in the sense that sectarianism has been ended – quite the contrary. So where can we seek meaningful resolution?

While for Shirlow and Murtagh, there are principled and steadfast 'individuals and groups' who seek to break down sectarian divisions, 'such efforts do not challenge wider narratives of resistance and interpretations of segregated living that point to the legitimacy of segregation as a rational mode of habituation'.[35] This agenda – the new social and institutional ossification of sectarianism – arising out of the Belfast Agreement, and which it sustains, in any case makes 'peace' intractable in as much as 'the insecurity and political mayhem that came about forged new versions of victimhood and risk at the hands of the ethno-sectarian other'.[36] The major consequence of this, from the point of view of social and political leadership, is that the middle classes, and the middle wayers (our term), the source of 'more pluralistic political codes' based upon 'alternative political discourses',[37] have been frightened by the (sectarian) political entrepreneurs. The latter sustain a frightened civil and wider political society from new cross-sectarian forms of leadership: '[the political entrepreneurs have a] capacity to encourage those whose lifestyle and identity is pluralist and secular to generally remain silent or to become apolitical.'[38] In some respects, it is difficult to dispute this pessimistic account of the rise of fear and the exclusion of varieties of opposition; the suggestion that the only space for 'pluralism' can be found amongst those who can culturally, politically, and pluralistically, rise above the sectarian society out of which they thrive, in however limited a form.

Yet there are problems with this perspective and not the least being our difficulty seeing just where this ideological and political leadership might arise from, if not from the sectarian society in which it is founded. The problem is also therefore one of diagnosis. For us, a new pluralistic leadership in society will be based upon those who are, relatively speaking, the major losers in the Belfast Agreement: the Protestant and Catholic working and lower middle classes. Despite the blind eye turned to the organised labour movement, to some extent with justifiable reason, the sorts of injustices and privations now well-catalogued require profound social and economic challenges and of the sort that cannot be delivered by individuals or groups who have been the significant beneficiaries of the period since 1998 – or not by them alone. The labour movement needs to engage in a new form of struggle to break the new sectarian state. The insurgency, led by the Provisional IRA, eventually brought the repressive apparatuses of the Orange state to a standstill while forever compromising the ideological and institutional power of the Unionist government to rule, but it was unable to break the new sectarian state for the reason that this new state was premised precisely on the cross-sectarian compromise deemed necessary to end the war itself. We shall deal with the ramifications of this for a new opposition in the conclusion to the book. The new sectarian state requires sectarian cross-class solidarities when what the labour movement and those otherwise excluded in the new state require is less sectarian and more class solidarity. If we were to argue, for example, that we will forever let our differences about the 'Border' divide us, then prospects for a properly developed opposition to neo-liberalism will be hopeless. But what if we agree to disagree about the Border while attending to those other fundamentally vital social, economic and political issues that potentially unite us?

1
Police Batons Respond to Demand for Civil Rights

THE GENESIS OF NORTHERN IRELAND SOCIETY AND THE SIX-COUNTY STATE

Frankie and his father had mixed views about the value of their trip as they travelled towards Derry that Saturday morning in October 1968. The Unionist government had never shown any inclination to listen to reasoned argument during the 48 years it had ruled over Northern Ireland. Nor had it ever shown any inclination to treat all of its population equally. In fact, it had always displayed a robust enthusiasm for discriminating against its minority by whatever means it felt appropriate or convenient.

A determination to preserve its position had been made clear over the preceding months when the state's armed police officers had overseen a violent eviction of squatters from local government-owned property in Caledon, Co. Tyrone. The incident had drawn considerable interest in Northern Ireland. A married couple with several young children, the Goodfellows, had finally lost patience with Dungannon Rural District Council authorities and along with Nationalist Party politician Austin Currie and members of the local Republican Club[1] occupied a house in the newly built estate. The family were natives of the area and had been on the council's housing waiting list for years, only to be turned down once again for a tenancy. On this occasion, Dungannon Rural District Council had decided to overlook the Goodfellow family in favour of a young single Protestant girl, Emily Beattie, who worked as secretary to a Unionist-supporting local government official. As a subsequent British government inquiry noted:

Miss Beattie took possession of her house on the 13th June. She was 19 years old, a Protestant, and secretary to the local Councillor's Solicitor, who was also a Unionist Parliamentary candidate living in Armagh. The Councillor's explanation for giving her the house was that in effect he was re-housing her family who lived in very poor conditions; also he had expected her to be married before she took possession of the house. In fact she did marry soon afterwards … In concentrated form the situation expressed the objections felt by many non-Unionists to the prevailing system of housing allocations in Dungannon Rural District Council. By no stretch of the imagination could Miss Beattie be regarded as a priority tenant. On 18th June, within a few days of Miss Beattie taking possession, the Goodfellow family, squatting next door, were evicted with full television coverage. Mr. Currie[2] had protested at all levels against the allocation to Miss Beattie, and raised the matter on the adjournment in the Northern Ireland House of Commons on 19th June 1968. He received no satisfaction, and accordingly formally occupied Miss Beattie's house with two others on 20th June, until in the presence of policemen, a few hours later they were evicted by Miss Beattie's brother who, himself a policeman, was to become a resident in the same house.[3]

The squatting and subsequent eviction was such a blatant piece of discriminatory housing allocation that it provoked a 3,000-strong protest march from Coalisland, Co. Tyrone, which was planned to culminate in Frankie's hometown of Dungannon. Unlike a more normal democratic society that had been alerted to wrongdoing among its public servants, the Northern Ireland government did not respond to the Dungannon march by ordering an investigation to be followed rapidly by correction. Instead, the minister with responsibility for security ordered the police to stop the protest march entering the town, ostensibly in case it might provoke a violent reaction from a right-wing counter demonstration organised by the Revd Ian Paisley.

There appeared little likelihood that a follow-up protest march organised for Derry to highlight similar behaviour by the local authority there, would achieve any greater success than that in Co. Tyrone. Frankie and his father were not typical of the main body of the protesters gathered in Duke Street in Derry. They were old school Republicans sceptical of the ultimate value of a totally democratic and constitutional attempt to change the fundamentals of the Northern Ireland state and society. As far as they were concerned, the Unionist regime had an unshakable commitment to retaining power at all costs and would not listen to a well-presented case for democratic reform if for no other reason than that it had never done so in the past.

As the pair moved towards the assembly point in Duke Street, they fell into conversation with others on their way to join the march that, drawing inspiration from the United States, was being billed as a civil rights demonstration. The fundamental weakness of the Stormont regime, they were saying, was its inability to accommodate democratic reform. A well-supported campaign demanding that everybody in Northern Ireland receive the same standard of treatment as people in the rest of the UK would prove impossible for a regime claiming loyalty to London to refuse. As far as Frankie and his father were concerned, this was only ostensibly a plausible argument, because the Unionist government in Belfast was not known to subject itself to so-called British standards of behaviour. More to the point, they said, what happens if the march is banned and we just go home as we did in Dungannon? Does anybody in Britain, or America, or even our neighbours in the Republic of Ireland care what happens in the northern part of Ireland?

An hour later, as the police riot squad began to viciously beat the marching demonstrators, it seemed to Frankie that his fears and scepticism were well justified. Perhaps it even appeared to the RUC men carrying out the beating that everything was as it should be within their perceived remit, as they lashed out at those that dared defy the ruling authority. The Catholic minority, they believed, tended to get out of control from time to time. Those given responsibility for protecting the state were, they understood, called upon from time to time to administer the type of punishment and retribution that would remind the minority that they remained in Northern Ireland on sufferance of the province's political ruling class – the Unionist Party.

All might well have been as normal in Northern Ireland that Saturday if a camera crew from RTÉ[4] in Dublin had not turned up unexpectedly to cover the event and subsequently broadcast around the world, scenes of unrestrained police violence in a part of the United Kingdom. Among those being beaten by the police was a Westminster MP, Gerry Fitt. Amazingly, at the time, Unionism and its police force did not recognise the damage it had inflicted upon itself. Only a truly reactionary ruling clique could be so unaware of the message it was sending to the rest of the world, but that was what the old Unionist regime was – a backward-looking group, more typical of the nineteenth-century era of empire than of 1960s Britain. The scenes of state brutality on that October day in Derry were a public manifestation of the nature of the Northern Irish state and just as important, much of what was wrong with Northern Irish society.

Northern Ireland was an anomaly, an aberration and a relic of empire. Constitutionally, it was an integral part of the United Kingdom yet, alone among the regions, it had its own parliament and one in which, by custom and practice, central government neither interfered nor advised. This arrangement meant that London had a duty of care for an area over which it did not exercise control and held final responsibility for an administration that could and did practice governance of a kind that was far from the norm in other parts of the United Kingdom.

Northern Ireland's ruling class at the time was a mixture of businessmen, retired military officers and landed aristocrats. The Government of Ireland Act established Northern Ireland as a political entity in 1920 and for the following 53 years, its government was composed almost exclusively of Unionist Party members. Their method and style of governing during that period had been established by practice during the previous century, when an unwritten and perverted form of social contract between a Protestant elite and a Protestant working class had evolved and developed in the aftermath of the turbulence of the revolutionary 1790s. In order to wean Northern Irish Presbyterians away from supporting the type of democratic Republicanism that had caused them to come out in open insurrection against the Crown and the local ruling class at the end of the eighteenth century, the Northern Irish establishment practiced systematic discrimination in favour of Protestant workers and the rural poor. This did not mean that all Protestants became wealthy or even comfortable. What it did mean was that they received first refusal on what little was available in terms of employment, housing and local government influence.

As part of this process, there existed a regular practice of visiting 'disciplinary violence' on the Catholic population if they showed any sign of questioning the status quo.[5] Andrew Boyd, writing in *Holy War in Belfast*, pointed out that 'Of the 3,000 workmen in the Belfast shipyards at that time [1886], not more than 200 were Catholics. Most of the others were Orangemen who believed that if Ireland got Home Rule the Catholics would persecute the Protestants. This is what Randolph Churchill meant by the "Orange Card".'[6]

The demands of capitalism, which required a compliant and cheap workforce, ensured that Northern Irish society did not become exclusively Protestant. A significant Roman Catholic minority in the North East acted as a reserve army of labour, filling vacancies at boom times and holding down wages at other periods. As a result, labour costs in Northern Ireland remained lower than in Britain. Unsurprisingly, this source of cheap labour alienated Protestant workers. Coupled with their ancient fears of Papacy, this led to a situation of deep and growing hostility between two groups who would surely, under different circumstance, have found common cause in the pursuit of improvements in working conditions.

Ongoing hostility between the two groups of workers in Belfast created a situation where Protestant working-class areas became redoubts of Unionism and opponents of any move towards home rule in Ireland. Violent Protestant working-class opposition to Home Rule served a twin purpose for the ruling establishment. On one hand, it raised the spectre of widespread civil disturbance in the event of Home Rule being enacted without the dominant political class having to dabble in illegality. On the other hand, it established one of the unspoken rules of life in Ulster: the Catholic residents of Belfast and surrounding districts were to be held hostage to the 'good behaviour' of their co-religionists elsewhere in the province.

In spite of the deep and obvious hostility between sections of the Belfast working class throughout much of the nineteenth century, the ruling elite in the city could not be absolutely sure of the permanency of this situation. Worryingly, from their point of view, was the very real evidence of the working class finding common cause. Their worst fears appeared to have been realised in 1907 when Liverpool trade unionist James Larkin organised dockworkers and carters in the city and called a general strike. If the sight of thousands of Protestant and Catholic workers joined in unity frightened the ruling order in the early days of the strike, the refusal thereafter of the Royal Irish Constabulary (RIC[7]) to protect strike-breakers drove them to panic.

Significantly, the ruling class found it necessary (not to mention possible) to have the regular British Army called in to regain control of the city. Equally significant and with little justification, the British Army sent a cavalry patrol on to the Catholic Falls Road resulting in a confrontation that led to the death of three residents and the wounding of many others. The inevitable riot that followed was quickly deemed a Fenian[8] uprising by the Unionist press and propagandists. Protestant workers, believing the press reports, withdrew support for the strike and thus ended an opportunity to overcome divisions within labour ranks in Belfast.

The ruling class was relieved by the collapse of the 1907 strike but undoubtedly realised the risk to their position posed by any diminution of the prevailing order in Ulster. These fears were not assuaged in 1919 when 40,000 Belfast engineering workers went on strike for a shorter working week.[9] When the Six-County state was established a few months later in 1920, Unionist founding fathers were greatly concerned about the possibility of working-class unity. This was very evident in July 1920, when a coordinated assault was launched on Belfast's Catholic workers. Over a brief few days, 11,000 Catholic workers were evicted from their places of work in what was the beginning of a calculated drive to subdue that section of society. Significantly, at the same time and by the same forces of reaction, approximately 1,850[10] Protestant trade union activists were expelled from their workplaces in order to ensure that there would be no effective element within the workforce attempting to overcome sectarianism and unite Belfast's working class. The lessons of 1907 and 1919 had not been forgotten by the Unionist hierarchy and measures were put in place to reduce the possibility of working-class unity recurring in the new Northern Ireland. With hundreds of people killed in civil disturbances and thousands more forced to flee their homes, there would be no early reconciliation. The bloody events surrounding the northern state's foundation guaranteed that Unionism's wealthy ruling elite would remain in charge for decades afterwards.

The new Northern Ireland state was built upon a society that had developed its divisive characteristics throughout the nineteenth century and was governed by a local ruling class sharply attuned to playing the sectarian game to its own advantage. This, coupled with a fear of their southern neighbours and a nagging suspicion of the intentions of the government in London, meant that the new state and its government were aggressive but edgy, arrogant yet unconfident.

Northern Ireland's governing class believed that their state would only survive as a separate entity if its Protestant population remained unified and politically committed to the union with Great Britain. Any dilution of the bond between working-class and ruling-class Protestants would risk the future of the state. At a distance of only 13 years after Belfast's 1907 general strike and at a time when Bolshevism was undermining old certainties across Europe, Northern Ireland's founding fathers felt it necessary and prudent to reinforce well-practised tactics of discriminatory behaviour in order to retain the loyalty of a majority within the working-class and rural poor. By granting privileged status to one section of the population, the ruling Unionist Party enjoyed a comfortable majority that it would not have had if normal class politics had prevailed in the region.

At the time of Northern Ireland's foundation in 1920, the government of its first Prime Minister James Craig wanted an army to protect the new state. Central government in London refused to allow the raising of a second army within the UK and was unwilling to have its regular force 'sub-contracted' out to a regional parliament. James Craig was forced therefore to retain the old RIC practice of a police force acting also as an armed militia for the defence of the state. To guarantee the loyalty of its new police force, now known as the Royal Ulster Constabulary (RUC), the Northern Ireland government quietly ensured that recruits were overwhelmingly Protestant and Unionist. The full-time regular force was backed up by an exclusively Protestant, 20,000-strong, armed reserve officially named the Ulster Special Constabulary but widely known as the 'B Specials', who were less tightly controlled, were often undisciplined and offensive and were on occasions willing to use lethal force to curtail the Catholic population.

A system of control through discriminatory practices that had begun in the immediate aftermath of the foundation of Northern Ireland was adapted and refined in the years that followed the Second World War. Britain's post-war Labour government had introduced sweeping social reforms that led to increases and improvements in the social welfare system. Programmes of state-funded social housing, free health care and education and improvements in benefits to the unemployed altered the nature of Britain and of Northern Ireland.

With local government being responsible for the provision of social housing and central government providing social security for the unemployed, the Unionist leadership feared that its carefully crafted and balanced system of structural discrimination would be endangered. As the programme was being rolled out in Britain, the Stormont regime worked to ensure that its grip on local government would not be threatened. Its local government agencies initially stalled as best they could the implementation of the package and thereafter allocated houses and other assets on a sectarian basis.

Nationalists in towns such as Derry, Dungannon, Armagh, Newry and Enniskillen found that local authorities were not building sufficient quantities of houses. Alternatively, when houses were built, they were being granted in disproportionate numbers to Unionist supporters. Catholics found that they were being housed in high-density, inferior buildings in areas where their presence did not threaten the balance of power in district council wards.

Nationalist areas across the Six Counties experienced the frustration and bitterness that was generated by unfair housing allocation and the restrictions of selective awarding of planning permission to favoured builders. In the Co. Tyrone town of Dungannon, active non-violent opposition to this practice had been organised by a young married couple, Con and Patricia McCluskey. Two general practitioners, they had been disturbed to see at first hand the impact of inferior housing conditions on the health of their patients, particularly among the young and the elderly. Many of their patients lived in dilapidated buildings that had been converted from temporary Second World War army billets. Accommodation that had once proved adequate for transient soldiers on their journey to war were, by the 1960s, long past their best. So miserable were conditions in Dungannon that a disused prisoner-of-war camp was used in the 1950s as accommodation for families on the local council's housing waiting list.

Local Catholic people were painfully aware of the discriminatory decision making process in relation to housing allocation. This was particularly so in those areas where the balance between parties was close. Near Dungannon is a small village known locally as The Moy, where the sectarian head count immediately post-war was becoming uncomfortably close for Unionist Party officials. A local government building programme was undertaken in the early 1950s, which resulted in Unionist supporters obtaining over 80 per cent of available properties and that in a population broadly equal in political make-up. Nor had local Nationalists the straightforward option of building on land to which they had access. Local government officials in the councils' planning departments regularly ruled against any such building proposal and even some among the more liberal Unionists complained about the subtle pressure exercised by the Orange Order on decision making.

Housing allocation was important to the ruling Unionist party in terms of maintaining the local status quo. Determining where people lived allowed for shrewd local political ward management and the old practice of gerrymandering. Some areas were therefore designated as suitable for Catholics to live or indeed to increase their population. Elsewhere, in areas where the sectarian headcount was more finely balanced (such as in the village of Caledon where the evictions took place), it was made difficult for Nationalists to access housing. Gerrymandering local government constituencies guaranteed control of planning and housing allocation departments and this, in turn, allowed the system to replicate itself.

Local government also enjoyed crucial powers of employment. Local councils employed a significant number of people and it was in their gift to say who would and who would not work in their areas. This was a major factor, particularly in rural areas. At a time when intensive mechanisation was leading to a sharp increase in the minimum size of an economic farm holding, part-time employment was immensely important for the survival of many small farms. For a century after the Famine, an Irish family could expect a decent standard of living from a 40-acre farm. By the late 1950s, this was being challenged as tractors, running water and electricity made the cultivation of larger units possible and provided the economies of scale that began slowly to undermine the old routine of mixed farming and partial rural self-sustainability.

Small-farm families found that to live in an acceptable level of comfort, someone in the household had to supplement the family income with an off-farm job. There was a dearth of such work in rural areas west of the River Bann in Northern Ireland during the 1950s and 1960s. One employer, however, had access to a pool of work. Local government was able to say who would find a wage as school-bus drivers, ambulance drivers, bus drivers, firemen, rates collectors, local government civil servants, census collators, dustmen and a number of other occupations. And west of the Bann, those who voted Unionist filled a disproportionate number of these positions.

Not that religious and political discrimination was confined to the rude rustics of Fermanagh and Tyrone. Queens University in Belfast was not above bending the rules and was still being found guilty of such practices into the 1990s. The BBC in Belfast was to all intents and purposes blind to what was going on around it and lived in a world more resembling the English Home Counties than the Irish Six Counties. When County Down won the All-Ireland Gaelic football final in 1960 and 1961,[11] GAA supporters who could not travel to Dublin's Croke Park were unable to see the match on television. In contrast, however, they were treated to extensive coverage of the two cup-final victories of London club Tottenham Hotspur in the same years. And in the arts, a similar burying of heads in the sand was evident when Sam Thompson's play *Over the Bridge*,[12] which dealt with sectarianism in the Belfast shipyard, was refused a performance by the Ulster Group Theatre in 1958 in order ostensibly to 'keep political and religious controversies off our stage'.

The Irish language, while not extensively spoken by Catholics, was viewed by Unionism as both potentially seditious and an unwelcome symbol of a different culture to that of the dominant Unionist culture. In 1933, Northern Ireland's first Prime Minister James Craig asked contemptuously:

> What use is it here in this busy part of the Empire to teach our children the Irish language? What use would it have to them? Is it not leading them along a road, which has no practical value? We have not stopped the teaching; we have stopped the grants, which I think amounted to £1,500 a year. We have stopped the grants simply because we do not see that these boys being taught Irish would be any better citizens.[13]

Even by 1965, when Unionism appeared to be at its strongest, Stormont still rejected efforts to promote Irish culture. Dr Feargal Mac Ionnrachtaigh's paper 'Resisting and Regeneration through Language in the North of Ireland',[14] sets out the extent to which the Northern Ireland authorities were prepared to go to prevent a modest initiative to teach the language when he tells of the difficulties placed in the way of a group of Irish language enthusiasts of the time:

> The Shaws Road activists had succeeded in setting up the North's first Irish medium nursery school for their children in 1965 before subsequently following this up by meeting with the Stormont authorities to explore the possibility of setting up an Irish primary school (Mac Seáin 2006: 4). In its aftermath, they received a threatening letter saying 'that teaching through the medium of the Irish language would not be deemed to be proper instruction for young children' and that if the school was formed then 'the law would be allowed to take its course' (Ibid.). This threat, which, according to Mac Seáin (Ibid.), effectively translated as 'set up a school and you go to jail'.[15]

Half a century after its foundation, Northern Ireland had grown into a political entity that could not reform itself. Its prime minister, Captain (Rtd) Terrence O'Neill, knew that something had to be done but had come to realise that even minor reform was almost impossible. Many factors combined to lock the state into a condition of sectarian inertia, blocking whatever opportunity existed for making progressive change.

A majority of working-class Unionists were unwilling to countenance any concession to the Catholic population that would threaten their position of relative privilege. Moreover, they were coming increasingly under the influence of the populist, right-wing clergyman Ian Paisley, who was placing O'Neill under constant pressure, preventing him from introducing even the mildest of reforms. The apparatus of state was equally tied into the miasma of mismanagement. With its upper echelons disproportionately peopled by Unionists, the civil service found it nigh on impossible to be even-handed – the *sine qua non* of a proper functioning bureaucracy. Policing too, with its emphasis on protecting the state as opposed to maintaining civil order, was deeply flawed and incapable of providing an agreed service to the public. And no section of Northern Ireland's Unionist population, constantly fearful of encroachment from the Catholic population, could be neglected without the governing majority feeling that its delicately balanced hegemony was under threat.

Northern Ireland's ruling class realised that to attempt reform in any area risked alienating not only some particular group but also triggering a chain reaction across Unionism. As in one of the old Soviet satellite states, removing one block from the wall threatened to undermine the entire edifice. Northern Ireland was in that wretched condition where to survive it had to make reforms but due to the nature of the state and the composition of its ruling culture and ideology, it could not itself bring about the changes necessary for a peaceful transition.

Northern Ireland was a hostile place for its Catholic population in those years. A widespread sense of alienation from the state permeated most of the Nationalist population. The depth of one's alienation, however, often depended on a person's social class and status. It was easier to put up with relative discrimination if someone was prospering and had a comfortable middle-class lifestyle. Those at the bottom of the scale and dependent on public housing found the impact of discrimination more immediate and much more difficult to cope with.

Alienation from the northern state had created a situation where the Nationalist population lived not invisibly but in a quiet, and at times, almost parallel world. Nationalists had their own schools, often lived in separate areas, sometimes worked in different occupations (if at all) and on occasion, even appeared to have a different culture of Gaelic football, Irish music, history and literature. This culture did not though appear on the 'official programme' where lord lieutenants, royal visits, state-sector education and Eton-educated prime ministers created the picture of a society seamlessly integrated into the British system. Deep bitterness and resentment was common among many Nationalists. Yet for decades, an all-pervading fear had kept much of this anger bottled up, typified by the local expression, 'Whatever you say, say nothing.'

Figure 1.1   The RUC attack a demonstrator in Derry on 5 November 1968.

Unsurprisingly, therefore, when the RUC cleared Derry's Duke Street of peaceful civil rights protesters on 5 October 1968, Frankie and his father felt a bitter sense of resignation. It reinforced their long-held belief that it was impossible to change or reform the northern state. It was pointless even engaging with it, they thought. They both believed the only viable alternative was the old dogmatic Republican policy of smashing the state, but this they believed to be something verging on the impossible. Southern Ireland was hostile to the notion of a northern uprising and the recently failed IRA campaign[16] showed that a majority of northern Nationalists were reluctant to take on the well-armed and aggressive regime in Stormont. There appeared to be an impasse.

Travelling back to Dungannon, their assessment might not have been wrong, but it failed to account for the impact television pictures of gratuitous police brutality would have upon the situation. They did not recognise it then but they were living at the beginning of a new and different era where events and conditions were bringing about rapid changes. Years of silent humiliation forcibly contained by an authoritarian administration were going to have an airing on the world's stage. In this new era, that type of exposure was bound to have consequences.

The Unionist government was trying to stop the world turning, but the new world that the people marching in Derry aspired to was asserting its gravitational pull. Many thousands of people hitherto unwilling to get involved in political struggle were about to join the campaign for change in the six counties of Northern Ireland.

2
Unionist Determination to Deny Democracy

The two Eddies were revelling in the excitement. In their early twenties and unusual for Catholics of the time and area, the pair were employed. Both worked hard in the building industry and it brought in a modest wage. Single men with few family commitments, they were able to enjoy life. As with many of their contemporaries in that milieu, they had modest expectations in a Northern Ireland that was designed to ensure they rarely exceeded the unexceptional goals reserved for them.

They were well aware of existing conditions in the Six Counties and during their early years had shared the prevailing attitude among most Catholics of resigned but passive resentment. The civil rights movement opened opportunities for contesting the authority of the Stormont regime that would have been unimaginable in earlier decades. They attended almost every protest march and demonstration that was organised and were just about willing to adhere to the instructions of the civil rights movement's stewards not to attack either police or Unionist counter-demonstrators.

In time though, they grew increasingly impatient. Unlike earlier generations of Catholics in the Six Counties, they felt a sense of empowerment in the surging level of protest. Growing crowds in the streets, peacefully protesting for democratic rights, had drawn attention and even approval from many influential people in Britain and abroad and left the Stormont regime ideologically out-manoeuvred. Why then was there no real progress if so many people could see what was wrong?, they thought. They knew too that many other Catholics shared their feelings. The civil rights movement with its marches and protest meetings had created an incredibly charged atmosphere. Those who attended and participated and even those who only watched from the sidelines spent hours talking and speculating on the possible course of events.

In August 1969, the two Eddies met with a few friends in Dungannon. They did not have anything planned or organised. They wanted to do something about the siege of the Bogside in Derry but had no idea what action to take. Their dilemma was resolved when the local police decided to send patrols into Catholic streets, apparently to 'command the area'. Almost spontaneously, local youngsters began to stone the patrols and before long, petrol bombs were being hurled. Throwing Molotov cocktails at the RUC and B Specials was an easy step for the two men to take as they joined in the attacks. A step made all the more easy before the night was out when B Specials opened fire with live ammunition on the petrol bombers, wounding several young men during the course of the evening.

Many of the B Specials were local men and well known to the Eddies. They had worked for, and even with, some of them on different occasions and for the most part had little difficulty doing so. The fact that these men, who recently had been ordinary neighbours, were now emerging as armed agents of a violent state reinforced for the two Eddies much of what they had heard their parents say over the years: 'There's no point asking for fair treatment here because when you do, they'll send in the "B" men to smash us. Your own neighbours will shoot you.'

Watching an armed Protestant militia acting as the first line of defence for Protestant privilege had a deep impact on the Eddies. Without knowing it, they were identifying one of the main bastions of Unionist power that had to be combated if the state were to be changed.

Trouble in Derry was hardly a surprise to many northern Nationalists and Republicans. Scenes of police brutality were not uncommon. Four years earlier, in September 1964, the RUC had used force to remove an Irish tricolour flag from a Sinn Féin election office in a Catholic part of Belfast. In the mid-1950s, the people of Pomeroy, Co. Tyrone, were subjected to widespread intimidation and state violence when Stormont's police force baton-charged a parade of local people trying to stage a welcome home event for a recently released Republican prisoner, Liam Kelly. What did surprise the viewing Nationalist population, though, was the notice taken by the national and international media in what had happened. Of particular interest and astonishment was the attention shown in particular by British-based broadsheets, such as the *Guardian*, *Observer* and *Sunday Times*. One journalist stood out by taking a very keen interest in the events of that day: the *Guardian*'s Mary Holland filed reports of police brutality during the civil rights march in Derry that shocked the paper's liberal readership. They were especially interested and disturbed to read that Member of Parliament Gerry Fitt had not only been beaten but had quite clearly been selected for special attention by the RUC.

For a people unfamiliar with having their views aired by any media other than their own local newspapers, the experience was new and exciting. For the first time in living memory, the British ruling class appeared to have learned of their existence and Dublin opinion, too, seemed to have been awakened by television coverage of events in Derry. The interest taken by outsiders in their story created exhilaration within the very confined world of Northern Ireland's Catholic community. People who might otherwise have dismissed the march as naiveté at best, or a dangerous and irresponsible act of provocation to Orange hegemony at worst, began to feel that change was possible.

Those who had questioned the wisdom of tackling Stormont through a peaceful and democratic strategy, proclaiming strict adherence to Martin Luther King's principles of non-violence, were now seen as faint hearts. They were relegated to the status of bystanders who had been bypassed by the new wave of optimism and action. Here was proof positive that a new and vibrant strategy existed. Proof too that younger, alternative figures now emerging had a capacity for delivering the type of serious challenge to Stormont that the older, more traditional leaders had failed to achieve.

Paradoxically, and in spite of all that has been said about the self-inflicted injuries sustained by the Unionist regime as a result of televised scenes of police brutality, the old Nationalist Party was the first casualty of the day. The Nationalist Party in 1968, under the cautious and conservative leadership of Eddie McAteer, had held sway in the North for almost a century. It was the remnant of the once great political machine led by Charles Stewart Parnell and John Redmond. After the Government of Ireland Act 1920 which partitioned Ireland, the party emerged (with considerable assistance from the Roman Catholic hierarchy and wealthy Catholic businesspeople) as the dominant force among northern Catholics. In spite of its obsequiousness, the party had little impact on the day-to-day workings of the Stormont parliament, being treated with contempt by the ruling Unionist government.

The Nationalist Party did, nevertheless, serve as a type of political lightning rod for the safe filtering and defusing of its constituents' discontent. Often acting in close concert with the Catholic clergy, Nationalist Party representatives would make 'humble' representations to the ruling elite and would occasionally gain token reward for their humility. Interestingly, at that time, the Catholic clergy were one of the few institutions within the minority community able to obtain limited concessions from Stormont. The Catholic hierarchy was able to obtain separate Catholic schools, limited planning permission for domestic housing construction and occasional grants for small industry from a Unionist regime that was bigoted but not unaware of the value of having a reliable and restraining influence on the minority. The hold that the Nationalist Party had exerted for 50 years was maintained largely through inertia, due to the absence of a credible alternative. The party was effectively rendered obsolete by fall-out from the RUC brutal handling of the civil rights march in Derry on 5 October events. A new generation of clever, articulate young politicians and activists came to prominence and brushed aside the staid old men of the Nationalist Party.

Sinn Féin (at that period, using the name 'Republican Clubs'[1]) was also a presence but its policy of abstaining from taking seats in parliament and its close connections to the IRA meant that usually only the most strident (or some might say foolhardy) supported it. Republicans suffered, moreover, from Catholic Church opposition who saw them as troublemaking radicals with sometimes suspect connections on the left. The infrequent excursions of Sinn Féin into the electoral arena were usually followed by an attempt at launching an IRA campaign that invariably ended in demoralising failure. Memories of the IRA's failed campaign in the years 1956–62, codenamed 'Operation Harvest'[2] by the organisation, were still fresh in many minds. This meant that while many younger Northern Irish Catholics viewed the Nationalist Party as bumbling and effete, Republicans were seen by many as folk caught in a time warp. The traditional Sinn Féin view, that nothing would change without violent insurrection, appeared to have been patently wrong as momentum gathered around the peaceful civil rights alternative.

With the two major political entities of northern Nationalism and Republicanism found seriously wanting in the turmoil that was created by the civil rights movement, the vacuum was filled by a number of political trends. Some were old school and some were new to the politics of confrontation. There was general consensus among those opposed to the status quo that change had to come but there was little agreement on how exactly this should come about.

Among the new recruits to protest were middle-class Catholics and many of those aspiring to that status, who constituted an influential and powerful body of opinion within the new movement. They were anxious to have a limited programme of reform implemented, but were determined to ensure that it would not go farther than they felt necessary; they were entirely unwilling to risk anything that might cause undue upheaval to their lifestyle.

A new departure in politics is, nevertheless, rarely filled by entirely different opinions. There is usually an input from older schools of thought, if only via a re-reading of established texts or the counsel of veteran activists. So it was too in the days after 5 October 1968 when street activists played an important early role. Some old leftists argued that there was an unacceptable danger in pushing the Stormont regime too far and into the use of widespread repressive violence. Their decades of bitter experience at the hands of the northern state told them that Unionism was not to be carelessly trifled with. They advised caution and urged the youngsters to 'hasten slowly'. There may have been more than a grain of wisdom in their advice, but on occasion the tide of human expectation and impatience sweeps prudence aside.

Influenced by events in continental Europe and the US, others believed that the proper course of action was to press ahead with some urgency lest the momentum be lost. On a notable and undoubtedly seminal occasion in Derry, this division between old and new leftists came into stark contrast. A civil rights march (not the 5 October 1968 march) approached the Craigavon Bridge and was halted by an RUC cordon. Initially, taking the advice of veteran trade union leader and Communist Party activist Betty Sinclair, the marchers sat down in the street and began to sing. After a few minutes, a young student activist stood up and began counting the police. She estimated that the sedentary marchers had numerical superiority and could overwhelm the police ranks and push their way into the city if the crowd charged forward. She began to address the gathering, urging them to ignore the older woman and to move forward. After a few minutes, people began to stand up and to push against the cordon. In a few minutes, they burst through the RUC ranks and poured into the city. Leadership of radical street protest in Northern Ireland had passed from the generation guided by Betty Sinclair to a new generation of activists inspired by Bernadette Devlin, the young woman who had called for the advance. There was, however, no single figure like Martin Luther King capable of imposing a unitary plan of campaign on the protest in the Six Counties. No matter how many efforts were made to forge one unified movement, the pace was set by smaller rather than larger groups and, frequently, natural enthusiasm alongside the vim and vigour of youth determined the shape of the next round of events.

With the publicity generated by the Duke Street events, the civil rights movement gained enormous buoyancy and a momentum that brought it to almost every Catholic town in Northern Ireland. Meetings were held in areas that had experienced the frustration of discriminatory Unionist rule for generations and drew large crowds of supporters. Present outside every civil rights meeting were raucous Paisleyite counter-pickets. The Reverend Ian Paisley[3] and his team of travelling supporters were Protestant fundamentalists who had set up their own Free Presbyterian Church after having split from mainstream reformed churches. In Ireland, north and south, clergy of all denominations had long been involved in party politics. In the North, Protestant clergymen had taken an active part in both the Orange Order and in the Unionist Party and it was not unusual for them to contest elections or enter into contentious debates or disputes about constitutional or constituency issues.

Ian Paisley's behaviour was unusual only in that he came from and represented a different group of northern society than did most of those sitting on the government benches in Stormont. The leader of the Free Presbyterian Church was from relatively humble origins and while he and his supporters were determined to maintain the privileges enjoyed by Protestants in Northern Ireland, he was also articulating a muted and often subliminal feeling amongst his peers and supporters that they were not receiving their due reward from the wealthy Unionist ruling class.

The process of counter-demonstration was a tactic well understood and practised by Ian Paisley and his supporters. From the late 1950s, he had repeatedly made the strange claim that an alliance between the Dublin government, the Papacy and the IRA was working to smash the union between Northern Ireland and Britain. Moreover, he claimed that, mystifyingly, the orthodox Unionist leadership was unwilling to take the steps necessary to counteract the threat. In order to prevent his predictions coming to fruition, he maintained it was necessary to contest each and every sign of what he perceived as Catholic/Republican rebellion and loudly proclaimed that the civil rights movement was not a genuine, legitimate and democratic expression of people's concerns, but was instead a preparation for widespread rebellion against the Protestant people and the Crown.

The Paisleyite presence was not, however, the only cause for tension at civil rights marches and meetings throughout the remaining months of 1968 and indeed in the years to follow. To the outside world, the civil rights movement may have looked like a homogenous mass movement but internally there was a barely concealed power struggle for leadership of the protest campaign. Underlying differences and divisions within the wider civil rights movement were grounded in the complexities of Northern Irish society with middle-class Nationalists, largely working-class Republicans and a small but determined bunch of socialists all trying to guide the movement in their favoured direction.

Different figures within these conflicting politics were beginning to gain popular support and all were offering their own ideas and advice. With broad-based civil rights committees springing up all over the North, meetings were not easily controlled by any one tendency and were usually too important for any prospective leader or group to ignore. Platforms were shared and points were gained and lost by appealing to the audience's sense of what they wanted and understood. It was a period when the marketplace for ideas among the Catholic population was more open than it had been for many years and for decades afterwards. As a result, partly due to its unenlightened and unrealistic decision to forbid safe and economical methods of contraception and partly due to a more widely educated populace, the Catholic hierarchy was beginning to lose its grip over many of its younger members. The expansion of education that threatened the autocratic mandate of the Roman Church also posed a threat to that old unordained Catholic hierarchy of publicans, bookmakers, lawyers and large-scale farmers.

Thanks to the Education Act of 1949, a generation of working-class Catholics was then emerging from third-level education with ambition to match their ability. They were usually articulate, passionate and energetic. In time, the vast majority would succumb to the lure of middle-class comfort and conformity, but for a period almost all were willing to challenge the status quo while some went so far as to argue for fundamental social and economic change. Among the radicals, people such as Bernadette Devlin, Eamonn McCann and Michael Farrell were emerging. Austin Curry, Gerry Fitt and the Maynooth-educated schoolteacher John Hume guided the more cautious and conservative element, which eventually formed the Social Democratic and Labour Party.

Debate within the broad civil rights constituency was largely between those who wanted to accelerate the pace of change and those more conservative elements arguing for caution – the old contest between revolution and reform. Many Republicans participated in the movement and in the debate, but they were usually from the new school that believed in the need to prioritise social and economic struggle. Old-style 'physical-force' Republicans were to a large extent sidelined in these deliberations, as their views and analysis were practically irrelevant to the unfolding situation that posed questions about tactics and strategy outside their remit of physical-force anti-Partitionism. In spite of these contesting ideas and sometimes acrimonious debates, the increasingly threatening behaviour of the counter-demonstrators helped conceal any sign of the diverse schools of thought within the protest movement.

Therefore, when a follow-up to the Derry civil rights demonstration of 5 October 1968 was planned for Armagh City on 30 November, it appeared to outsiders that the movement was not just united but almost monolithic. A Paisleyite counter-demonstration was organised and, while the RUC had promised to allow the original march to proceed, information was leaked to Protestant demonstrators of police intentions to block the town from early morning. Ian Paisley and his assistant Major Ronald Bunting gathered their supporters, armed with cudgels and iron bars, into Armagh shortly after midnight. The RUC was then allowed to claim that in spite of its intention to allow the civil rights march and rally to take place, they had no option but to prevent it entering Armagh, ostensibly to preserve law and order. The day did not end entirely peacefully, however, as a Loyalist demonstrator used a cosh to knock an ITN cameraman unconscious while an RUC officer used his baton to smash a BBC camera.

It is intriguing to note that the British government's assessment of these patterns of police behaviour was invariably to ignore structural or underlying misconduct. Lord Scarman, who reported on the conflict in 1969, while regretting police partiality where he perceived this to be an issue, always defined it in terms of either individual complicity or police incompetence (usually due to being overstretched). Scarman's report was one of the better, albeit complacent British establishment attempts, to explain to a UK constituency what everyone bar the most blinkered understood to be police partiality and brutality.[4]

The RUC's supposed inability to permit a legal civil rights march to pass through Armagh was in stark contrast to the police determination to assist Ian Paisley to march wherever he chose. Two years earlier, in 1966, Paisley had insisted on his right to march with his supporters through Catholic districts on his way to demonstrate outside the Presbyterian General Assembly in central Belfast. The Stormont government and RUC acquiesced with his demand and thereafter faced up to the inevitable riot.

As Andrew Boyd described it:

The march, which was held on the evening of Monday 6 June, was intended to be both insulting and provocative, yet the Minister of Home Affairs and the RUC allowed it to take place. Moreover, they gave permission for Paisley to proceed to the Assembly Building by way of Cromac Square, a predominantly Catholic part of the city, which had been the scene of sectarian riots in other years ... Although the riot at Cromac Square was short and sharp the material damage caused was extensive. Cars and taxis parked in the vicinity of the square were wrecked and the plate-glass windows of shops and of Cromac Square Post Office were smashed. Eventually the Paisleyites, flanked and protected by RUC men, got through the square and proceeded along May Street and Howard Street to where the General Assembly was in session and awaiting the arrival of Lord Erskine, Governor of Northern Ireland.[5]

The stalled Armagh civil rights' demonstration drew an estimated crowd of 5,000 people. Such sizeable numbers indicated to Northern Ireland's prime minister, Captain Terence O'Neill, that the protest movement was not going to fade away quietly. To the population of Northern Ireland, O'Neill delivered a broadcast which was to become known as the 'Ulster at the Crossroads' address. He appealed for calm, promised to address grievances and warned that Ulster was at the eponymous crossroads, from which the people could either take the path to peace and prosperity, or opt for violent confrontation. While Paisley and his supporters viewed the broadcast as a crass surrender to rebellion, O'Neill's address was generally well received by both the Catholic and Unionist middle class. Some of the local newspapers organised a petition in support of the prime minister and sections of the civil rights movement under the direction of John Hume offered the Northern Ireland government a cooling-off period during which there would be no more demonstrations or rallies.

Not all civil rights activists were, however, as willing to pull back from confrontation with the state. The newly formed student organisation known as People's Democracy announced its intention to hold a march from Belfast to Derry in the early New Year of 1969. Many of the middle-class professionals who had gained prominence in the aftermath of the October demonstration in Derry were opposed to the student initiative, but were forced to alter their public position after the march was viciously attacked by Paisleyite supporters at Burntollet Bridge in County Derry.

The students had left Belfast on New Year's Day and made their way slowly towards Derry. Their journey was not straightforward, having to make a number of detours as Major (Rtd) Ronald Bunting commanded the Paisleyite faction in a series of disruptive counter-demonstrations. Those early attempts to disrupt the march were only a forerunner to what was to happen at Burntollet. An estimated crowd of 400 Paisleyites (including many off-duty members of the B Specials[6]) under the direction of the major staged a planned and well-organised ambush on the students. As the Cameron Report stated:

> The place was well chosen for an ambush; ammunition in the shape of supplies of stones and other missiles including pieces of old iron had been provided and, in case of stones, piled in the adjacent fields ready for use; and the wearing of white armbands – presumably for identification – had obviously been arranged beforehand among the attackers, many of whom were armed with cudgels or clubs of various kinds.[7]

Local farmers sympathetic to Ian Paisley had used their tractors to deliver rocks by the trailer-load for use against the young civil rights activists who suffered many injuries as a hail of stones rained down on them. This barrage was followed by Paisleyite supporters charging the procession and wounding a group ill prepared for the ferocious assault.

An equally dangerous series of events had occurred the evening before the Burntollet ambush, albeit one not recorded by television cameras. A Paisleyite rally had taken place in Derry's Guildhall, which led to sectarian fighting on the edges of the Catholic Bogside area. The RUC launched a raid on the area and, using batons and boots, inflicted punishment on a large number of residents. The attack was severe.[8] Policemen did not confine their attack to pedestrians but entered houses, smashing furniture and assaulting people in their own homes. As civil rights activist Eamonn McCann described it:

> The area was peaceful and deserted at 2 a.m. when a mob of policemen came from the city centre through Butcher Gate and surged down Fahan Street into St Columb's Wells and Lecky Road, shouting and singing:
>
> > Hey, hey we're the monkees.
> > And we're going to monkey around
> > Till we see your blood flowing
> > All along the ground.
>
> They broke in windows with their batons, kicked doors and shouted to the people to 'come out and fight, you Fenian bastards.'[9]

This wanton use of police batons was to continue and led eventually to fatalities.

Tension and resentment was naturally very high in Derry, as the beaten and battered parade made its way into the city later the following evening and as the full extent of the attack became clear. The RUC had failed abjectly to protect the students and worse, many maintained that the RUC had hemmed in the marching students in order to facilitate the attack. Few among the Catholic population were prepared to accept that the police had no knowledge whatsoever of Major Bunting's intentions. Their conviction that the RUC had allowed the marching students to walk into an ambush was reinforced, when it emerged that members of the B Specials had been identified among the Paisleyite mob. Suspicions were heightened during a final assault on the students as they entered the city when a named B Special commandant was identified among the attackers.

The reaction from Northern Ireland's prime minister caused further resentment within the Catholic community when, bizarrely, he attempted to blame the students for starting the violence at Burntollet, describing them as 'foolhardy, irresponsible, hooligan civil rights marchers'. To make matters worse, he threatened to mobilise the B Specials. This was in order to restore law and order, he said. A strange claim, since credible reports were circulating that up to a quarter of those who attacked the People's Democracy at Burntollet were members of that very force. The events of January were to set a pattern for the days to come and reinforced the view held by many in the Catholic community that the state was not a series of discrete components, but was in fact a seamless and coordinated whole. Few in the Catholic community viewed the state as merely the official apparatus made up of executive, judiciary and public servants. To the Catholic community, it seemed clear that the state apparatus also reached across into quasi-official institutions such as the Orange Order, sections of the media and significantly, to also incorporate, albeit unofficially, the street fighters who claimed to draw their inspiration from Ian Paisley.

This is important since this book argued at the beginning that the Northern Ireland state was constituted from quasi-autonomous elements within the Unionist community and moreover, that the early state had relied upon a form of mobilisation that would be both internal and external to the official state apparatuses, namely, the A, B and C Specials. Many of those who formed the B Specials had fought in the Great War and played an important role as the local eyes and ears of the nascent state. These individuals worked in and out of the state in everyday life. They were indeed, as their designation made explicit, the state's auxiliaries. Effectively, they acted as the state's night watchmen and this perspective defined absolutely the continuing form and character of the B Specials throughout the state's history. What we are arguing in effect is that everything the B Specials did they did entirely in character. And of course, the social and other associational relationships with the official regular police force, the RUC, formed and reinforced part of a culture of anti-Nationalist condescension, if not outright contempt.

It was hardly surprising therefore that policemen had been seen to mingle happily with Paisleyite crowds along the route of the People's Democracy march and had been accused of diverting the march into the ambush and thereafter hemming in the students in order to prevent their escape. From a Catholic standpoint, it was difficult to see any real difference between rioting mobs of Paisleyites, and B Specials participating in riots, while assisting the mobs and rampaging bands of policemen bludgeoning Catholics in their homes.

In reality, the northern state depended upon a complex interaction between the different layers of its supporters. There seemed little real difference between the roles of those who practised unofficial violence in order to maintain the status quo and those who used their positions within the official apparatus of state to carry out unofficial operations for the same purpose. Until the cataclysm of 1968, this had worked fairly well for the regime, but this edifice of state-civil society repression had of course been built upon a quiescent, defeated Catholic population. Mass action by a discontented minority, while the stuff of 'ancient' Unionist nightmares, was not actually supposed to occur; that was what the 'night watchmen' were supposed to be there for: to nip it in the bud.

In the early months of 1969, the Ulster Volunteer Force (UVF) introduced explosives to a fragile situation when it bombed public utilities carrying water and electricity supplies. The Loyalist organisation concealed its involvement in the campaign and attempted to have the IRA blamed for causing the explosions. While few Catholics believed that Republicans were responsible for the damage, the destruction allowed the Stormont government to talk darkly about subversion adding to the tension and apprehension within the community. Yet the ruse of IRA responsibility was one which even the British government at the time recognised to be a fiction.[10] In total, the UVF carried out bombings on six different occasions in 1969. The Provisional IRA was not formed until the very end of 1969.

Events did not improve as the months rolled on and the Orange marching season got under way. Orange Order spokespeople usually now describe the Order's activities as purely cultural and religious. In the past however, Northern Ireland's Catholic population viewed it as an organisation dedicated not so much to protecting Protestantism as to the violent suppression of its opponents. The Order marched where and when it wished and did so with enthusiasm in all but a handful of areas. It acted as an umbrella organisation for the Protestant population, providing a mechanism that at once covered over natural class differences and helped facilitate the unofficial management of affairs in Northern Ireland.

When one of the Orange Order's sister organisations, the Apprentice Boys of Derry, decided to go ahead with its annual march on 12 August 1969, there was apprehension that it might lead to an escalation of the simmering violence. The march did indeed cause tension but did not lead to a direct confrontation. That happened later in the evening as Bogside residents set up barricades to prevent the RUC making another incursion into their small district. Initial attempts by the RUC to enter the area were repulsed and what had started out as a desultory confrontation between police and locals was soon transformed into a major issue over who governed. The authorities deemed the resistance by the Bogside population as a threat to its authority and ordered ever-larger numbers of policemen into Derry.

The RUC faced two major disadvantages in its efforts to dominate the Bogside on this occasion. The police were not permitted to use live ammunition and did not have equipment to deal with a coordinated attempt by civilians determined to prevent them gaining control. The Bogsiders also had the advantage of the area's physical geography. Young men had occupied the flat roofs of high-rise buildings commanding the centre of the area. They continued to pour a steady hail of Molotov cocktails and rocks onto the attacking police below. It soon became obvious to onlookers that the men on the roofs and elsewhere were being supplied with a large and steady supply of ammunition by residents of the area.

RUC men were fighting a fatiguing and losing battle against the Bogside residents and doing so before the eyes of the world's television viewers. It was a demoralising and frustrating experience for a police force that had exerted such control for so long. It was also a bitter experience for the Unionist masses who expected any show of revolt to be put down with alacrity and without any hesitation or reluctance to use whatever force was necessary. The situation in Derry was reaching stalemate when Bogside supporters from other parts of Northern Ireland decided to lend assistance. In an effort to spread the RUC thinner on the ground and force the prime minister to declare a halt to the siege of the Bogside, demonstrations were organised in other towns across the Six Counties.

3
The Violent Storms of August '69

There was a time when evening brought calmness over city districts and residents would relax. It was especially so in older industrial towns where residential and commercial quarters were closely integrated. As day gave way to evening, traffic calmed, businesses closed for the night and inhabitants enjoyed a few hours' peace before the clamour returned with daybreak. This was not always the case, though, in Belfast and it was certainly not so on the evening of 14 August 1969. For over a century, there had been a history of dangerous inter-communal riots in working-class areas of the city. The 1920s had been a particularly awful time when hundreds were killed and the memory of those terrifying days was fixed in the mind of every Belfast Catholic. So, as the battle for the Bogside in Derry was drawing to a climax, a sense of dread began to seep through the households of the small streets off the Falls Road.

The Falls and Shankill roads do not converge at any point, but both thoroughfares draw closer to each other as they near the city centre. In 1969, the lower parts of these thoroughfares were accessible to each other by a series of small streets and walkways running at right angles to the two main roads. In Belfast's troubled history, this ground had often been the scene of sectarian conflict and death.

Richard was 15 years old and knew the story of Belfast's past as well as any other youngster of his time. What he did not understand was the exact nature of the danger he was in by insisting on remaining with his father and grandfather in their small terraced house on Peel Street. A few hours earlier, his mother and sisters had been sent to the relative safety of their relatives' home in the Beechmount area, some distance away. He refused to move with the others and eventually his father relented.

Belfast Catholics had learned over many painful decades to recognise the signs of trouble brewing. All day long, the men had been boarding up windows and reinforcing the doors of their small red-brick houses. Richard and his father had moved the furniture and linoleum out of the front room so that there would be less to burn if incendiary materiel was poured through the front door or window. They had bought a few strong planks of timber that morning and used them as a wedge to prevent the front door from being easily smashed in. They turned off all lights and waited in the back kitchen with the grandfather, who sometimes fingered his rosary beads and occasionally put his hand to a hurley stick.

By early evening, the streets were silent. Time passed slowly and tension grew in the little back room as daylight hours drew to a close. They heard a gunshot. Richard had never heard shots fired in anger. Before he had time to check with his father and grandfather, his doubts were removed. Another shot and another, and within minutes he knew that he was listening to intense gunfire and it was close by. Then the shooting stopped. Richard was nervous and uncertain. The old man said quietly, 'Wait 'till you see, the police will come now.' And so they did. Police came in armoured cars, careering through the narrow streets, firing first at random and then with deliberation at the street lighting.

He did not notice at first that the police vehicles were no longer racing through the street. Again it was the old man who identified what was happening. 'Do you hear them?' he asked, 'Do you hear them any longer?' Richard did not understand. 'Can hear what?' he said. 'Listen', the old man said, 'when you can't hear the police it means the others are coming.' And he set aside his rosary and took the hurley in both hands: 'Just hope that there's someone out there to stop them or we'll be in trouble.'

The old man knew what was about to happen. With the streets cleared and in darkness, Unionist incendiaries would invade the area and systematically burn the houses. It was a pattern that he had experienced before. In the distance, they could hear the noise of an advancing crowd. Richard wanted to go out and see what was happening but on this occasion his father forbade him to leave the house and there was no ambiguity about the seriousness of the command. Richard stayed and listened. As the noise of cheering and shouting drew closer, his apprehension changed to outright panic.

Richard knew the district well and knew instinctively where the yelling was coming from. He could tell that the attack was not focused on any single point. It was as if the attackers were making a broad-fronted assault with the intention of penetrating wherever a weakness presented itself. He slipped away from the back room and crept upstairs and peering through the skylight saw flames rising from neighbouring streets. A wall of flame and smoke separated the entire length of the lower Falls from the Shankill.

Just when it seemed that the whole district might be destroyed, a few single shots rang out. Other gunshots immediately followed and while he wasn't a firearms expert, it seemed to him that gunfire was being exchanged. Very quietly, the old man climbed into the small space beside him and together they watched across the rooftops.

'Listen to the pattern of the shooting,' the old man said. 'Shooting from near the edge of the fires and more from the dark. That means someone is fighting back. Can you see flames around Divis Street and the fires all along the back of us? If they get right out onto the Falls, this will be worse than the Twenties.'

Richard's father remained downstairs with a short handled 'billy-hook' that his brother had bought at a country fair some years before. Throughout the night, the old man or the boy would come downstairs and join him, reporting on what they believed was happening all around. The old man was sanguine. 'They are in the area but not able to get onto the Falls', he told his son, 'and so long as that stays the case it means we'll not be driven out of this part of the city. We'll just stay here and pray for daylight.'

As dawn broke, Richard knew from his father and grandfather that the worst had passed; for that day at any rate. They were lucky still to have a house. Many of their neighbours were not so fortunate.

Figure 3.1   British Army soldiers survey the ruins of Bombay Street in August 1969 (© Gerry Collins and Red Barn Gallery, Belfast).

Unlike other parts of the United Kingdom, Northern Ireland had a quasi-colonial tradition where one section of the community participated enthusiastically in policing the other. It required no conspiracy to bring great numbers of Protestant people into action for what they perceived as defence of the regime. And as in other parts of the world, where one community takes it upon itself to police the other, the consequences are typically destructive.

With hindsight, it should have been obvious that the Stormont-governed state would use lethal force to crush protest if it appeared to have the potential to challenge or undermine the power structures. State violence had always been unleashed on those deemed to be posing a threat to the established order. To a certain extent, it matters little whether the state officially authorised the reaction of August 1969, or whether it happened spontaneously. Ultimately, Northern Ireland was incapable of coping with a movement demanding democratic rights and the response to such a campaign was entirely of the state's making and its responsibility.

The B Specials had come to epitomise the essence and ethos of the Northern Ireland state in the eyes of its Catholic population. They were integral to the management of the state and had ingested the theory of a ruling order that utilised one section of the population to contain the other. There was an unquestioned assumption among members of the force that they had a right and a duty to bear arms against their Catholic neighbours. They had played an important role in the establishment of the Six-County state and had assisted in its maintenance in the intervening years.

The B Specials were nominally under the control of a district police division and ultimately responsible to Stormont's Ministry of Home Affairs. They were, however, organised in local units and usually paraded and trained in their own dedicated drill halls. In rural areas, the B Specials were often trusted to store personal weapons in their homes so that they could mobilise at short notice. This granted B Special platoons a degree of autonomy that enabled them not just to muster quickly but also to act independently of headquarters. B Special platoons were not uniform in outlook but certainly reflected the collective opinion of the Unionist population of the district from which they originated.

There was in Northern Ireland a long tradition of an armed Protestant community guarding its position against hostile and sometimes rebellious Catholic neighbours. Thanks to a special relationship with British governments, Protestant Ulster had for centuries been a heavily armed community. Thanks too, to this special relationship, influential elements of the British establishment had on occasions turned a blind eye to illegal importation of arms as had occurred in April 1914. Twenty-five thousand weapons and four million rounds of ammunition were landed without opposition at Larne, in order to foil Westminster's decision to grant home rule to Ireland.

The situation in Northern Ireland over the nights of August 1969 cannot be compared with that of the Second World War when Waffen-SS attacked Jewish ghettos. In reality, it resembled more the type of racist-inspired behaviour witnessed in the southern states of the US before the civil rights era of the 1960s, than a genocidal pogrom. The key difference between the situation in Belfast and that south of the Mason-Dixon Line was that in the latter instance, the besieged African American community had (in theory at any rate) a right to bear arms in their own defence and unlike Westminster; the US federal government made some serious attempts to redress underlying grievances.

The first fatality of August 1969 happened in Armagh city when John Gallagher, a Catholic civilian, was shot dead by B Specials during street disturbances on Cathedral Road. There was no evidence to indicate that Mr Gallagher was anything other than a Catholic working man on his way home to his wife and family after having a few drinks in a local bar. He was not a participant in the disturbances and even if he had been, he posed no threat to police in the vicinity. In reality, there was little to contradict a widely held view in the area that the shooting was simply a result of indiscipline by trigger-happy rural B Specials.

Ominously, vicious riots also erupted in Belfast on 14 August. Some time during this outbreak of violence, the RUC sent armoured cars with heavy-calibre Browning machine-guns onto the Falls Road. Following the RUC incursion, Unionists from the Shankill Road supported by B Specials launched an attack on the lower end of the Catholic Falls Road, burning houses as they went. It was during this raid that the only Protestant to die that night was shot in the Catholic Divis Street, leading many to conclude that he had been a member of the incendiarists.

In Divis Street, off the Falls Road, RUC personnel fired a number of bullets from one of their Browning machine-guns into the nearby flats and tower block. One of these bullets killed a 9-year-old Catholic boy while he lay in bed. Other shots from police weapons killed a local Catholic man who was serving in the British Army and happened to be home on leave. The Browning machine-guns used on that occasion by the RUC were and remain weapons of conventional warfare. These guns have a lethal range of approximately one mile with their large-calibre rounds giving them such devastating power that they are capable under certain circumstances of penetrating brickwork.

That any police force in the United Kingdom would be equipped with such a fearsome weapon was astonishing. That it would be used during civil disturbances in a built-up area could only be deemed irresponsible at best if those authorising its use knew of its capability. There is little doubt that RUC headquarters and personnel understood only too clearly what kind of damage a heavy-calibre Browning machine-gun could do when fired under such circumstances. They did, nevertheless, authorise its deployment and use.

Across the city, on 15 August, the scenes of bloodshed were repeated in the Catholic Ardoyne,[1] where RUC personnel charged into the district followed by a Unionist crowd, which burned down much of Hooker Street. During the incident, RUC men opened fire with submachine-guns, killing two men. Rioting continued the next day in Belfast, with the city experiencing the worst outbreak of violence in decades. In the Catholic Clonard area, Unionist incendiarists burnt down all of Bombay Street. During this attack, a 15-year-old member of the IRA was shot dead. In the Ardoyne area, another violent confrontation took place leading to the death by shooting of a Protestant man.

Over the course of the two nights, six people were shot dead in Belfast. Four of the victims were Catholic, all shot by the RUC, two of whom died in their homes. A huge number of houses were burned down. The impact of this was to lead to one of the largest displacements of people in Belfast since the 1920s. According to a report delivered later at the Scarman Tribunal, of the 1,820 families that fled their homes, 82.7 per cent were Catholic.[2] The same report calculated that over the period 5.3 per cent of all Catholics in the city were displaced, as compared to 0.4 per cent of the Protestant population.

While Belfast had clearly witnessed the worst of the violence, shooting incidents occurred in other parts of the Six Counties. Dungannon, Coalisland, Dungiven, Newry all reported shooting incidents with people being shot and wounded by either the RUC or the B Specials. The Catholic population might have been in a state of agitation and rebellion, but they were for the most part using stones and Molotov cocktails against a state deploying live ammunition and weapons of war in order to quell a demand for civil rights. Set against subsequent events in Northern Ireland, seven deaths and some streets burned out might not appear to have been a particularly significant happening. It would be impossible, however, to underestimate the impact of those August days and nights on the psychology of the Catholic population of Belfast and their reaction to them.

For many, it was a new and horrifying experience, but for others it was the third time that they had witnessed their homes burned by Unionist mobs.[3] In the years 1920–21, Belfast and its hinterland had experienced civil strife on a frightening scale when its Catholic population was subjected to intense and systematic attack.[4] The violence served two purposes: Belfast's Catholic population was cowed into accepting the new state, while they were also compelled to rely on the good behaviour of co-religionists elsewhere in the Six Counties. During July 1920 in Belfast, 11,000 Catholics (out of the city's population of about 93,000) were forcibly expelled from their jobs and 23,000 were driven from their homes. A military curfew declared on 30 August 1920 lasted until 1924. Although affecting all sections of the community in theory, this order did not apply to the thousands of A, B and C Specials who enjoyed unrestricted movement during the curfew when many of the house invasions and sectarian murders took place. As the local MP Joe Devlin said in Westminster after one such murder: 'If Catholics have no revolvers to protect themselves they are murdered. If they have revolvers, they are flogged and sentenced to death.'

Destructive civil disturbances again occurred, albeit on a lesser scale in the 1930s, when the same pattern of death and house burning took place.[5]

The pattern of violence in the 1920s and 1930s impacted ominously on the generation of 1969. The 1920s and 1930s were, after all, still within living memory in 1969; the victims of that onslaught were determined that they would not be left so vulnerable again. Their trauma was great and would inevitably find some form of tangible expression.

With events in Northern Ireland having reached crisis point, the newly elected prime minister of Northern Ireland, James Chichester Clarke, was summoned to London. He emerged from his meeting in Downing Street having conceded that the B Specials would be replaced by another force. Crucially, however, he was able to guarantee to his supporters that the constitutional arrangement whereby Northern Ireland was ruled by a Unionist majority would remain in place. The communiqué stated clearly in the first paragraph:

1) The United Kingdom Government re-affirm that nothing which has happened in recent weeks in Northern Ireland derogates from the clear pledges made by successive United Kingdom Governments that Northern Ireland should not cease to be a part of the United Kingdom without the consent of the people of Northern Ireland or from the provision in Section I of the Ireland Act 1949 that in no event will Northern Ireland or any part thereof cease to be part of the United Kingdom without the consent of the Parliament of Northern Ireland. The Border is not an issue.

Its second paragraph confirmed that the Unionist Party would remain firmly in control:

(2) The United Kingdom Government again affirm that responsibility for affairs in Northern Ireland is entirely a matter of domestic jurisdiction. The United Kingdom Government

will take full responsibility for asserting this principle in all international relationships.[6]

This was a decision of enormous importance. Northern Ireland was a dysfunctional political entity in which the ruling majority justified their undemocratic actions by adopting a nineteenth-century British Empire mentality. The Orange state treated Catholics as if they were inferior people. The Orange state could not change. It had to be ended or it would continue along its repressive sectarian path. When Britain failed to act decisively, it ensured that violence would erupt again.

4
Widespread Conflict Looms

Kevin had been a member of the IRA since the half-centenary celebration of the Easter Rising in 1966. His family was not untypical in Belfast of the period. His mother came from a staunchly Republican household, but two of his father's younger brothers had enlisted in the British Army while unemployed in England in the 1950s. In a strange way, his paternal uncles had a stronger influence on him than his mother's relatives, as the ex-service men's experience in England left them with a strong Labourite outlook, which they imparted to their nephew.

Kevin certainly accepted the basic IRA position on Partition and the Union, but his views on social justice and the working class were largely informed by the days he spent with his uncles. As a result, the new left-wing direction taken by the IRA in the aftermath of the 1956–62 campaign made a lot of sense to him and the Republican movement seemed to be the best vehicle available through which he could advance his political views. He had backed the organisation's decision to support the civil rights movement and had helped enforce the IRA policy of ensuring that no member broke ranks and used arms during the civil rights campaign. However, the events in August 1969 undermined his confidence in his own analysis of political progress, leaving him with conflicting emotions.

There was little doubt in his mind that making the IRA part of a popular people's struggle had been a correct strategic decision in the early 1960s. He was intellectually and emotionally of the left and did not subscribe to the hysterical anti-Protestantism that was then sweeping much of Catholic Belfast. Yet the blunt assault by the state's forces on his locality had shaken his faith in the line being advocated by the IRA leadership. The events of August had been a crucial watershed in his native city and his neighbours were not only demanding guns but appeared utterly determined to obtain them and to fight.

It seemed to him that the IRA leadership was wedded to a theoretical schema that made little allowance for developing reality on the ground in Northern Ireland. The civil rights era had aroused a latent anger and resentment among the Catholic community that was not going to be easily contained or assuaged. The IRA was correct in its commitment to the broad-based civil rights campaign, he felt, but had failed abysmally to gauge the consequences of a challenge to the Unionist regime. As a result, the IRA was under-prepared and poorly resourced for the state's onslaught and the subsequent loss of credibility among many working-class Catholics in Belfast.

The largely Dublin-based leadership had taken over in the aftermath of the failed 1956 campaign and had striven long and hard to restore morale and direction to a beaten and depleted organisation. They recognised the futility of depending on a spontaneous uprising motivated by sentimental patriotism. Being working-class men from poorer areas of the capital, they saw the merit in advice being offered by an articulate and persuasive group of Marxists who were advising the leadership. What Kevin now believed, though, was that the IRA leaders held a Dublin-focused outlook and viewed Belfast as a secondary theatre of operation – a serious misjudgement in the light of events.

In a normal political party, such a disastrous miscalculation would result in a change in leadership. The IRA was not, however, a normal political party nor did its leadership respond easily to pressure from the grass roots. Kevin worried that the fundamental change required in the movement's ruling structures was being frustrated by that same governing body, with the inevitable outcome that the organisation would split.

The events of 14 and 15 August shocked the Catholic population in Northern Ireland, but left those in Belfast particularly distraught and traumatised. Throughout the latter part of the nineteenth century, devastating assaults had been launched on Belfast's Catholic population on a number of occasions and especially whenever Irish home rule was being debated in Westminster. Again at the beginning of the twentieth century, during the crucial years of 1920 and 1921, hundreds were killed when the issue of independence for Ireland was on the British parliament's agenda.

So precarious was the position of Belfast's Catholic population considered to be that even 30 years after the creation of the northern state, the IRA had decided during its 1956–62 'Operation Harvest' campaign not to engage in any offensive actions in Belfast. Their decision appeared justified when Ian Paisley and his supporters provoked a major riot in the Divis Street area of the Falls Road by demanding the removal of an Irish tricolour flag from a Sinn Féin office window during an election campaign in 1964. The trepidation felt by many Belfast Catholics meant that while they also experienced discrimination as practised across the rest of Northern Ireland, they had hesitated to organise civil rights demonstrations in the city.

When Northern Ireland's Prime Minister met with British Prime Minister Harold Wilson in Downing Street in August 1969 on the Tuesday after the Belfast burnings and shootings, there were mixed feelings in the Catholic community. Two questions dominated their thinking: would the British government finally recognise its responsibility for the Six-County state that was constitutionally an integral part of the United Kingdom, and do something about the profoundly corrupt governing authority in Stormont? Their second question, and by no means of lesser urgency, was to ask how they could ensure their own security?

Long experience of the violent nature of the Northern Irish state gave them little reason to believe that the system would easily change. And while they welcomed the breathing space offered by the arrival of the British Army, they were reluctant to place absolute faith in the armed forces of a government that had turned a blind eye to the situation in Northern Ireland for decades. They wanted protection that they could rely on under all circumstances, and that meant getting weapons into their own hands. For many years, there had been an assumption in working-class Catholic districts of Belfast that in the event of major civil strife, the IRA would have the capacity to arm and defend them in their own city. Events did not justify their expectations. The attacks of August 1969 had caught the IRA poorly prepared; subsequently, the organisation was overstretched during the burning and shooting.

After the failure of its 1956–62 'Operation Harvest' campaign, Republican leaders had taken a conscious decision to move away from simple militarism and engage in a broader course of action. The largely Dublin-based leadership understood the hopelessness of trying to build a broad, island-wide movement on purely anti-Partitionist policies and had concentrated on developing a new and distinctly left-wing profile and politics. It was this decision that led them to support the campaigns for social justice that were eventually to crystallize into the civil rights movement. They were rightly concerned that any breach of internal IRA discipline would have had very damaging consequences for both the Republican and the civil rights movements. Understandably, with so much emphasis on peaceful agitation, they were not inclined to concentrate resources on buying arms nor, with so much riding on their participation in a new and successful popular wave of agitation, were they prepared to risk sending extra weapons into volatile areas. However reasonable their assessment was from a political point of view, it made no sense at all to many people on the ground in Belfast. One of the first lessons outsiders learn about the political geography of Belfast is that it is not a cleanly separated entity such as old East and West Berlin or the divided Cypriot city of Nicosia. Working-class Belfast is a patchwork of divided districts where often only local residents can tell where one begins and the other ends. Moreover, many Belfast Catholic areas such as the Markets, Short Strand and Ardoyne were to all intents and purposes surrounded by what the inhabitants viewed as hostile communities.

This balance was unstable at best and required little to disturb the precarious equilibrium. The clear perception in Catholic Belfast in August 1969 was that the state, in the form of its armed police supported by B Specials and abetted by armed civilians, had launched a pogrom on their districts. Many now claim that but for the action of a small number of ageing and disaffected IRA men who had disregarded their leadership's orders and held on to a small number of weapons, the Catholic population might well have been driven from the city. In reality, there is more to the story than this. Undoubtedly, the intervention of Republican veterans had a major impact and prevented Unionist gangs from inflicting significantly higher casualties. There is compelling evidence, however, that the IRA, although under-resourced, played a significant part in this defensive operation in spite of the fact that the Republican movement did not see itself as a Catholic defence organisation. It is also the case that had the RUC acted in concert with B Special platoons and UVF units to butcher the city's Catholic population, many more would have been shot dead at that time.

The purpose of the Unionist attack had a more limited, albeit calculated and brutal objective. Launching a vicious punitive assault on Catholic Belfast was intended to intimidate that community and to send a clear warning signal to their co-religionists in other areas of the Six Counties. There was a certain cynical logic to this strategy. Unionism knew London was reluctant to interfere with or irritate its ally in Northern Ireland. A brief bout of violence with modest casualties would be tolerated by Westminster. Mass slaughter would have entirely different consequences and would undoubtedly have led to intervention on some scale by the sovereign parliament.

Without doubt, the period following those August days had a more telling impact on the next 40 years than almost any other phase in the time to come. The Catholic population of Northern Ireland listened anxiously to reports of the meeting in Downing Street between the British and Northern Ireland prime ministers on the Tuesday after 14 and 15 August. They were not reassured by what they heard.

Ten days later, British Home Secretary James Callaghan visited Northern Ireland in order to investigate and advise. He received a joyous reception in the Bogside where he was cheered heartily by locals who saw him as a liberator. He would not have been so rapturously welcomed had the people known that his commitment to change was superficial and confined to greater British state interests.

Before leaving Northern Ireland, he issued a communiqué. Again, it began by reiterating London's commitment to Unionism and to the Stormont parliament and only thereafter mentioned reform. On this occasion, there was a little more meat on the bones, but the first clause carried an ominous message that reform was to be partial:

Par 8.
(i) Equality of opportunity for all in public employment, without regard to religious or political considerations.[1]

Equality for all in public employment was, undoubtedly, a progressive step but it would only address part of the problem. In 1969, Belfast shipyard Harland & Wolff employed 7.5 per cent of Northern Ireland's industrial workforce directly and a further 10 per cent indirectly, only a few of whom were Catholic.[2] Moreover, this private company was kept afloat by government subsidy and MoD orders. After all that had happened, the British government was still not willing to go to the heart of the problem and take decisive action against the Stormont government and its Unionist party. In his memoirs, Callaghan has made it clear that he insisted then that any settlement had to come within that very same Stormont framework. In other words, similar to the old Henry Ford formula of giving the public any colour of car it wanted so long as it was black, Northern Ireland could have any settlement going, so long as it meant retention of the Unionist regime in Belfast.

London's reluctance to make root-and-branch change to a patently flawed system appeared inexplicable to many in the Catholic community. Not so, though, to some of the older Republicans who were now finding an audience for the first time in several years. The British government, they argued, had little interest and no sympathy for the cause of Northern Irish Unionism, Ulster Protestantism, or the Orange Order. Nor for that matter was London hostile to Catholicism or even Irish Nationalism *per se*. What Britain *did* have, Republicans told their communities, was what a former British Prime Minister Lord Palmerton had once said: no permanent allies, only permanent interests.

Britain's interest in Ireland lay not in promoting Protestantism but in a very calculated determination to protect its western flank by maintaining a physical military presence in Ireland. With the Second World War having ended a mere 25 years previously, an overwhelming majority of cabinet members, senior civil servants and top flight military personnel had very clear memories of the strategic importance of Ireland in the war with Germany.[3] Nor were they likely to change their mind on this matter being, as they were then, in the midst of an ongoing cold war with the Soviet Union. Moreover, this was six years after the Cuban missile crisis, and Britain's political and military establishment was not blind to the possible risk posed by small, potentially volatile islands.

Republicans argued that in spite of what the government might say in public, Britain had an overwhelming strategic interest in remaining in Ireland and moreover, that its NATO allies viewed Northern Ireland as a strategic asset that had to be kept within the Western alliance.[4] This viewpoint was to find an echo two decades later when Britain's government wished to enter into negotiations with the IRA. The then Secretary of State for Northern Ireland Peter Brooke issued a statement on 9 November 1990 saying that Britain had 'no selfish strategic or economic interest' in Northern Ireland.[5] Significantly, Brooke refused to accede to Republican requests and insert a significantly important comma between the words 'selfish' and 'strategic', indicating that what ever about the morality of Her Majesty's Government's interests, the British state most certainly did retain a strategic interest in Ireland.

In the post-colonial world of the second half of the twentieth century, London would have found it almost impossible to justify remaining in any part of Ireland had it not been for Northern Ireland Unionists' willingness to support the Union. In order to maintain its strategic base in Ireland, Britain therefore had to ensure that it did not alienate Unionism. Britain faced a dilemma of its own making. Abolishing a corrupt administration and granting thoroughgoing civil rights could upset Unionism to such an extent that Unionists might have been tempted to follow Ian Smith's lead in Rhodesia and make a unilateral declaration of independence (UDI). This was not an entirely fanciful fear in light of the position, favouring an independent Ulster, adopted a few years later by former Stormont cabinet minister Bill Craig and his Vanguard Party, prominent among whose ranks were two former leaders of the Ulster Unionist Party, David Trimble and Reg Empey. The alternative was to soft pedal on reform and risk alienating the less strategically important, albeit more deserving, Catholic population. Cynical *raison d'état* would lead Britain to opt for the former. There is more than Irish Republican conspiracy-making in this account. Noted historian Paul Bew, in an article in *History Ireland*, quoted a British civil service source as saying that Home Secretary James

Callaghan was recommending to the cabinet a 'talk Green, act Orange' strategy in 1969.[6]

It was for this reason and not because Britain was sympathetic to Unionism, much less that successive British government and their intelligence agencies were unaware of what was happening in Northern Ireland, that nothing was done to improve conditions. While no questions were being asked on the world stage, as was the case prior to October 1968, British governments were content with the status quo in Northern Ireland. The fear in Catholic communities was that as soon as attention moved away from the region, British governments would again turn a blind eye to the situation. It was a bleak assessment, but one that began to make a lot more sense to younger Catholics as the year wore on. With the immediate concern for most being their safety, the sequence of disappointing initiatives from London led them to consider the need to provide for their own defence. They wanted guns and they started to search for them.

For decades, the only group within the Northern Irish Catholic community conversant with the use of clandestine arms was the IRA. When that organisation failed to provide adequate protection for these areas, small groups began to form local citizens' defence organisations and send their representatives out to procure arms. This fact was recognised by the British government at the time. In seeking to dispel the myth that the events of August 1969 were the result of an armed Republican uprising, the Scarman Report said:

> Undoubtedly there was an IRA influence at work in the Derry Citizens Defence Association (DCDA) in Londonderry, in the Ardoyne and Falls Road areas of Belfast, and in Newry. But they did not start the riots, or plan them: indeed, the evidence is that the IRA was taken by surprise and did less than many of their supporters thought they should have done.[7]

> 2.7 There is evidence, however, of preparations for 'defence' by the DCDA in Londonderry, a body that certainly included some IRA members. But, as our review of the Londonderry disturbances reveals, the basic pattern was reaction to, and not the initiating of, the course of events. The DCDA did not organise the disturbances: but it made quite elaborate preparations to keep the police out of the Bogside, if necessary by violence, in the event of disturbances erupting on the streets. The true difference

between the IRA in Belfast and the DCDA in Londonderry was that the DCDA was ready, while the IRA was not.[8]

However influential the defence committees were in the days after August 1969, they were a fragmented collection of localised groups. There was an objective need for coordination, which was to emerge in a very traditional form. With fear and tension simmering in Belfast, a group of veteran IRA men and their young supporters decided to confront the local leadership of their movement in order to ensure that the events of August would not be repeated. Some of the older men had had misgivings since the mid-1960s. Many of them were politically conservative; they feared the influence of communism, were suspicious of anything resembling conventional politics and resented generational change of leadership. However, without the events of August 1969, they would have had little impact on militant Republican politics. It was the presence of the young men who had grown disenchanted with what they viewed as a national leadership that had lost touch with the reality of events in the North that made this schism so important. Unable to reconcile their differences, the two groups split in late 1969. The smaller breakaway group took what they expected to be a temporary title of the 'Provisional' IRA. With few supporters outside of Belfast, the new organisation might well have withered away as just another Republican splinter group. Circumstances were to ensure that in time it became the IRA.

Fearing a fresh attack, two different groups from within the Catholic community began to search for arms. One group was composed of the old Republicans in the newly formed Provisional IRA who were no longer restricted by a cautious headquarters' policy. The other group was something new: a disparate constituency of working-class Catholics who had little previous contact with Republicanism. So much had changed in the post-August 1969 climate, that while on one level the two groups were competing for the same resource, there was little friction between them.

South of the Border, televised scenes of ongoing police brutality and the behaviour of Paisleyite mobs had generated a heightened sympathy for victims of the troubles. Moreover, in this atmosphere, support for 'the people in the North' came from Southerners of different political backgrounds. For a brief period, old animosities that had developed after the Irish Civil War were set aside as a wave of solidarity swept the Republic of Ireland. With feelings running so high in the South, Nationalists and Republicans from different parts of Northern Ireland began to search out any contact they could find in the Republic and ask for guns. The response was astonishing, as weapons of varying ages and quality, sporting guns as well as military weapons, were unearthed from the most unlikely of places and sent north.

Veteran Republicans in the Provisional IRA drew on old contacts to conduct a concerted trawl for guns. The IRA had not been a large or successful organisation since the 1920s, but its many attempts at insurrection had created an extensive old boys' network of former prisoners and retired IRA activists. Men who had seemingly long given up the militant dreams of their youth and settled into the mundane normality of life found old comrades they hadn't seen in decades, quietly visiting and asking for a 'favour'. In those incredible heady days, Fianna Fáil members and even Fine Gael supporters donated weapons, but by far the greatest number were guns held surreptitiously by old and retired IRA men who over the years had quietly hidden away firearms without the sanction or knowledge of the movement.

Among this grand old arsenal were Thompson guns from the 1920s, Lee Enfields from the earliest to latest models and a range of pistols that could only be matched by a well-stocked museum of antique firearms. Less well-connected groups found that, for the most part, they were only able to acquire sporting weapons. Nevertheless, these guns were accepted with gratitude and taken back to areas traumatised by the troubles.

In spite of this, the balance and quality of arms remained firmly in favour of the Unionist community, which had over 100,000 legally held firearms excluding those held by the RUC. The Catholic population's trawl for guns had garnered only a fraction of that number and most of what had been collected was, for the most part, unlicensed. The Catholic community's arsenal had to be concealed and therefore was not as easily accessed in an emergency and was always subject to confiscation. Nevertheless, confidence was returning to Catholic areas. Barricades were in place, and with even a small arsenal, the sense of total defencelessness gradually dissipated.

Although the reforms introduced by the Wilson government did not threaten the constitutional position of Northern Ireland, they proved too much for many Unionists who had grown accustomed to uncontested dominance. Ian Paisley continued to raise the political temperature and made the implementation of reform measures difficult for the Stormont government. As was his style, he regarded even the mildest of measures as a betrayal of the Protestant cause. Some of his supporters were willing to take direct and violent action to prevent reform. One such person, intent on resisting any concessions, was a quarry foreman from County Down, Tommy McDowell, a Free Presbyterian, a member of Paisley's Ulster Protestant Volunteers (UPV) and a member of the Ulster Volunteer Force (UVF). On 19 October 1969, he and a number of other UVF members travelled to Ballyshannon, Co. Donegal in the Republic and attempted to dynamite an electricity power station. Their mission went disastrously wrong when McDowell accidentally electrocuted himself and was abandoned by his colleagues. Locals were alerted by his scream and took him to the local hospital where, although unconscious, he lived for a further 24 hours. During his time in hospital, he was visited by a Free Presbyterian minister. A large number of Free Presbyterians and known members of Paisley's many organisations attended his funeral in Kilkeel, Co. Down.[9] Among those present were members of the Ulster Protestant Volunteers and the Ulster Constitution Defence Committee. After months of official statements accusing the IRA of responsibility for the bombing campaign, it was clear that Unionists had been responsible.

As Scarman explicitly made clear:

> On the last day of March and during the month of April there occurred a number of explosions at electricity and water installations in the Province. We are satisfied that, though the perpetrators of these outrages cannot, with one exception, be identified, they were the work of Protestant extremists who were anxious to undermine confidence in the government of Captain O'Neill. At the time it was widely thought that the explosions were the work of the IRA, though it is quite clear now that they were not.[10]

The crisis continued to escalate during the first months of 1970 as a power struggle intensified within the Unionist community. The leader of the official Unionist Party and prime minister of Northern Ireland, James Chichester-Clarke, was accused by Paisley and his supporters of having allowed London to dismantle the B Specials,[11] disarm the RUC and introduce a raft of concessions, including permitting Catholics to retain barricades erected in the aftermath of the August violence. Chichester-Clarke found his position further undermined when members of his own party also attacked him opportunistically, allegedly for the same weaknesses.

Grass-roots Unionist feeling was hardening and this became obvious when, on 16 April 1970, Ian Paisley and his colleague William Beattie defeated Unionist Party candidates in by-elections for two Stormont government seats. A further election was held on 18 June 1970 and this time it was a British general election that not only saw Ian Paisley elected to Westminster but the Tories returned to government in Britain. With Ted Heath and his Conservative Party ruling Britain, Unionists believed that they would have a more sympathetic hearing from London.

As the Orange marching season was drawing to its July climax, the loyal orders insisted on marching through sensitive areas of Belfast. With the events of August 1969 still fresh in Catholic minds, it was inevitable this would re-ignite civil disturbance. As rioting intensified, gunmen began to attack the Short Strand, a small and isolated Catholic district in East Belfast, seemingly with the intention of burning down a local church. It appeared that the drums were beating out the same old message of 'Croppy lie down'.[12] Republicanism had always been built upon the need to address political, social and economic repression and a new wave of Republicanism was now to emerge in Northern Ireland.

5
An Emerging Force

They had only returned to Belfast a matter of weeks after they had married in England, when her brother asked them to do a wee job for the movement. Bernie and Tony did not look, at first glance, to be typical Falls Road residents. Having spent their student years in the heady atmosphere of 1960s London, they had picked up an outlook that seemed to match their hippy lifestyle. Although both had graduated, they were dedicated followers of the contemporary popular music scene and while in Britain, had travelled to as many concerts and festivals as they could afford. To indulge their passion, they had bought an old camper van that allowed them to travel extensively and, with a few friends to share the costs, relatively cheaply.

It was the camper van that first drew them to the attention of the IRA. Bernie's brother and his mates realised that the vehicle and its owners would provide them with a fine means of transporting a consignment of guns and ammunition into Belfast. The van had English licence plates, was painted in the hippy style of the time and Tony even had a London-issued driving licence. In time, such a cover would not mislead British Army or RUC patrols, but in the early 1970s, the perception of IRA operatives were stereotyped in the minds of the state's forces as grim-looking men in slouch hats. The idea that hippies from England might be working for the IRA never occurred to them.

The IRA had, nevertheless, to persuade the newly wedded couple to risk a substantial slice of their future on a gun-running operation and that was not an easy task. Fun-loving hippies with very real career prospects might be laid back and relaxed about social mores but could be quite practical when asked to jeopardise their freedom. Nevertheless, when Bernie's brother eventually agreed to accompany them on the journey and assured them that, in the event of their being intercepted, he would accept full responsibility for the arms cache in the vehicle, the pair acquiesced.

The plan was simple. The three would make a trip south of the border starting off the day before a bank holiday weekend and spend time in the Republic before meeting their contact. With the weapons concealed on board, they would return north on the bank holiday Monday, ostensibly to attend a rock concert in Belfast that night.

Bernie and Tony were, nevertheless, deeply apprehensive as they crossed into the Republic and were unable to take any pleasure from their days parked in a camping site close to a small seaside town a few miles north of Sligo. Every time they saw a couple of tough-looking men, they imagined that they were about to meet their contact and expected to see guns and bullets being piled high on the camper van's table. Only Bernie's brother seemed able to enjoy the break, drinking in the evenings and flirting with every girl who glanced in his direction. And nothing happened.

On the Monday morning, Bernie's brother suggested that they move on, going home via Fermanagh where they could enjoy the scenery. Bernie and Tony grew tense. So this was how it would happen. They would collect materiel somewhere near the lakes and somebody would surely see them. They were so nervous that when Bernie's brother told them to stop for lunch at a small hotel in Co. Leitrim, they could barely eat. The tension grew as they crossed over the border and drove through Fermanagh. They drove on, joining the motorway to Belfast outside Dungannon and still no rendezvous. With Bernie's brother sleeping in the back of the camper, she leaned over to Tony and explained that the IRA had apparently organised a dry run to test the pair. It seemed obvious and their spirits lifted immediately.

As they drew closer to Belfast, Bernie's brother woke and asked them to take the airport road. It would be easier to get into Belfast that way, he said. A few miles further on they drove into a checkpoint manned by the locally recruited Ulster Defence Regiment. Tony and Bernie were relaxed – they had nothing to worry about. The UDR patrol asked where they were going and after a casual glance into the van, waved them through.

About five miles from the outskirts of Belfast, Bernie's brother said he needed to relieve himself and asked Tony to pull the vehicle over to a nearby gateway into a field. As the camper parked, a car that had been following stopped and two men got out. As their car moved off, they walked towards the camper and quickly opened the doors. Using screwdrivers, they prised open the door panels and took out several parcels.

'Two long and one small in each door', Bernie's brother called to the men. In seconds, they had the materiel removed and the panels replaced. The two men carried the materiel over the gate and behind the hedge. Bernie's brother advised Tony to move on and they travelled the last few miles into Belfast in complete silence. They parked outside Bernie's parents' house and after a long pause Tony asked, 'How did that happen?' 'You're better not knowing,' Bernie's brother replied.

By 1970, Belfast's Catholic working class had acquired a mixed view of the British Army over the decades since Partition. Older and more traditional Republicans still viewed them as an army of occupation and retained a measure of hostility towards Britain's armed forces that no amount of reform would soften. Their views were not, however, a majority opinion by the mid-1960s. British regular soldiers had not been actively deployed in Northern Ireland against any section of the local population since the 1920s. Folk memories remained but the Second World War had provided for a large influx of troops who were not aggressive in the local context and whose presence brought a certain degree of prosperity to the city at the time. Equally important in the post-war years was the fact that due to high levels of unemployment among Catholics in Belfast, a significant number had served in the British Army during the 1950s and 1960s. In fact, one of the first groups to organise for the defence of Catholic Belfast was the Catholic Ex-Service Men's Association, which was composed of former members of Britain's armed forces. When the British Army was deployed in 1969, the welcome was not as universally warm and all-embracing as London's media portrayed it at the time. There was, nevertheless, a willingness to be persuaded that on this occasion the English could behave even-handedly and with impartiality in Ireland.

The conflict in the Short Strand on Saturday, 27 June 1970, was a turning-point for more parties than the nascent Provisional IRA. It was to set in motion a chain of events that brought an end to the brief period of détente between Belfast's Catholic population and the British government and its army. The gun battle at St Matthew's Catholic church (and gun battles elsewhere in the city at that time) and its immediate aftermath was to restore Britain to its more customary role in Irish history, as far as most non-Unionists were concerned.

Unionism reacted to the gun battles with apoplexy. Its spokespersons did not ask why a group of armed Protestants had launched an offensive against a Catholic church and condemn them for doing so. Instead, they demanded to know why so many guns were in Catholic hands and clamoured that these guns be removed. There was more than a whiff of hysteria about these calls and for many Catholic people it was a voice that echoed back across many decades, if not centuries. The Orange Order had been founded in rural mid-Ulster at the end of the eighteenth century to combat the influence of the democratic United Irishmen movement. Its earliest activities were to carry out a sustained campaign of intimidation against local Catholics through use of a (by then obsolete) section of the Penal Laws that forbade them to own firearms. On the pretext of searching for weapons, Orange gangs would invade Catholic homes, wrecking them and terrifying families in the process. Although these raids gradually declined as the nineteenth century progressed, ongoing isolated acts of 'disciplinary violence' continued to be visited upon Ulster's Catholics more or less regularly.

The fact that the expected result had not been delivered in the Short Strand and elsewhere in the city caused huge concern among Unionists. With a newly elected Conservative government in London, Unionists immediately demanded that the British Army, which had failed to intervene while the attack on the Short Strand was happening, be immediately dispatched to search for Catholic weapons. On Friday, 3 July 1970, the British government responded to Unionist demands for action to disarm Catholics in Belfast and ordered its army to carry out house searches in the Falls Road area of Belfast. The seal-and-search operation lasted until the Sunday morning, during which time a significant number of arms were discovered and confiscated. However, the British Army operation provoked stiff resistance from local Official IRA units. During the 34-hour curfew and search, enormous damage was done to residents' homes and possessions.

Figure 5.1 Young man arrested by the British Army in Coalisland, County Tyrone, 1971 (© John McGuffin).

When the curfew ended, the British Army had killed four civilians. The Catholic population of Belfast in particular and Northern Ireland in general had been thoroughly alienated by the events of that weekend. Any doubts they had about the nature of the government in London were dispelled as they watched William Long and John Brooke, two Unionist government ministers, being driven through the area in British Army vehicles.

When the British Army had finished, there was no parallel follow-up to deprive Unionist areas of weapons – not that removing illegally held weapons from the Protestant community would have made any significant difference to the situation. Over 100,000 firearms were licensed in Northern Ireland, and the vast majority of these were already in Unionist hands. What the unilateral action did appear to indicate was that Unionism had not accepted the need for change and that Britain was not going to compel them to do so. Moreover, any hope of assistance from Dublin was wishful thinking. While the Falls Road curfew was not the only incident that alienated the Catholic population, it was nevertheless the culmination of a series of events that altered their evaluation of the situation. The great fear in Catholic communities across Northern Ireland, felt most sharply in Belfast, was that of being outnumbered and abandoned in a dangerous, hostile location. The events of August 1969 had reinforced old fears and re-ignited memories of the worst aspects of their status in the Unionist state.

And as the British government was being pressurised to disarm the Catholic population, another typically tragic Belfast action was taking place on the Sunday after the Short Strand gun battle. Around five hundred Catholic workers at the Harland and Wolff shipyard were forced by Protestant employees to leave their work. Most of the Catholic workers were unable to return and lost their jobs. There was a clear gulf between the British Army's brutal handling of the Falls Road siege and its apparent inability to protect workers in the shipyard. This discrepancy did not go unnoticed.

When the Dublin government under Jack Lynch arrested two cabinet ministers in May 1970 for allegedly attempting to import arms to the North, there was an ominous feeling of *déjà vu*. The South had gone its own way in 1922 and while its politicians had been happy to use Partition as a vote-catcher at elections, Dublin offered no material help during the intervening years. So when Jack Lynch arrested his ministers for gun-running, it mattered little whether there was any truth in the allegations or not. As far as many northern Catholics were concerned, he had prevented arms from reaching them and deepened their conviction that they had to look to their own resources for protection and defence, or once again submit to the Orange state.

The perception that forces were working to isolate the Catholic minority was given added credence shortly thereafter when civil rights leader and Member of Parliament Bernadette Devlin was arrested for helping organise resistance in Derry during August 1969. Her arrest took place on 26 June and was in stark contrast to the lack of action taken against leading Unionist politicians who had participated in the conflict. Not only did her arrest reinforce an impression that the government was not impartial but that it also had a plan to settle Northern Ireland by siding with the Stormont regime and its supporters in order to crush the campaign for social justice and democracy.

After all the bright hopes of a peaceful and democratic civil rights movement winning the day for democracy by the self-evident justice of its case, a different perspective began to emerge in many quarters. There was a prevailing argument in working-class Catholic districts that the old IRA men had been right all along and those who wished to see change needed to get in contact with them as soon as possible. Not only was uncompromising Republican rhetoric looking more valid but in practice it seemed that its advocates alone had a useful template of action that appeared to meet the demands of the situation. They had a readymade plan matching the temper of the time.

Insurrection is not, as the Russian master of revolution Vladimir Lenin has pointed out, a game to be played by amateurs. Learning how to fire a sub-machine gun or prime an explosive device is relatively easy. How to do so from within the underground and thereafter to coordinate that activity among many hundreds of people is an art that does not come to groups or individuals overnight. Nor can guidelines for how to do so be found in a book. Over many decades, the IRA had acquired a certain experience in the arts of guerrilla war, insurrectionary activity and operating within a clandestine underground. The organisation was by no means infallible nor was it beyond adopting futile tactics, or recruiting incompetent commanders and followers. Nor had it succeeded in removing Partition. In contrast, however, to youthful intellectuals and prevaricating middle-class Nationalists, they had a clear advantage. They were in no doubt as to what had to be done and how they should go about doing it.

After a century of clandestine activity, Irish Republicans had a multi-layered network of supporters and activists. It was not as large as they would have liked but it existed and following each incident in the Six Counties during the crucial years at the end of the 1960s and early 1970s, the network grew. Old activists joined with ageing comrades who had been persuaded to come out of retirement and together with a young generation, a new movement began to develop.

The IRA's 'old boys' network extended over the country. Often these men were no longer actively involved with the movement and therefore were usually not under imminent threat of arrest. They were, however, often well known in their communities and districts as men with Republican connections and thus provided a readily available point of first contact for those wishing to join the organisation. In those chaotic days, no other group had its 'stall' so well set out to make initial contact with the angry young men manifesting the fear and outrage of their communities.

Those groups who did have a public presence and who might have considered the need to organise armed resistance had little knowledge of the means and techniques of doing so, the first requisite of which is to train the personnel volunteering for action. The IRA, with its long years of experience and having emerged less than ten years previously from its 'Operation Harvest' campaign, was able to establish and maintain training camps south of the Border. To the ingénue, it might seem a relatively simple task to locate a quiet rural setting in which to train armed men, but in practise it can prove surprisingly difficult to find a spot where even a few local people are not prepared to keep the authorities informed.

An underground army needs weapons; while the average reader of the popular press believes that guns and explosives can be bought and smuggled into a small island such as Ireland with ease, those who try soon learn that it is never as straightforward as they believe. Wherever guns are available for purchase, the authorities are invariably determined to monitor their distribution and sale. It is in their own very real interest to know who has arms and no ruling authority can take the risk of being unaware of a potential armed threat, no matter how small. All states, therefore, ensure that they are kept informed when even a relatively small amount of weapons with military capacity is being bought.

If a country were friendly with Britain, as was the US for example, they would endeavour to intercept the shipment and inform the British government where possible. If the country had a difficult relationship with Britain, as the Soviet bloc did, they were even more careful about upsetting sensitivities. Even had the Soviets viewed the IRA as being within their own ideological camp (and they did not), they had to carefully weigh the benefits between having the IRA as a friend, or making an enemy of Britain and its allies. Therefore, the few states that did offer support to Irish insurgents had to be prepared to pay a stiff price doing so.

In spite of such difficulties, an insurrectionary movement must have access to a basic arsenal in the first place and thereafter have the ability to activate long-standing and well-placed networks of people capable of accessing weapons in quantity and shipping them back to base. The capability to do so requires the use of carefully acquired and cultivated contacts in the various fields of arms sales and transatlantic transport. No organisation acquires that type of expertise and range of contacts overnight. In those crucial days of 1970, the Provisional IRA, with people in the US who had been sending arms to Irish Republicans from as far back as the 1920s, was able to deliver what people believed they needed: guns and ammunition.

Other elements of insurrectionary warfare are still more difficult to acquire in a hurry. Structures and tactics and rules are as important for an underground army as they are for a regular military machine. The difference is that without a barracks and parade ground, discipline and coherence must be implemented in a manner that suits the time and the place and the culture of the insurgents. Moreover, when men volunteer their services and can leave whenever they wish (as IRA members can), the nature of command is qualitatively different from that of a regular army. The IRA has a tradition and a culture of managing men that had evolved over long years. While their system was far from perfect, it had the enormous advantage of already being in place, was at least workable and was widely understood as carrying the stamp of approval granted by time and history.

And it was this stamp of time that enormously accelerated the pace at which the Provisional IRA was able to gain control of an insurrectionary situation. When others retreated, armed Republicans moved forward with certainty. If they had not worked out a comprehensive strategy (and they had not), they still appeared to act with assuredness and certainty. While others advocating reform were trying to gauge whether to appeal to Britain or attempt to pressurise the London government from without, the Provisional IRA simply said that they intended to arm and fight. As Britain behaved more brutally, it appeared to many that the Provisional IRA option alone matched the situation.

In time, they would opt for an uncompromising stance, demanding a complete British withdrawal from Ireland and saying that they would replace both states with a 32-county socialist republic. No matter how difficult or even impossible it might appear, there was a degree of logic to the position. Without Britain, Stormont would collapse and in a new dispensation, Unionists would have to negotiate as equals. Objectively, it had its flaws in practice, but it was simple and positive and in light of their experience, made more sense to a lot of working-class Catholics than asking Unionism to reform itself or the Tory government to act progressively.

6
Training People for Insurrection?

'A wise volunteer is prepared for each and every eventuality,' the veteran training officer (TO) told his charges, 'and bringing pyjamas and a dressing gown to my training camp shows that this volunteer is clearly prepared for each and every conceivable eventuality, no matter how remote that possibility might be.'

The team of IRA recruits were standing in the backyard of a deserted and remote farmhouse 'somewhere in the southern part of Ireland'. It was after dark before they were set down on a quiet roadside and led by scouts over a mile-long muddy lane to their training ground. In spite of the cold drizzle of a mid-winter night, the group was told to fall in for parade and instruction. All baggage was examined as a security precaution to ensure that an enemy agent hadn't attempted to smuggle in recording, photographic, or broadcasting equipment (or, almost as subversive in the old training officer's mind, pornography or whisky). It was during this exercise that the contents of Kieran's suitcase were exposed to view.

More knowing recruits had brought cigarettes and chocolate, but not Kieran. He was unprepared for the rigours of life in one of this old man's camps. The IRA did not provide conventional bedding – sleeping bags were laid out on straw in the barn. Nor did anyone need a dressing gown to visit the bathroom – an al fresco arrangement at the rear of the hayshed. A toothbrush was handy although shaving on site was optional. And just when a sensitive soul thought he had experienced the worst the IRA could devise for him, the TO arranged an evening meal of porridge and Calvita cheese sandwiches. It was the evening meal because it was evening. It was also the morning meal and the mid-day meal and the afternoon meal and any other meal that the IRA cared to cook because there was nothing else to eat on the camp except porridge and cheese sandwiches.

After an uncomfortable night's sleep and an appallingly unappetising breakfast, Kieran was contemplating the damage that the TO's latest manoeuvre might have on his hernia if he were asked to try it. What made the whole thing worse from Kieran's point of view was that he could not begin to imagine the circumstances that might have him moving forward on his hunkers, carrying a Lee Enfield rifle with a penny balanced on its foresight blades.

Yet his turn came and worse, he had to operate the rifle bolt while performing the exercise. Kieran stumbled and fell forward, dropping his weapon – an unforgivable error. Kieran pitched backwards onto his buttocks, holding on to his weapon but almost stuck the TO with the gun's barrel. Kieran was eventually excused the drill – the only man on the camp to win such a concession.

Kieran remained a member of the IRA but never became a member of one of its basic operational squads, which were known within the organisation as Active Service Units, or more commonly referred to as ASUs. It had taken him some time in fact to recover from his experience with the TO and his only experience of handling a gun was during the spell on what he always recalled as 'that detestable training ground'. Nevertheless, his work as an organiser of back-up for the organisation in his locality was to prove crucial for years afterwards. He knew the area he lived in and its people. He could access safe houses and transport and as a shrewd observer of the opposition and its stratagems, he could ensure that peripatetic ASUs were safe in his district. Safe that was until GHQ started sending its agents to visit him and his network of supporters, because somewhere among the senior officers was an agent of the Crown.

With the involvement by state agents in the onslaught of August 1969, most Northern Irish Catholics took seriously the threat of an intense and systematic offensive by supporters of the Stormont regime. Before long, the Provisional IRA, which was willing to contemplate almost any scenario, was offering to train the entire Catholic population in the use of arms. In its earliest days, the Provisional IRA developed most rapidly as an organ of defence and as a reaction against physical violence carried out by the state and its supporters. For approximately three years after its formation, the organisation offered training in the use of arms to local defence committees and groups of individuals without asking them to commit to joining the IRA. Many hundreds of men (and not a few women) from Catholic districts crossed into the Republic and travelled to IRA-run training camps in order to receive instruction in the use of firearms.

The service provided was not purely altruistic. Older Republicans knew the value of drawing large numbers into their zone of influence and identifying people who might prove valuable to them at a later stage. The breadth and depth of this engagement with a great mass of the Catholic community impacted on the movement as it sought to keep on board people who were not necessarily dedicated to more traditional Republican goals. During this period, the Provisional IRA's outlook was an odd mixture of traditional military authoritarianism coupled with an acknowledgement of the need to win a measure of popular approval. Two factors forced the Provisional leadership to adopt this pragmatic attitude. For a time after its formation, the movement was not sufficiently confident of its own capacity to resist assault on Nationalist areas and therefore welcomed help from almost all quarters without making overly onerous demands on its assistants. The second factor encouraging the Provisional IRA to keep its door open to as many as possible was the struggle for supremacy in Catholic communities with the rival Official IRA from which it had split.

Running secret training camps, with a large turnover of people, usually poses major issues of security for those charged with ensuring that the centres remain operational but undetected. Each and every attendee is a potential intelligence leak, so the need to move participants into a location without them knowing exactly where they were, was important and required experience that the IRA had. Assembling a number of people in a quiet rural setting without making their presence obvious or known also required skills not commonly found among the general public in peacetime. And even when people learn these skills, they still need local knowledge of geography and family loyalties and a trust that only comes after years spent serving a common cause. It takes decades to build networks of sympathetic local people and in this respect the veteran Provisional IRA men had a head start over all others, with the exception of their rivals in the Official IRA.

Induction into the IRA typically went through a number of phases. Initially, a member of middle-ranking seniority would meet a new applicant, preferably someone not known personally to the candidate, which lessened the risk of a rejected candidate knowing the recruiting officer's identity. Pressure of events sometimes made this precaution impossible, with occasional damaging consequences for the organisation.

For those applicants who were accepted, the movement would arrange training. Initially, this often involved no more than a series of discussions of varying intensity with a middle-aged veteran who would outline the customs and practices of the IRA and offer advice on how to avoid detection and, failing that, how to cope with surveillance and interrogation. They would also send their charges on minor but challenging intelligence-gathering missions, in order to assess their enthusiasm and commitment. The reasoning was simple: if a young man was unwilling or incapable of enduring a couple of hours standing and watching in the cold or wet, he was unlikely to measure up to the more rigorous demands inevitable at a later stage.

Once satisfied with the new recruit's willingness and ability, they would be trained in the use of explosives and firearms. With the British and Dublin authorities aware that training was taking place in the Republic, it grew increasingly difficult, as time passed, to move groups of men from one area of the Six Counties into the South without detection. To get around this difficulty, training was arranged on a graded scale in order to minimise time spent south of the Border. Basic instruction in the use of pistols and sub-machine guns was often carried out in sympathisers' homes in the Six Counties. The IRA, nevertheless, viewed this practice as an unsatisfactory substitute for properly organised training camps where more detailed instruction could be delivered.

In order to prevent new and untested people acquiring too much potentially compromising information about its personnel at a very early stage, the IRA tried not to have people from different areas training together in camps in the Republic. In practice, this meant organising numerous sessions in many different locations. In the early 1970s, most IRA training camps were situated in remote areas close to the Border with each one being effectively managed by different regional units of the organisation. Training in those days was seldom centralised and was not therefore standardised. Although not perfectly satisfactory, this afforded a degree of security that later practice could not provide.

At first, this arrangement was convenient for rural units in areas close to the Republic where the practice of crossing over and back for business or entertainment was well established. British and Irish intelligence agencies had difficulty, for example, determining whether a group of young men travelling from South Tyrone to Monaghan after work on a Friday were merely out for the evening or making their way to an IRA training camp. Obviously, this system was not always suitable for the large numbers of Belfast volunteers and the IRA, therefore, set up training facilities for them far from the Border. In time, increased Garda numbers and pressure forced the IRA to move almost all of its training camps away from Border areas and further south. This provided for a more standardised mode of instruction but since so much was now in one system, it was also more vulnerable to security leaks.

More often than not, instruction took place inside a barn or hayshed out of sight of curious passers-by or policemen. Weapons for basic training purposes, that is, stripping and reassembling guns, were often old or malfunctioning. This was deliberately so, in order to minimise losses (and to lessen possible legal implications) in the event of a police raid. Training in the use of explosives for most IRA volunteers was almost always done by explaining circuits, timing devices and simple detonating fuses. Only in exceptional circumstances were recruits shown real explosive materiel at this stage. Firing live rounds on a training camp would usually take place at the end of a session and at a location some distance from where the instruction took place. Since ammunition was always scarce, for much of the campaign most recruits were fortunate to have the opportunity to fire more than five or ten live rounds before being sent out to operate.

The Provisional IRA had, however, taken a much more crucial strategic decision on training in the early 1970s. By late 1972 and with its ranks greatly increased by a series of events – internment without trial, Bloody Sunday and the downgrading of the Official IRA's armed campaign – the Provisional IRA leadership decided to cease providing training for defence to non-members, in order to tighten control over manpower and access to weapons.

In the short term, the plan had some merit. In the long term, though, it deprived the organisation (and the Catholic population) of the means and the concept of a broad, ground-level defence against Loyalist attack. The IRA as an organisation may have been able to deal with a 1969-style assault on its supporters. This was not, however, the type of threat posed in the 1980s and 1990s by Loyalist death squads. UVF and UDA gangs attacked random or isolated homes, defenceless customers in pubs, or punters in bookmaker's shops. Only those with the capacity to remain in situ around the clock could protect these targets from attack. IRA units constantly avoiding British Army and RUC patrols were not best placed to perform this role. The lack of defence in depth against a Loyalist onslaught became, in time, a significant element in the IRA's decision to end its campaign in the 1990s. To a large extent, deciding to tighten control over the armed insurrection illustrated a fundamental dilemma facing the Provisional IRA – it needed popular support yet felt uneasy about placing unregulated trust in the masses. This was and remains an unfortunate feature of insurrectionary Irish Republicanism.

In spite of this strategic weakness, the Provisional IRA in the early 1970s had a plan and, whatever outsiders may have thought, it was following it. Historically, it had an identifiable pedigree. This was a vitally important distinction between opposition movements in Ireland and other western European countries. By the late 1960s, insurrection was no longer widely practised in western Europe. Small groups of urban guerrillas had emerged on the Continent, but their campaigns were minor in comparison to that of the IRA. With the possible exception of the Basque group ETA, none of these isolated insurrectionary currents won broad, popular support. The IRA, on the other hand, while small and marginalised, was part of the political fabric in Ireland and this gave it an advantage when conditions developed in its favour.

With history conferring a degree of familiarity on the IRA that was not available to others contemplating insurrection, and a long and established infrastructure allowing them to train and equip an underground army, the organisation only needed the momentum of events to take it into all-out offensive. There was nothing inevitable about the emergence of the Provisional IRA. In reality, the greatest contribution to its emergence was not so much the actions of diehard irreconcilable Republicans but the utter intransigence of reactionary Unionism supported by London, cynically guarding its selfish and strategic interests in Ireland.

As previously outlined, Northern Ireland had been created in a period of trauma and was designed to provide favourable treatment for just one section of the people. The nature of the Six-County state effectively prevented its governing class from improving this system over the decades, even had they wanted to do so. There was, however, one authority that had the power and ability to alter the situation for the better in Northern Ireland had it chosen to do so and that was the British government. That London knew of the situation in Northern Ireland is beyond doubt. In the early part of the 1960s, the Co. Tyrone-based Campaign for Social Justice had been in contact with Britain's Labour Party leader Harold Wilson to brief him on the range of injustices being routinely practiced within a region of the UK. His response: 'I agree with you as to the importance of the issues with which your Campaign is concerned, and can assure you that a Labour Government would do everything in its power to see that the infringements of justice to which you are so rightly drawing attention are effectively dealt with.'[1]

In a pamphlet published in 1969 by the same group, they pointedly reproduced Wilson's reply and also printed a section of the 1920 Government of Ireland Act that had established the Six-County state and which made the London government's responsibility abundantly clear. The pamphlet stated:

Section 75 of the Government of Ireland Act, 1920, by which the Parliament at Westminster set up the Northern Ireland State, says:

'Notwithstanding the establishment of the Parliament ... of Northern Ireland ... or anything contained in this Act, the supreme authority of the Parliament of the United Kingdom shall remain unaffected and undiminished over all persons, matters and things in Ireland and every part thereof.'[2]

This paragraph made it clear that there could be no ambiguity about where ultimate authority lay: Britain was responsible for Northern Ireland. By its determination to protect its strategic interests through calculated inertia and indifference to Unionist misconduct, Britain was not just culpable for the Stormont regime and its practices but was the one authority that could alter it by legislation.

7
Attempting to Quell the Insurgency by Bloodshed and Blandishment

Bloody Sunday was carried out with one objective. The British Army decided coldly and deliberately to shoot the risen people off the streets. We were shot with our backs turned, in some cases with our hands in the air as we went to rescue the wounded. We were killed on the barricades, in the courtyards, and a few died god knows where. The vultures picked them up first. But the siege goes on. The 808 acres of Bogside, Brandywell and Cregan remain free. And 40 of the 42 entrances to Free Derry remain barricaded. Sunday, Bloody Sunday was a fine day and a foul day.

Nell McCafferty, writing in *Starry Plough*
and cited in *Nell: A Disorderly Woman*[1]

Cathal's aim was to bomb the town's RUC station, but he was faced with some serious difficulties. By the early 1970s, most Northern Irish town centres had been turned into pedestrian-only zones as the authorities erected barriers on roads around the outskirts of urban centres to prevent car-bombings. In some towns, such as Belfast, this measure was enforced with permanently manned checkpoints around the periphery and heavily patrolled inner areas. This practice was manpower intensive and barriers were left unmanned overnight in many country towns, with the authorities relying on random patrols and covert surveillance for deterrence.

Whenever a chink appeared in the system, IRA Active Service Units would move to exploit the opening. Often they would smuggle a satchel charge through unmanned pedestrian access points in the barriers and manually plant a bomb in a selected target. To an extent, this tactic undermined measures taken to stymie the bombing campaign, but the task facing Cathal required a much larger amount of explosives than an individual or even a few men could carry.

It seemed, however, that an answer to his problem had presented itself when one of his team spotted an opportunity. British Army engineers had replaced original security fencing with large concrete bollards linked together by several tubular steel poles embedded in the bollards. There was no chance of moving this barrier quickly, or without heavy lifting gear. Consequently, British Army and RUC personnel were reassigned away from the perimeter and sent to concentrate on guarding commercial premises in the town.

What Cathal's intelligence gatherer had spotted was simply a Royal Mail box inside the barrier. How was the mail collected? He read the collection times and waited. A red Royal Mail van with a uniformed postman came driving up the street inside the barrier, stopped his vehicle, parked beside the box and collected the mail. With this done, the postman moved on to finish his round and deliver the contents in his van to the town's post office – situated invitingly beside the RUC station.

The plan was straightforward. As darkness fell, Cathal's IRA unit used a pick-up truck to ferry a half-ton of home-made explosives to a yard behind a disused shop outside the barrier but close to the mailbox. It was a large quantity of explosives but Cathal's team knew that they would only get one chance to deliver this operation. Nevertheless, as they set out the bags of explosive behind the yard gate, the team quickly realised that it was going to take them longer to effect their plan than originally envisaged.

The team of five had arrived a good twenty minutes before the collection was due. As they waited for the mail van to come, they scanned the area for any sign of enemy activity but were happy to see only a group of youngsters playing outside on the street. As time passed, the IRA continued to watch for the van and for any sign of unusual activity. In their heightened sense of awareness, they failed to see the increasing number of youngsters at play outside the gate.

The van turned the corner and parked as expected at the mailbox. Two members of the unit walked quickly and quietly from their position and ordered the postman at gunpoint to accompany them back to the yard. One member of the team took the postman's jacket and cap and sat behind the wheel of the mail van while one man held the postman prisoner. As the remaining IRA men began carrying bags of explosive to the van, Cathal realised that they might have over-estimated their capacity. There were over twenty bags of explosive to be loaded, all of which had then to be linked with detonation cord and finally connected to the timing device. There was a limit on how much time they had to spare before the van's absence was noticed. It would only be a matter of time before a foot patrol came to investigate the missing van.

Cathal was in the back of the van desperately taping detonation cord and willing his small team to hurry when he saw an amazing sight. The youngsters, the eldest of whom could not have been more than thirteen, were dragging bags of explosive towards the van. Not one of them was able to lift or carry a bag. Two or three per bag and frantically pushing, pulling, shoving the slimy, oily contents towards the van. He was asking himself whether to chase them off or accept their help when he realised that they were facilitating his operation in a way he could not have done with his own team. Reluctantly, he allowed them to continue and told his team to stand at the rear of the van and load. The vehicle was filled in minutes, driven and parked beside the post office close to the RUC station. The IRA driver then walked quietly to a waiting car and drove off to make a warning phone call.

The rest of the team began to climb into their pick-up when the children gathered around them. The youngsters wanted to travel with the ASU on the truck. Cathal was in a dilemma because he certainly couldn't take a group of children in the get-away vehicle. He was dumbfounded momentarily but then had a flash of inspiration. A whip-around among the team managed to raise

£3.50. He told the youngsters that he intended returning to bomb the town the following week and that he might need them again but only those who obeyed 'orders' would be called upon. They were to take the money, go to the local shop for crisps and remain tight-lipped.

Twenty-five years later, Cathal returned to the town and by chance met one of his old team who was a native of the district. Recalling old times, they reflected on the night of the post van bomb. Cathal asked about the 'ancillary staff' as the team had later named the children. 'There was a lot of talk about it in the months afterwards', his friend said, 'and then it died away but you know something, not once in the years since has anyone said to me that he was one of them or have I ever heard a name mentioned. They took you at your word to stay tight-lipped.'

Britain had a clear legal responsibility for what happened in Northern Ireland but did not interpret this obligation as a duty to do its honest and even-handed best for all its subjects there. British governments instead regarded the Irish appendage to the United Kingdom as a strategic asset that had to be maintained at whatever cost necessary. An important advantage in Britain's determination to retain a foothold in the area was the fact that a majority in the Six Counties favoured maintaining the Union. If retaining this support meant declining to confront Unionism, London was prepared to accept that situation.

As mentioned previously, this was apparent in the aftermath of the August 1969 assault on Catholic districts of Belfast, when Harold Wilson's government refused to take decisive action against the Stormont regime. Less than a year later, Edward Heath's Conservative government authorised the siege of Belfast's Lower Falls in an effort to appease Unionist demands for punitive action against a community that was just recovering from a traumatic and murderous assault the previous year. If serious doubt surrounds the British government's motivation, it is only necessary to examine the sequence of events as they unfolded through the 1970s.

Having taken unilateral action against the Catholic population in June 1970 by laying siege to the Lower Falls, the British government permitted Northern Ireland's Prime Minister Brian Faulkner to introduce internment without trial in August 1971. The measure was one-sided and directed against the Catholic community. As journalist and historian Tim Pat Coogan was to write, the British government was content to allow the Stormont regime to instigate a swoop that

… included people who had never been in the IRA, including Ivan Barr, chairman of the NICRA [Northern Ireland Civil Rights

Association] executive, and Michael Farrell. What they did not include was a single Loyalist. Although the UVF had begun the killing and bombing, this organisation was left untouched, as were other violent Loyalist satellite organisations such as Tara, the Shankill Defenders Association and the Ulster Protestant Volunteers. It is known that Faulkner was urged by the British to include a few Protestants in the trawl but he refused.[2]

Figure 7.1 The British Army in Ardoyne, Belfast after the introduction of internment in 1971 (© John McGuffin).

As a subsequent BBC account of the action was to note, when then Prime Minister Edward Heath was interviewed, he admitted that the UK government had agreed to the measure in order to maintain the Stormont regime.[3] 'We were all very loathe to do this,' Heath said, 'but as we were faced with the collapse of the whole government of Northern Ireland, we said yes. But when they had taken these steps, one realised that so much of it was unjustified.'[4]

The cabinet in London agreed that those arrested and interned should be subjected to torture at the hands of the British Army. A BBC investigation, following the release of cabinet papers in 2002 under the 30-year rule, revealed the contents of a cabinet minute from a meeting attended by Prime Minister Heath, with senior cabinet members and military chiefs, which heard that the methods of interrogation used in Northern Ireland had not differed greatly from those used against insurgents in Cyprus or Malaya:

Techniques designed to isolate detainees, to prevent them from obtaining any exact sense of time and location, and to impose fatigue by exposure to insistent and disturbing noise were regarded as proper ... while it was important that methods of interrogation should not overstep the proper bounds, it had to be remembered that the lives of British soldiers and innocent civilians depended on intelligence. We were dealing with an enemy who had no scruples, and we should not be unduly squeamish over methods of interrogation in these circumstances.[5]

Anger in Catholic working-class areas erupted into violent anti-government demonstrations. In the 48 hours after British troops made their initial raids at 4:00 in the morning on Monday, 9 August, 17 people were killed, ten of whom were Catholics. And as so often was the case with the outbreak of civil disturbance in Belfast, many people began to fear attack by neighbouring communities, with the subsequent flight to safer areas. A report compiled by Hywel Griffiths, director of the Community Relations Council in September 1971 concluded that 'Although we were not able to record an exact religious breakdown we have estimated from origin and destination addresses that of the total number of movements 40% were Protestant while 60% were Catholic.'[6]

In the ensuing hysteria, the Provisional IRA was almost overwhelmed with a flood of recruits. In County Tyrone, for example, Republicans had been relatively slow to respond to the split in 1970. By mid-1971, while the Provisional IRA had established a basic skeleton organisation in the county, they were still a minority in comparison to the Official lRA. When several key personnel were arrested on 9 August, a veteran IRA man who escaped the swoop claimed that the Provisional IRA in Tyrone had only one operational ASU left in the county. By Christmas 1971, that number had increased at least ten times, and the leadership's biggest problem in the area was not finding manpower but accessing sufficient arms to equip its newly recruited fighting units.

The story was repeated throughout working-class Catholic areas across the Six Counties. Any ambivalence about Britain's responsibility for the mess that was around them had evaporated and in its place was a certainty that only an end to British rule in Ireland would rectify the situation. The rapid expansion of the Provisional IRA did not happen in isolation. Others were organising and none more so than the still vibrant NICRA. Internment without trial had sent shock waves through all civil libertarians in Ireland

and was a rallying point for thousands. A series of protests continued throughout the remainder of 1971 and into 1972 and drew huge crowds onto the streets to protest the British government's violation of a basic norm of democracy. With the Provisional IRA intensifying its operations by the day and a mass movement of people on the streets, it was clear that large parts of Northern Ireland were becoming virtually ungovernable.[7]

When a protest march organised by the civil rights movement against internment took place in Derry city on Sunday, 31 January 1972, the British Army opened fire on the crowd, killing 14 people and wounding many others.[8] Within minutes of the shootings, the British Army and its government were issuing a comprehensive yet entirely false account of what had happened. The marchers were accused of possessing bombs with intent to use them against British troops. Elsewhere it was said that IRA personnel hiding among the demonstrators had shot at British paratroopers who had, it was claimed, very carefully shot and killed their attackers. The participants on the march knew that the British authorities were lying. The Catholic population knew that the British were lying and so did a majority of the Southern Irish population.

Almost four decades were to pass before the British government publicly accepted the outcome of an inquiry by Lord Saville of Newdigate that those shot dead on the civil rights march were unarmed civilians and that the British Army opened fire without justification. In June 2010, Lord Saville issued his report into the events of the Bloody Sunday killings and concluded that British soldiers fired without provocation and gave no warning.[9] His report ruled that all 14 who died and the others who were injured almost four decades previously had been unarmed and were completely innocent.

He further found that British troops had continued to shoot as protesters fled or lay fatally wounded on the ground. The 5,000-page report states, 'As we have said, none of the casualties was posing a threat of causing death or serious injury, or indeed was doing anything else that could on any view justify their shooting.'[10]

Whether the British Army had acted with or without calculated reason is another question altogether. In spite of the still larger crowd that attended a subsequent civil rights march in Newry a week later, the result of the massacre was to incapacitate the mass movement of peaceful protest. At a stage when it could have led to a widening and deepening of the mass struggle, the shootings on Bloody Sunday curtailed street protest for a number of years. The negation of the mass movement, to be replaced with a focus on armed struggle dovetailed with other aspects of historical development. A large number of Northern Irish Catholics believed that the British Army action on Bloody Sunday was not accidental but was designed to channel anti-government mobilisation into a single arena that its military could deal with: armed conflict.[11]

No similarly resolute action was evident from Britain's armed forces two years later when Unionists decided to overthrow the power-sharing Sunningdale Agreement. The British government had published a White Paper, 'Northern Ireland Constitutional Proposals', outlining plans for a Northern Ireland Assembly in March 1973. The proposed Assembly would be elected by proportional representation (PR) with 78 members sitting at Stormont. In addition to having a power-sharing executive the White Paper also proposed a 'Council of Ireland' to deal with matters of mutual interest between Northern Ireland and the Republic of Ireland.

Representatives of three parties – the Unionist Party, the Social Democratic and Labour Party (SDLP), and the Alliance Party of Northern Ireland – subsequently met for talks about the possible formation of an executive to govern Northern Ireland. On Wednesday, 21 November 1973, agreement was reached on the formation of a power-sharing executive, to be composed of 11 voting members (six Unionists, four SDLP, and one Alliance Party) and four non-voting members (two SDLP, one Unionist, and one Alliance Party). On Thursday, 6 December 1973, a conference was held in Sunningdale, England, at which final agreement was reached between the three parties on a power-sharing administration for Northern Ireland incorporating the Council of Ireland.

The Executive met for the first time on 1 January 1974 and was widely hailed in London and Dublin as the answer to the 'Northern Ireland Question'. All was not rosy however, and in May 1974, a coalition of hard-line Unionists declared their opposition to the recently established power-sharing administration and the Council of Ireland. They launched a general strike under the auspices of the Ulster Workers Council on 15 May, demanding an end to the cross-party administration in Stormont.

There followed a 14-day general strike during which there was widespread intimidation and bloodshed. British Prime Minister Harold Wilson described the strike as 'A deliberate and calculated attempt to use every undemocratic and unparliamentary means for the purpose of bringing down the whole constitution of Northern Ireland so as to set up there a sectarian and undemocratic state, from which one third of the people of Northern Ireland will be excluded.'[12]

In spite of Wilson's concerns about the outcome of the strike, his government and its army were unable to bring it to an end before the Executive had collapsed. Some commentators also said Wilson's understanding of why the strike was taking place was somewhat odd, since Northern Ireland had been a sectarian state excluding one-third of its population since its foundation.

In *The Point of No Return*, British journalist Robert Fisk described the strike thus:

> ... the fifteen unprecedented, historic days in which a million British citizens, the Protestants of Northern Ireland, staged what amounted to a rebellion against the Crown and won ... [during which] ... a self-elected provisional government of Protestant power workers, well-armed private armies and extreme politicians organized a strike which almost broke up the fabric of civilized life in Ulster.[13]

The IRA had not supported the Sunningdale Agreement, nor did its volunteers mourn the collapse. In private, leading members of the organisation had recognised that the agreement placed a serious question-mark over the viability of the armed campaign. They were certainly not satisfied with the contents of the deal, but were sufficiently pragmatic to understand that if Northern Ireland appeared to function normally while enjoying cross-party endorsement, there would be much less support for continuing with an armed insurrection. When the Sunningdale Agreement with its power-sharing administration collapsed, the IRA's analysis – that Britain was a partisan player in the conflict rather than an honest broker – was powerfully reinforced.

The organisation pointed out that the Unionist population was clearly not prepared to tolerate a working compromise and the British government was unwilling to compel them to do so. The only realistic alternative they said was to continue fighting. By the time the Sunningdale Agreement collapsed in May 1974, less than six years after the first civil rights march from Coalisland to Dungannon, the British government had presided over a series of events that only the most partisan of its admirers could deem as an even-handed management of affairs in Northern Ireland. Retaining Stormont governance after the trauma of August 1969, laying siege to the Lower Falls in June 1970, introducing internment without trial in 1971, committing the Bloody Sunday atrocity in 1972 and conducting the pointless Border poll in 1973, recording a totally predictable Unionist majority, were not designed to do anything other than reinforce the status quo.

The IRA viewed the British government's capitulation to the Ulster Workers Council strike as evidence of London's partisan approach. When faced for two weeks by a stubborn but not all-powerful section of the Unionist community, the British government tamely surrendered the one initiative that could conceivably have addressed the underlying difficulties. The British were not prepared to employ the type of decisiveness that helped break the Soviet blockade on West Berlin less than 25 years earlier during the period June 1948 until May 1949. Nor did Britain employ the type of decisive action favoured by its army when faced by disobedience from the Catholic community in Northern Ireland.

Sunningdale was Britain's proffered solution to the Northern Irish question. The plan was qualified and contained a major caveat. Britain's qualifications were that London had decided that Northern Ireland was to remain firmly within Westminster's control, albeit somewhat better managed. Catholics would be forced to accept the constitutional position of Northern Ireland within the United Kingdom and Unionists would be required to accept reform. The caveat was that none of this was to take place at a pace that might cause Unionists to contemplate a rupture with London. With Unionism having so clearly demonstrated that it was not prepared to consider anything less than a return to the Orange state and London unwilling to discommode Unionism, the IRA saw little reason to reconsider the armed option.

8
Irish Republicanism and Class

Men make their own history, but they do not make it as they please; they do not make it under circumstances of their own choosing but under circumstances existing already, given and transmitted from the past. The tradition of all dead generations weighs like a nightmare on the brains of the living. And just as they seem to be occupied with revolutionising themselves and things, creating something that did not exist before, precisely in such epochs of revolutionary crisis they anxiously conjure up the spirits of the past to their service, borrowing from them names, battle slogans, and costumes in order to present this new scene in world history in time-honoured disguise and borrowed language.

Karl Marx, *The Eighteenth Brumaire*
of Louis Bonaparte, Chapter 1[1]

In the broadest sense, Republicanism has enjoyed a wide support base in Irish society for over two centuries. Approximately four in every five persons now living on the island accept it as their standard form of government and many of them could not even imagine accepting a monarch as head of state in Ireland. That is not to say, though, that Republicans in Ireland are of one mind on what constitutes best Republican practice or indeed on what the essential ingredients of the philosophy might be. There is an understandable tendency among all Republican parties to define the philosophy in terms best suited to their own needs at any particular time. For example, politicians with views as diverse as former leader of the now defunct Progressive Democrats, Michael McDowell, and Republican Sinn Féin's former president, Ruairi O'Bradaigh, both insist that they are true Republicans.

There have always been differing interpretations of Republicanism in Ireland, but it is fair to say that one of its enduring characteristics has been the existence of an insurrectionary, armed constituency. What is also an enduring feature of Republicanism in Ireland has been the steady separation from its militarist part of different interest groups and classes. Some of the more dogmatic adherents of Republicanism describe this tendency as betrayal, seeing it simply as a sell-out to what they often describe as constitutionalism. The reality may be more prosaic.

Contrary to what some may think, the philosophy of Republicanism was not introduced into Ireland, at the end of the eighteenth century, in order to secure political unification of the island if for no other reason than that the country was not divided into different jurisdictions at that time. Nor was it concerned purely with national independence, since that could conceivably have occurred under an Irish monarchy or dictatorship, forms of governance that were anathema to those who first advocated the Republican message in Ireland.

Irish Republicanism has its roots in the late eighteenth-century United Irishmen movement which was influenced by democratic currents present in the radical wing of the Parliamentary Army of the English Civil War, by the American War of Independence and later and most importantly by the French Revolution. The French Revolution was not a war for national independence but rather an intense and bitter power struggle between different classes and alliances of classes. Originally led by the prosperous middle class, the French Revolution found admirers among the same class in Ireland. Wanting greater freedom for trade and commerce, a sizeable section of the Irish bourgeoisie saw merit in a republic and put their stamp on its early manifestation. Their enthusiasm for the concept was shared by Ireland's poor peasantry who, understandably, found the idea of eradicating aristocrats and dividing land among peasants an attractive concept.

The concept of replacing monarchy and installing a democracy, governed by an elected assembly, was a raw challenge to the Irish ascendancy at the beginning of the 1790s. Those advocating these ideas came to be viewed as a serious threat to the very existence of Ireland's ruling class and to the government of Britain when King George's armies went to war with revolutionary (and republican) France in 1793. People and organisations promoting the establishment of an Irish state modelled on the French republic were viewed as traitors propagandising on behalf of the king's enemy. When Irish Republicans made contact with the French to ask for help and counsel, Britain acted to crush what it recognised as a danger to its own security. Ireland was not to have additional autonomy and was certainly not to become a republic.

As the promotion of radical Republicanism in Ireland became increasingly dangerous, many of the upper and middle bourgeoisie drew back from conflict with Britain. When insurrection eventually broke out in 1798, it was the peasantry for the most part who fought and, naturally, died. State coercion and violence was used extensively and unsparingly by the British to crush Republican ambitions in Ireland. Over 30,000 died in the uprising of 1798, the overwhelming majority of them on the Republican side. Irish Republicans found themselves taking a view from an early period that their cause could only be achieved after breaking free from monarchist Britain. Moreover, many believed that separation from the Empire could only be attained through armed insurrection.

With its philosophical origins in a French revolution that for a period gave power to the Jacobins, Ireland's Republicans tended to be composed disproportionately of outsiders, the less well-off and the disaffected. Republicanism and its clandestine networks provided a vehicle for those sections of society unable to access the levers of power, or who believed their needs were either not being met or deliberately stymied by the powerful ruling class.

Growing out of the bourgeois democratic period at the end of the eighteenth century and early nineteenth century, Irish Republicanism was not and never has been a classically socialist philosophy seeking to base itself within an industrial proletariat. It has, however, usually reflected the class interests of its adherents, frequently including the most disadvantaged in society. As with any conventional Republican outlook, it has always had a fundamental distaste for monarchs and aristocrats. In Ireland, this was easily accepted into the indigenous manifestation of Republicanism. Throughout the eighteenth and nineteenth centuries, landlordism in Ireland was a byword for savagery, mismanagement and debauchery. It was held to be largely responsible by the Irish peasantry for the devastating impact of the Great Famine of the 1840s.

Irish Republicanism has never, though, had the same unambiguous attitude towards the business class as it had towards aristocracy. Yet the restructuring of the militant underground that began through Irish émigrés in France after the Famine years, leading eventually to the formation in 1858 of the Irish Republican Brotherhood (IRB), known also as the Fenian movement, drew its organisational inspiration from the Parisian radicals of the mid-eighteenth century. The first declaration by the Fenian movement, on 17 March 1858, underlined a commitment to the needs of working people,[2] saying that the organisation aimed 'at founding a Republic based on universal suffrage which shall secure all the intrinsic value of their labour'.

Figure 8.1   IRA volunteer in Derry, 1971
(© Eamon Melaugh).

The Fenian attempt at insurrection in 1867 was a military failure. It succeeded in mobilising only a miserably small number of fighters for the uprising and found that its efforts at the time lent more wind to the sails of parliamentary Nationalism than to radical Republicanism. What it did succeed in doing, however, was to establish an underground network of militant activists who were central to the agrarian struggle of the following decades. This prolonged campaign for peasant property rights involved a combination of tactics that included input from Nationalist Party parliamentarians, agitation through a mass popular movement and direct action against landlords' property.

In spite of an underlying identification with the less well-off, Irish Republicanism has always had a Nationalist element embedded within it. For so long as Ireland's Republicans viewed the task of breaking the political union with Britain as an essential prerequisite to the establishment of an Irish Republic, their path has run parallel to that of Irish Nationalism. As a consequence, there has often been a degree of ambivalence about the nature of Irish Republicanism. There were those who understood it to be a radical and democratic movement that sought to create a democratic republic while others viewed it exclusively as a militaristic version of nationalism in which struggling for democratic rights was of less importance than national independence.

This confusion became particularly marked when, at the beginning of the twentieth century, IRB-led Republicans organised a large popular volunteer force to counter Unionist threats to the passing of a Home Rule Act through the British House of Commons. Although the Act would only give Ireland limited autonomy, Unionism prepared for war. The IRB initiative to counter Unionist preparations was popular and successful, so much so that the Nationalist Party joined the newly created Irish Volunteers and assumed control, imposing its party leader John Redmond as head of the organisation.

When the Irish Volunteers split on the outbreak of the First World War, it was not along class lines but rather over the issue of whether to support Britain 'in her hour of need', or whether to adopt an old Fenian maxim and use Britain's difficulty as Ireland's opportunity to seize independence. One class-conscious activist did, nevertheless, align himself with the Fenian position albeit on the basis of his adherence to socialist internationalism. James Connolly, who by 1916 was general secretary of the Irish Transport and General Workers Union, had organised an Irish Citizens Army in 1913 to protect striking workers during a general strike in Dublin. Connolly was determined to launch an insurrection come what may.

Connolly's execution in 1916 robbed the Irish labour movement of its only remaining strong leader (James Larkin was in the US). Those who remained in the leadership of Ireland's labour movement accepted a minority position in Republican and national politics during the war for independence and struggled to assert labour interests in later years, allowing others to dominate the agenda. In spite of positive sounding insertions into the 'Democratic Programme',[3] of the first Dáil,[4] the cause of Labour almost disappeared from the national programme in the post-1916 period, when eventually, the Irish middle class settled for an improved version of Home Rule in 1922, which they imposed by ruthlessly prosecuting civil war.

Ireland's civil war was fought out between the middle class-led Free State and uncompromising Republicans drawn largely from small farmers supported by many urban workers. The Irish Labour Party and official trade union movement supported the Free State and acted as its loyal opposition through the first decade of the state's existence. This decision was to cost the Labour Party the loss of a significant number of Ireland's working class and practically all of its small farmers to the constitutional Republican party Fianna Fáil. This situation was to last for several generations after the Irish civil war had faded into history.

As late as 1977, Michael O'Riordan, the then general secretary of the Communist Party of Ireland was lamenting that:

> From 1973 until 1977, the Fine Gael party – of which O'Duffy was elected leader in 1933 – was the dominant party in a coalition government with the Irish Labour Party … The unnatural political and governmental alliance of the Irish Labour Party with Fine Gael brought out, once again, some of the traits that characterised the weakness of the Irish Labour Party during the pro-Franco campaigns of the 1930s … A latter day Roddy Connolly co-chairing a joint Fine Gael meeting in support of the Presidential candidate of Tom O'Higgins, one time 'Blueshirt' … Labour deputy Sean Treacy in Madrid in 1976 congratulating the Francoists on the occasion of their takeover of Republican Spain's capital.[5]

Labour was to continue propping up Fine Gael in the decades that followed. Prior to the 2007 general election, it appeared that Fine Gael was threatened with irreversible decline when its total membership in the Dáil was smaller than that of the combined opposition deputies. Labour refused to forge an alliance with Sinn Féin and other left-leaning TDs and instead drew up an accord with its old partner Fine Gael, thus not only guaranteeing the survival of the Blueshirt tradition,[6] but undermining attempts at creating a broad, albeit social democratic, left movement in the Republic.

In the aftermath of the civil war, Republicanism in Ireland was to go through a series of mutations over the course of the twentieth century. For 20 years after the establishment of the Free State, Republican hard-liners focused their efforts on 'restoring the republic' that had been allowed to lapse with the acceptance of the Treaty in 1922. Their efforts appeared to have achieved a measure of success when, in 1949, the Fine Gael leader John A. Costello declared the 26-county state to be a republic. Although the island remained divided, one of the most contentious aspects of the treaty appeared resolved and significantly, the Irish middle class accepted and endorsed the concept of a Republican form of government.

It could then be argued by many that the Republican goal had finally been achieved. There remained the question of the northern Six Counties, but that appeared more of a purely Nationalist ambition than a broadly democratic Republican principle. In some quarters it was argued, for example, that the IRA campaign of 1956–62 had more the appearance of an irredentist operation than a struggle for the promulgation of the Declaration of the Rights of Man. When the Dublin government organised an extensive and elaborate series of celebrations to commemorate the fiftieth anniversary of the 1916 Easter Rising, it seemed that Republicanism in Ireland was so well embedded within the conservative establishment that it no longer possessed the potential for generating revolution or social progress.

Events in Northern Ireland in 1969 prompted a review of old-style militant, insurrectionary Republicanism's historic role in Ireland. The original organisers of the civil rights movement had thought outside the paradigm of insurrectionary Republicanism on one hand and passive parliamentary Nationalism on the other. They had identified the structural weakness of an administration that proclaimed boundless loyalty to a government and its monarch, yet refused to abide by standards pertaining in what they viewed as the mother country. The organisers of the civil rights movement in Northern Ireland had identified the value of likening their movement with the great struggle for justice in the United States and drew some accurate parallels between the behaviour of the Stormont regime and that of segregationists in the southern United States. Their critique was devastating and damaging, and triggered the process that caused the old Unionist system to impale itself on its own contradictions and ultimately to lead to its destruction.

What those behind the civil rights movement had failed to anticipate was the reaction of the Northern Ireland government and the society it presided over and the violence that grew out of this volatile arrangement. More disastrously, they had underestimated the British government's willingness to tolerate injustice and foul play within its own state. And when Northern Irish Unionism and the Six-County state it produced reacted with bloody violence to a campaign for democratic rights, the leadership of the civil rights campaign was left floundering. They were, in reality, invited to accept the limited reform package offered by London with its details to be implemented by Stormont's Unionist government or to go home quietly and sulk.

The rise of local defence committees would thereafter change the terrain of struggle for everyone and reveal the need for organisational and ideological clarity. As even the British state recognised, the local defence committees were semi-spontaneous autonomous local movements. As such, they constituted a basis for mass community participation and represented the kind of mass social movement the Left had always sought and about which militaristic Republicans had always been suspicious. Neither was able to see the originality of what was happening. For this reason neither the IRA, as it was then constituted, nor the 'Left' were able to take this semi-spontaneous movement forward. And yet people from the Left and Republicans were closely involved with the defence committees. Under the circumstances, it was inevitable that a new organisation would include veteran republicans and young militants with left-wing ideas and before long, this new manifestation of Irish Republicanism would come to be known as the Provisional IRA.

Unionist gunmen and their politicians were soon to make it obvious that they had learned nothing from the civil rights movement and had forgotten nothing from their days of unchallenged rule, demonstrating in practice their determination that the second-class status of Northern Irish Catholics was not to be fundamentally changed. This seemed evident as Unionist gunmen attacked St Matthew's Catholic Church in Belfast's Short Strand in June 1970, intent it appeared, on implementing an old imperialist policy of using force to clear and dominate the streets, and only then to set the parameters of political debate.

Despite Unionism's inability to forget, they would surely be slow to learn that things had indeed changed and would never be the same again. A middle-aged, veteran IRA man with a small handful of helpers would confirm that assessment when they organised a ferocious defence of the church, leading to several fatalities among the attacking Unionist gunmen. The defensive action came at no small cost to the Republicans, with one of their number losing his life and Billy McKee, the veteran IRA man in charge, receiving serious gunshot wounds.

The importance of the battle at St Matthew's was twofold. In the first instance, since the British Army was close by but did not intervene to prevent the onslaught on the Catholic Short Strand, many Republicans could argue with some justification that London had demonstrated its partiality in favour of Stormont.

The only definitive solution to the problem, they were able to say, lay in breaking the connection with Britain and creating a 32-county republic.

On the other hand, the battle heralded the emerging Provisional IRA as a potent force capable of contesting the ground with Unionist gunmen. Within a period of months, non-violent pacifist methods had been incapacitated and insurrectionary Irish Republicanism had emerged robustly from what had seemed, only twelve months earlier, to be on an irreversible path towards terminal decline. This fresh manifestation of insurrectionary Irish Republicanism emerged from among the Catholic working class, the unemployed working class and the small-farming community. This was to be of enormous significance. Eventually, the class composition of the Provisional IRA, holding with what was at first a dystopian view of Northern Ireland, was to shape the intensity of their war and the nature of their settlement. Many antagonistic to the IRA attempted to overlook or misinterpret the class composition of the IRA. Some southern Irish journalists even suggested at one period that a significant number of Provisional IRA members were from the affluent middle class and that there existed a reservoir of well-heeled IRA supporters both north and south of the Border. As with much else that emanated from the Republic's tightly controlled media during the years of the northern conflict, this was pure agenda-driven propaganda.

The Provisional IRA was, for the most part, from the class Wolfe Tone described as 'the men of no property'. Their class make-up, which included large numbers of long-term unemployed workers, blue-collar workers and small farmers, all made for a complex relationship with the state. Their place in Northern Irish society – the bottom tier of a community held in second-class status – was also an important factor in their reaction to their situation and to the terms of their ultimate reconciliation with the reconstructed Northern Ireland state.

Those areas that from the 1980 voted consistently for Sinn Féin can reasonably be identified as IRA strongholds. Marginalised and deprived urban communities in Belfast, Derry and other northern towns were where the IRA fought its urban guerrilla war. Less well-off rural areas and less well-off rural people, albeit not always farmers, made up the vast bulk of the IRA cadres that fought in the countryside.

Belfast districts such as Ballymurphy, Turf Lodge, the Falls, Poleglass, Ardoyne and the Short Strand were and are all solidly working-class areas. These are parts of Belfast that once supplied a reserve labour force for the mills, factories, transport and communication industries of the city. With the decline of heavy industry and textiles in western economies, Belfast also declined, and as is always the case, those in marginal positions were first to experience the brunt of unemployment. In the sectarian Northern Irish state, this meant that a disproportionate number of Belfast Catholics were out of work. By the time the conflict broke out, some of these communities had experienced long-term unemployment for several generations. There was real deprivation in areas where a majority of households depended on social welfare payments for survival and with it, all the side-effects that scarcity and few options inevitably bring.

Critics of the IRA used to claim that the organisation was able to recruit from these areas because young men had nothing to keep them occupied. It even became fashionable in some middle-class circles to say that the IRA was a form of alternative entertainment for some of its members. The reality was very different: real desperation and a determination not to go back to the miserable indignities of the past drove these people to levels of commitment that matched their plight.

The IRA profile in rural Northern Ireland was slightly different from that of their urban comrades, not in terms of the average volunteer's age or in terms of their experience at the hands of the Orange state, but in terms of their occupations. Catholic prospects were no better in rural parts, but unemployment there had traditionally led to emigration: those left behind ran small shops, or were tradesmen in the construction industry or small farmers.

Their environment tends to set a person's outlook and organisational style and this was reflected in the IRA structures and activities. In larger urban areas, where people had lived together for several generations and where larger numbers of men and women would either socialise or use common facilities such as church halls or clubs, greater numbers were involved in operations and in the size of the basic operational unit. In rural areas, the basic work unit was either the family farm or a work squad of no more than two or three men.

These differences were, however, largely technical. The Provisional IRA was largely a movement of the working class,[7] the unemployed working class and less well-off rural population. Its support base was made up of those who found themselves doubly disadvantaged, as they were excluded and marginalised both by reason of their class and community origins. As one old Provo was heard saying many years later at a friend's funeral, after a graveside oration by a well-spoken and clearly middle-class member of Sinn Féin: 'After having spent all my adult life in the Provisional IRA, I can safely say that in all that time I never met an architect, an accountant, a quantity surveyor or a bank manager who fired a rifle or made a bomb for us.'

9
The Political and Military Strategy of the Provisional IRA

The operation was going well until a premature detonation in the mortar-gun barrel caused devastation among the IRA attack team. The mortar crew had been operating from the back of a commandeered lorry with protecting cover fire from a group of riflemen who were gathered around them on the vehicle, when the lethal blast occurred. Within seconds, it became obvious that there were casualties among the team and original plans for withdrawing were going to have to change rapidly. The problem was that with two men dead and several others seriously injured, the team needed somewhere to regroup and attend to their wounded.

It would have been a difficult task under ideal circumstances and these were far from ideal conditions. The IRA had launched a gun and rocket attack on a British Army/RUC station before they began to mortar the outpost. Well before the accidental explosion, the outpost had signalled its headquarters for assistance and while the British Army would have been reluctant to rush out to the scene, local foot patrols and covert units would have been alerted and directed to the spot. The few uninjured men left on the lorry had to take a swift and bold decision. They gathered their dead and wounded onto the lorry and drove to a nearby village where they knew there was support for the Republican cause. The IRA parked in the main street of the village and as they began under cover of darkness to carry out the grim work of regaining control of the situation, the local civilian population joined them in their task.

Within minutes of their arrival, the entire village seemed to know what had happened and gathered to help. In the few hours before dawn, bleeding and shell-shocked men were taken into houses, washed, medicated and bandaged. Blood-stained clothing was removed and destroyed, and replacement outfits found for those in need. Villagers fed the IRA unit and assembled teams of car drivers and scouts who were dispatched to hospitals across the Border with the injured men who needed professional medical assistance.

Knowing that with daylight the British Army would launch a full-scale follow-up operation, men from the village began to lead uninjured members of the IRA party on foot overland to safer locations. The final action of the night was when the volunteer now in charge had to make a difficult decision about what to do with the bodies of his dead comrades. He knew that he could not take them with him and he knew that he could not leave them in the village and put the inhabitants at risk from Loyalist death squads. He had no option but to have the dead wrapped in sheets and left by a roadside some distance from the village and arrange for a phone call to be made to the local hospital advising them of the location of casualties.

The IRA experienced many painful days and nights.

Provisional IRA strategy must be viewed in the light of the concrete situation in which their battle was fought. To a large extent, the organisation faced an incredibly difficult if not impossible task from the outset. Neither leadership nor the rank-and-file can be faulted for failing to achieve what was politically or physically impossible. Nevertheless, there were strategic failures as well as considerable achievements. Due largely to the rapid and unplanned formation of the organisation, there was a sometimes eclectic adoption of strategy and tactics, especially at the outset. In some ways, this may have assisted the speedy take-off and development of the movement since it was not troubled by internal debates around esoteric ideological points. Absence of a clear theoretical framework, on the other hand, led inevitably to some directional misjudgement and ambiguity.

Geographically, Northern Ireland is a small place where a motorist can comfortably drive diagonally from one end to the other within a three-hour period. The population is a little larger now than in the late 1960s, but still has not exceeded 1.7 million people, just over 40 per cent of whom are Catholic.[1] Less than half of those who viewed themselves as Catholic could have been considered supporters of the IRA insurrection, although most volunteers (and police officers, if they speak frankly) will testify that relatively few Catholics actively cooperated with the authorities to the disadvantage of Republican fighters. Ranged against this small community of comparatively under-resourced people was a formidable opposition. The Unionist population, at approximately one million people, was significantly larger and with state assistance was invariably much better armed. The British state was and remains one of the leading military and economic powers in the world.

South of the Border, a majority of the Republic of Ireland's population was unwilling to assist the northern insurrection. Governments in Dublin quickly realised that involvement in northern affairs could potentially destabilise their state and from an early stage decided that instead of challenging Britain, Dublin would designate the IRA as the real problem rather than a response to it. This dishonest and pusillanimous position, nevertheless, gained majority support in the Republic for a number of reasons.

The Republic's ruling class had a vested interest in not disturbing the comfortable niche they enjoyed and ensured that every section of the southern establishment worked enthusiastically to reinforce the government stance. Almost without exception, broadcast and print media maintained a line that the Provisional IRA was responsible for the conflict and journalists who deviated from this stance risked being sacked or downgraded. To reinforce and emphasise the state's authority, the Republic's government dismissed the Raidió Teilifís Éireann (RTÉ)[2] authority on 24 November 1972 for protecting a source. This body was replaced with a compliant group who thereafter enforced tight censorship. A small group of journalists at the station opposed the direction in which they were forced to go but to little avail.[3] In spite of this and the fact that most who worked in RTÉ were opposed to the IRA, right-wing broadcasters felt the need to keep up the pressure and continued to rail against so-called 'Hush Puppy Provos'.[4] Even the Republic's education system was redesigned to reflect a purely southern Irish worldview and at a third level, praise and position was granted to those historians who revised the past to absolve Britain of blame for its mismanagement of Irish affairs during the centuries of rule from London. On a wider level, the state existed in a condition of ongoing emergency, practising a permanent anti-Provo witch-hunt. Many workers feared being deemed sympathetic to the IRA, as conviction under the Offences Against the State Act carried automatic disbarment from any form of publicly funded employment.

Faced with such formidable opposition, the Provisional IRA could easily have crumbled after the initial enthusiasm died down. That it did not subside easily indicated a depth of resentment and anger – not to mention commitment – that few outsiders readily understood. Passion, however, could be no substitute for an effective strategy in the long run.

The most basic problem facing IRA strategists was how to devise an operational policy for dealing with an enemy that was too powerful to be defeated in a conventional military sense. Britain was never going to suffer a rout similar to that inflicted on them at Singapore in February 1942, or on the French at Dien Bien Phu in 1954.[5] Without the option of driving its enemy into the sea, or to Republican-controlled POW camps, the IRA could only hope for total success by inflicting such pain on the British that London would lose its will to stay. The latter option obviously depended on Republicans having the capacity to deliver war on an intense scale; in the light of IRA resources, that was a huge undertaking.

In spite of this, many IRA volunteers at ground level in the early 1970s were carried along on a wave of optimism believing that they could indeed inflict a military defeat on their enemy. This misconception grew largely from the spontaneous nature of the organisation's founding and initial development. The IRA did not create the circumstances in which the organisation found itself. Nor could it anticipate the series of momentous and traumatic occurrences, such as internment without trial in August 1971 and Bloody Sunday shortly afterwards in January 1972, that caused its ranks to swell so rapidly. In practice, the Provisional IRA and its Army council was often responding to events that were happening with mesmerising rapidity.

As a consequence, the leadership frequently reflected (and often tried to reflect) the rank-and-file mood as much as moulding that outlook. Under such circumstances, it was nearly impossible to curb ambitious demands or make a pitch for pragmatism and, with the Irish Civil War still an issue for many Republicans of the era, it was difficult to explain the difference between a prudent compromise and unprincipled capitulation. This in turn, coupled with momentous circumstances, led the IRA to commit itself by 1972 to a stark objective of British withdrawal and an all-Ireland republic. This was a political stance, which made it difficult if not impossible to discuss or to contemplate an alternative, in the event that the organisation found itself unable to impose its own preferred solution.

It was, moreover, a position that tended to flounder on the question of Unionist opposition to a united Ireland on Provisional IRA terms. Unionism had a majority in Northern Ireland and for so long as the 26-county state and its population insisted that unity could only come by consent of a majority in the Six Counties, Britain was under no political pressure to accommodate the IRA demand nor under any administrative pressure to contain a hostile majority in its Irish territory. How to win over or accommodate a significant section of the Unionist community was a dilemma that continued to confound the Provisional IRA throughout its existence.

Due largely to the political and emotional turmoil that brought about the Provisional IRA, the organisation was not good at recognising qualified objectives. In the early 1970s, there was, for example, a political initiative that emanated from within the Unionist community, which might have unlocked the conundrum of how to engage constructively with the Unionist population. A number of well-placed Unionist politicians and paramilitaries mooted the concept of a confederation of Ireland. This proposal would have seen the Six Counties retaining very significant autonomy within an island-wide political entity functioning within the European

Union. Political union with the United Kingdom would have been dissolved without conceding total sovereignty to Dublin. With the IRA then supporting the Éire Nua[6] policy, which argued for a four-province federal Ireland, there appeared to be room for productive negotiation.

The initiative got as far as a meeting between representatives of the Provisional IRA and the UVF, but was sabotaged by a number of actions that may or may not have been concerted. At the meeting's outset, a Provisional IRA negotiator behaved aggressively and undiplomatically, leaving the Loyalists feeling distinctly uncomfortable. Their anxiety was compounded when Dublin government minister Conor Cruise O'Brien learned of the meeting and deliberately released word of it to the press, causing consternation within Unionist circles. Ian Paisley then read about the proposal and verbally attacked the entire notion and those examining it. As a result, the negotiations were quickly ended by Unionists and, deprived of momentum, the idea was relegated to the margins of political discourse. The concept, however, retained a certain currency in one format or another within certain Unionist paramilitary constituencies for many years afterwards, although the IRA made no attempt to pursue the option. In hindsight, it is possible to say that an opportunity to agree a new constitutional framework outside the UK was abandoned: eventually the Provisional IRA would settle for much less than confederation.

The option was not on the table, however, when the Provisional IRA felt compelled to increase the level of its engagement and move from its early organising and defensive phase into a fully offensive mode. In the aftermath of internment without trial in August 1971 and the death of 14 civilians in Derry on Bloody Sunday 1972, the political landscape was transformed. With hundreds of recruits flowing into the organisation, the developing strategy of the IRA leadership was both a response to the demand of the Catholic community and provided personnel to sustain the commitment to an armed struggle. The organisation believed that it had to respond to the situation, and threw its full energy into carrying out as many armed operations as possible. There was a 'push–pull' effect at work on the IRA in this instance. Many Catholic people desperately wanted to strike back at the British and pressurised the IRA to do so, while at the same time the organisation was unwilling to miss the opportunity presented by circumstances.

Early belief in a decisive victory was dimmed somewhat by experience but was replaced by an equally seductive premise that a sufficiently high casualty rate among regular British troops would cause the UK population to vote for withdrawal from Ireland. The Vietnam conflict with its anti-war movement in the US was sometimes quoted to reinforce this idea but, however plausible it seemed in theory, the reality proved different. Quite simply, the IRA did not have sufficient capacity to inflict the scale of casualties on Britain's army that might generate the type of broad anti-war movement that troubled the Pentagon. Moreover, because its army was not suffering excessive casualties, Britain's Ministry of Defence never had to ask for conscription (a draft), a principal reason for much of the anti-war resentment in the United States.

In a broader sense, single-minded concentration to the exclusion of all else on a strategy requiring British capitulation carried within it a political risk. In the first instance, it allowed British and Dublin governments to create and then cultivate a malleable tool – the SDLP – to oppose the IRA from within the Catholic community. Secondly, as this threat eventually dawned on the IRA, it drew the group into pursuing almost blindly a policy of overtaking the Nationalist party electorally, with little consideration given to the detrimental impact this was having on Republican principle and policy.

Along with its uncompromising position of 'a united Ireland or nothing', the IRA had an ambiguous socioeconomic outlook that was in essence poorly developed and even utopian, rather than ideologically or scientifically based. The IRA had adopted the goal of an Ireland-wide socialist republic early in its history. Apart from a small group of reactionaries who wielded a limited amount of influence at the movement's formation, there was little opposition to the slogan on the masthead. What was missing, however, was a coherent analysis and understanding of what it meant to be socialist or how it might be implemented, apart from a broad and sometimes uncertain view that the details could be worked out in the aftermath of an IRA victory. This 'all-right-on-the-night' attitude was prevalent among many volunteers: with young men and women engaged in an intense battle with the British state, perhaps it was hardly surprising that this was the case.

Throughout the twentieth century, Marxism had influenced Republican Ireland, but its impact was intermittent and failed to make a profound impression. The Marxist James Connolly remained a revered figure within the Provisional IRA and, by the early 1970s, Frank Ryan and the Irish contribution to the defence of Republican Spain was viewed favourably; however, there was a reluctance to embrace the workings of scientific socialism. The

Provisional IRA was composed largely of young men and women in a hurry, who were focused on prosecuting the insurrection and often viewed political education as an optional extra. Moreover, the posturing adopted by many of the left-wing parties and groups active in Ireland at the time exacerbated this unfortunate reality.

No matter how explicable the Republican grass-roots' attitude might be, it did not have a beneficial impact on the organisation. With a largely working-class support base open to a much more coherent left-wing political agenda, the Provisional IRA was in a position to influence the creation of a wider social and indeed socialist movement than it did. Developing a popular mass movement addressing social and economic issues would, in time, have given it a stronger base in the Republic. It would also have added to its prospects for attracting support from the left in Britain and could have created a foundation for class-based politics in Northern Ireland.

Conversely, refusing to adopt a more conventional model of socialist theory and practice, the Provisional IRA continued to depend upon a militaristic and hierarchical mode of organisation that remained suspicious of uncontained mass movements. This aspect of IRA behaviour not only impeded the movement's political progress but also had a stultifying effect on its military analysis.

Events and circumstances create conditions and set patterns of military activity in times of civil unrest and insurrection. Popular movements are often guided by what can be done as much as by what the actors and participants wish to do – and so it proved with the Provisional IRA. As described previously, the organisation was created hurriedly in response to the August 1969 assault on Catholic Belfast. It drew from the experience and traditions of veteran Republicans, but it came into being swiftly and under pressure of events rather than as a result of long and careful deliberation.

Concerned initially with a defensive role and responding to rapidly developing circumstances, the Provisional IRA did not follow a classic path of guerrilla warfare or an insurrectionary seizure of power. There was no master plan for insurrection prior to the situation in Northern Ireland deteriorating and descending into violent chaos. Under the prevailing circumstances, there was a demand, first for defence, then for reprisals as a deterrent, and finally all-out assault to overthrow the state. Given the circumstances, almost any organised group could have assumed the role, but history and the absence of alternatives meant that it was the Provisional IRA which emerged to fill the vacuum.

In contrast to a widely held contemporary view that the IRA was only ever concerned with uniting Ireland politically, the early Provisional IRA had a somewhat more limited short-term objective. As late as 1971 and after the introduction of internment without trial in August of that year, the organisation was insisting on a more modest package. On 5 September 1971, the organisation published a five-point plan it deemed as necessary before it would offer a truce. These points, which significantly did not mention a British withdrawal, were:

1) Ceasefire by the British Army
2) Abolition of Stormont
3) Free elections to a 9-county Ulster parliament
4) Release of detainees, and
5) Compensation for those injured by British Army actions.

The events of Bloody Sunday in Derry when 14 people were shot dead by British soldiers, changed the political climate; the IRA moved towards its now better-known position of total British disengagement, or in its own language, 'Brits Out'.

Unless warfare descends into mindless bloodletting, it usually follows certain logic. There is an objective to be achieved, something that requires a plan of campaign which necessitates identifying different milestones along the way. Insurrectionary struggle is no different and because it usually begins by being under-resourced, often makes even greater organisational demands on its practitioners.

In the tradition of the French Revolution, and mirrored throughout the nineteenth century and into the early years of twentieth-century Russia, insurgents usually sought to amass forces and seize a capital city. Success depended on revolutionaries' ability to hold their position in the face of counter-attack. In this scenario, large cities were of great importance and successful insurrections tended to spread from the centre to the countryside. With the passing of time, governing classes began to design cities to be more difficult for insurgents to capture and defend and, along with developing aerial capacity, insurgent strategies were forced to change.[7]

Mao Zedong, witnessing the destruction of urban Communist forces, reversed the insurrectionary orthodoxy practised over the preceding century and a half. Defying prevailing thinking, he went to the countryside and launched the process of strangling the centre from the margins. Whichever method was favoured, successful exponents of the arts of irregular warfare have all agreed that a campaign follows a series of phases. Guerrilla warfare theorists insist that insurgents should not escalate their campaign to a higher level until they are sure of their ability to succeed under the latter. Whether these periods are short or long depends on local circumstances, but steps have a logical progression. The first is a preparatory period when the message of insurrection is spread through the population, or at least that portion receptive to the call. The second is when insurgents strive for strategic balance with the opposition and finally, the third phase is when the insurrection is sufficiently strong to take the offensive and capture power.

Given the balance of numbers in Northern Ireland and the disparity of resources, the Provisional IRA did not have the option of contending for a 'strategic balance of forces'. There never was any possibility of inflicting a conventional military defeat on the British military. The IRA opted in practice for a campaign to make the Six Counties ungovernable and thus make a political resolution impossible within the context of a settlement internal to Northern Ireland. The rationale was simple. In the eyes of the IRA and its support base, Northern Ireland was a dysfunctional and failed entity, incapable of reform and maintained in this position by the British government. In order to overcome this situation, the IRA wanted to break the political connection with Great Britain, end Partition and bring all of Ireland under a unified political structure. While the aim was straightforward, the means for achieving it, in the absence of military victory, were not always so clear.

IRA strategy during the Black and Tan War of 1919–21 had been relatively simple. Its aim was to make Ireland ungovernable by the British and where possible, to facilitate the rule of Dáil Éireann, which had been established in 1919. The new parliament or Dáil was composed entirely of Sinn Féin members who had won seats in a large majority of the Irish constituencies during the British parliamentary election of 1918.[8] The strategy enjoyed a measure of success due to the fact that Britain found it difficult to cope with a war for independence, which was endorsed by a very clear majority of the Irish population at a time when the Empire had just fought a war ostensibly for the freedom of small nations. Moreover, although allied to Britain, the US was at that time content to allow the old Empire to suffer a limited humiliation, as the Americans sought to replace Britain as the world's premier economic, political and military power.

However, with no similar conditions pertaining in the Six Counties during the last quarter of the twentieth century, the Provisional IRA was not in a position to bring about 'dual power'. In any case, the existence of a Unionist majority foreclosed any such option. Consequently, IRA leaders struggled throughout the conflict to create a viable political alternative that would gain sufficient support to undermine Britain's administration in the North.

Many of the early leaders and influential figures in the Provisional IRA were veterans of the 1956 Border campaign. Most of these men had spent time in jail together either in Belfast's Crumlin Road or south of the Border in Mountjoy Jail or in the Curragh detention camp. Some had spent time in all three locations. As a result, they usually shared an analysis of the 1950s campaign. Significantly too, they always referred to this earlier engagement as the 'Fifties Campaign' and rarely by its official title 'Operation Harvest', signifying either subliminally or candidly that it was merely one more round in an ongoing fight. This cohort of senior Republican leaders did not necessarily attempt to recreate the methods and tactics of the earlier round of hostilities, but their outlook was informed by what they had experienced then.

The IRA's 1956–62 Operation Harvest campaign had come in the aftermath of a Dublin government-sponsored initiative in the early part of that decade, designed to end Partition by use of publicity and diplomatic pressure. Although these attempts to persuade the British government that it should leave Ireland failed to have any impact in Westminster, it stirred up considerable feelings among young Republicans in Ireland, especially south of the Border. With the coalition government of John A. Costello having proclaimed the 26-county state a republic in 1949, one of the old Civil War issues was removed from contention. The renewed IRA campaign concentrated, therefore, on what was described as 'unfinished business with England in the Six Counties'. This demand was in many ways part of a purely Nationalist agenda calling for an independent, unitary Irish state. With limited insight of concrete conditions in Northern Ireland and a poor appreciation for the need to identify with daily living conditions there, the 1956–62 campaign gained little active support in the Six Counties and less still south of the Border.

Lack of support did not, however, prevent the IRA leadership of the time from drawing up elaborate plans for its campaign. In many instances, these plans broke the cardinal rules of guerrilla warfare. With an outdated understanding of contemporary warfare, the IRA in the 1950s established Black and Tan War-style flying columns. The strategy quickly fell apart. Flying columns proved too cumbersome for serious action in the North against well-armed mobile RUC patrols that almost always knew the terrain better than the IRA guerrillas.

Compounding this misunderstanding of the role and nature of the RUC, the southern-based IRA leadership also failed to recognise the significance of the locally recruited B Specials. Operating in their own areas as an armed reserve to the full-time regular police, this force performed a function considered vital in every counter-insurgency strategy across the world. That is, its members provided a constant on-the-ground presence of men familiar with their native districts who monitored events, responded rapidly to incidents, and manned checkpoints at key locations. By preventing IRA personnel from moving freely, they contributed enormously to the campaign's defeat. The IRA leadership of the time ordered its units not to initiate attacks on the B Specials, believing naively that it could neutralise this force by appealing to its members' sense of Irish patriotism. Unsurprisingly, the B Specials treated the request with derision.

With patchy support in the Six Counties depriving the organisation of an adequate supply of safe houses and local intelligence, the IRA often resorted to making risky long-range sorties from south of the Border. In time and with its resources dwindling, the IRA was forced to resort to small local operations, such as cutting down electricity pylons and burning Border customs posts. With too few men, too little support and too strong an opponent, the campaign fizzled out amid demoralisation and recrimination in 1962. No matter which side they would take in subsequent divisions, those IRA men who came through the rigours of Operation Harvest drew powerful lessons from the experience that were to remain with them.

IRA veterans of Operation Harvest who created and led the early Provisional movement believed that, above all else, they must not repeat the mistakes of the past. From their point of view, and for men steeped in a militaristic tradition, this rarely included political considerations. All too often, their conclusions simply led them to believe that a better campaign meant a) avoiding organisational blunders and b) delivering bigger and more devastating blows to the enemy than previously.

These men were suspicious of a distant leadership living outside the Six Counties which was, in their opinion, prone to creating fancy but futile strategies. Moreover, having tasted the agony of defeat a decade earlier, they were determined not to be distracted by sentimentality or squeamishness on this occasion. These were sensible precautions but still required an additional rationale.

Crucially, the IRA needed realistic long-term political and strategic goals and not just demands, no matter how attractive these might be. The absence of such a strategy ultimately worked against the adoption of a planning timeline that might have allowed the organisation to create a process whereby the IRA could have set itself a series of objectives. Other successful guerrilla movements were aware of the need for such an overview but circumstances denied this to the Provisional IRA.

Learning from previous campaigns, the Provisional IRA developed cautiously at first. The organisation was determined not to engage in any large-scale, vainglorious gestures where it might lose men in significant numbers. After early gun battles with Loyalist snipers in Belfast in 1970, the Provisional IRA adopted a slow build-up in keeping with its limited numbers. Instead of launching an all-out offensive, the organisation opted for a policy of retaliatory strikes against British Army personnel and agencies connected either to the northern state or to British business.

When the British Army began shooting petrol bombers,[9] the Provisional IRA began to shoot British soldiers. When the RUC or the British Army raided Catholic houses, the IRA bombed British or Unionist-owned businesses. As a tactic for raising the organisation's profile and winning support among working-class Catholics, it was a major success. As a long-term strategy, however, it had its limitations. The IRA needed to find a way of using its limited military capacity to move the political situation along to its advantage. This would have entailed a very pragmatic and realistic view of what was politically as well as militarily possible; under the circumstances, the outcome was mixed.

With no realistic prospect of inflicting a decisive military defeat on the British state, the IRA found itself in a drawn-out war of attrition. Due to the origins of the Provisional IRA and the conflict that gave rise to it, the initial focus was in Belfast city. Between 1971 and 1975, the Belfast Brigade of the IRA flung itself at the British state, its army and at the commercial structures of a city that for more than a century had refused to grant its members and supporters full citizenship. To this end, the Belfast Brigade launched a series of campaigns simultaneously.

Over many decades, Irish Republicans had acquired a degree of expertise and confidence in the use of explosives. From an early stage, the newly emerging Provisional IRA recognised the power of a bombing campaign. In a region where private British and/or Unionist companies owned much business and a majority of the infrastructure was government controlled, a campaign of sabotage was viewed as a crucial tactic. From an IRA point of view, the destruction of commercial property, telephone exchanges, electricity sub-stations, courthouses, or motor taxation offices served several purposes. In the first instance, it undermined the local commercial and administrative infrastructure. More significantly perhaps, it demonstrated to the people of Ireland and the world beyond that the northern part of the island was a troubled area where an insurrectionary movement was engaged in conflict with the state.

The Belfast Brigade of the IRA bombed the commercial centre of the city in order to damage financially its overwhelmingly Unionist establishment. Bombing the city centre had other advantages from an IRA point of view. It tied up a considerable number of the opposition in guard duty and it made for spectacular television footage. The usual practice was to try and give a warning before the bomb exploded (an exercise that too often failed), a tactic which allowed cameramen to take the type of film footage that for a number of years typified news reports from Northern Ireland. Only the ideologically blinded could pretend that Northern Ireland was a normal part of the United Kingdom.

The Belfast IRA knew, moreover, that as the number of attacks increased, the enemy would find it virtually impossible to monitor and investigate every incident. This factor of British Army and/or RUC overload provided, in itself, a modicum of security for the IRA's Active Service Units. It even afforded the Republicans with a type of training ground for raw recruits, who were given the opportunity to gain experience on relatively safe operations. In a technical sense, the IRA was able to carry out these attacks with a limited number of personnel.

Throughout its campaign, the IRA made extensive use of explosives and trained its people in their manufacture and use. For the most part, training was basic. In a different context, it would probably have proven adequate for controlled demolition or quarry work. Difficulties arose, however, when they needed to use more sophisticated timing devices and were forced to resort to manufacturing homemade explosives. Paradoxically, as the IRA grew rapidly in strength after the introduction of internment without trial and the Bloody Sunday shootings in Derry, its problems with explosive manufacturing increased. Feeling obliged to increase its level of activity and with a huge influx of recruits, the organisation began to provide training through more junior individuals and entrust the manufacture and delivery of devices to less experienced people.

It is a matter of fact that a majority of bombs planted by the IRA were delivered with a warning in advance of detonation. In order to do so, the organisation's volunteers took greater risks with homemade timing devices than had they employed the crude but safer (and shorter delay) black smoking fuse. Under pressure to increase operations, many IRA units began to take risks with where and when they planted their devices. It took the IRA some years to devise a safe timing device and before its engineers were able to so, many civilians and IRA volunteers[10] died in premature explosions. Nevertheless, bombs in cafes and restaurants that took civilian lives, whether accidents or not, were understandably viewed by Unionists as murderous attacks on their community rather than military operations.

While the Belfast bombing campaign continued, IRA units in Catholic working-class districts fought a continuous battle with the British Army. Republican fighters enjoyed an early advantage as British foot-patrols found themselves in areas where they were unable to match local knowledge. British Army commanders were determined to hold and dominate the ground and insisted on maintaining a heavy and visible presence in all Catholic areas. In practice, the British Army found that it was patrolling a hostile region but without having the authority to destroy potential dangerous zones, as would have been the case in more conventional warfare. For reasons of domestic policy rather than morality, the British government was unable to employ the type of tactics used, for example, by the Israeli Army in Gaza. Obviously, the IRA never posed a threat to the British state's existence in a way that Hamas does to Israel, and London evidently believed that to use Israeli methods would have been counter-productive. Demolishing large numbers of Catholic homes and indiscriminately killing many civilians would have risked alienating the Republic of Ireland, undermining the SDLP, disturbing liberal British opinion and demolishing Britain's claim that it was a peacekeeper in a troubled area.

Contained by these restrictions, British soldiers in the early part of the insurrection walked into IRA ambushes time after time as Republican volunteers displayed an amazing level of ingenuity in finding new and unexpected avenues of attack. For a short period, it appeared as if the IRA could not be contained in Belfast and that the British Army might lose the upper hand in Northern Ireland's largest city. Gradually, though, the situation began to turn in favour of the larger force. IRA losses mounted as British Army commanders began to understand better the geography of Belfast. An armed cordon strung around the centre of the city blocked IRA access to its target and led in turn to the capture of a considerable number of ASUs attempting to penetrate the security zone.

Gradually, the British began to impose their strength on IRA districts. Unaware of the geography when they first arrived, foot-patrols soon learned the pattern of streets and roadways. More damaging still to the IRA was the accumulation of information and knowledge that was being gathered by the British Army and RUC. Where Republican faces and families had initially been a baffling mystery to the squaddies, constant house searches, coupled with non-stop checkpoints, meant that eventually the enemy became familiar with the areas they occupied and with their residents. By early 1974, the Belfast Brigade was under enormous pressure with a critical mass of its personnel in prison, a great number of British soldiers billeted on its territory, and intelligence leaking to the enemy at a disturbing rate.

It came as an unpleasant shock to both the IRA in Belfast and to the leadership of the movement overall, when together they realised that its largest and most hard-hitting brigade was vulnerable. Belfast had been, after all, the cradle of the insurrection. Curtailment of the Belfast Brigade's operational capacity was inevitable, nevertheless. It had nothing to do with the volunteers' bravery or determination, something they had in plenty. It had all to do with the relative size of the protagonists. Belfast was a relatively small city of 450,000 people, with its Catholic working-class making up less than a third of that number and most of that contained in distinct areas. Britain's army had strength and numbers to surround, squeeze and strangle the urban IRA – and that was what happened.

The British government had, nevertheless, been forced to deploy an incredible amount of its military and intelligence-gathering machine to gain the upper hand in Belfast, which had become a city under siege. And while a large number of Belfast Brigade personnel were in prison, Britain knew that to maintain its grip on the area it would have to retain a large garrison in the region. In spite of the apparent reverses suffered by the Belfast Brigade, its campaign of the early 1970s had transformed the political landscape of Belfast and indeed Northern Ireland forever. The century-long balance of power in North-east Ulster had been changed irreversibly as it had become clear that Unionism, on its own, could no longer hold Belfast's Catholic population hostage. The Belfast Brigade may have been seriously damaged but the community from which it sprang emerged confident and determined to assert itself. More than anything else, this proved corrosive to the existence of the Orange state.

If the Belfast Brigade was under pressure by the mid-1970s, it took longer for the British Army to gain a similar advantage over rural IRA units. Whereas urban IRA units in Belfast and Derry had larger numbers to draw on and the organisation reflected this fact with membership divided into companies, battalions and a brigade staff in overall charge, IRA organisational structures in country areas were different. With wider spaces and different terrain, the smaller rural ASUs proved more difficult to pin down. Moreover, ASUs operating in proximity to the Border often had the advantage of being able to evade capture by crossing into a different jurisdiction in the Republic of Ireland, where the IRA campaign had a measurable degree of hard-core support concentrated along the Border areas.

Southern Irish authorities did not by any means welcome Republican fighters into their territory and from an early stage collaborated with the British government in an effort to smash the IRA campaign. The coalition government of Liam Cosgrove that came to power in the spring of 1973 introduced heavy-handed legislation in conjunction with an increased level of collaboration with the British in an attempt to curb the IRA and was, eventually, only stalled by the electorate's refusal to countenance the type of brutal measures that might have achieved his government's purpose.

At the beginning of the Provisional IRA campaign, many rural units developed almost as a collection of self-contained semi-autonomous groups, rather than anything resembling conventional military structures. Small ASUs were usually located in a particular district or area and the membership was often made up of a handful of friends or workmates. That they shared some form of openly known contact with each other such as membership of a local football team, or part of a construction squad meant that (initially at any rate) it would raise little suspicion if they were to be seen frequently in each other's company. The downside of this, of course, was that if one member was exposed, the others came immediately under suspicion. Small groups of men working with a considerable degree of autonomy increased the security of rural ASUs. Indeed, some of these units had come together before joining the IRA. Frequently, their only contact with the rest of the organisation was when one of the group crossed the Border to meet with senior-level IRA officers in order to learn of broad policy directives, or to arrange for delivery of weapons and explosives. RUC and British intelligence found such groups particularly difficult to unearth and penetrate.

In some ways, the rural ASUs practiced a classic form of guerrilla struggle reminiscent of what Mao had named 'Sparrow Warfare'.[11] While rural Republicans had the capacity to maintain their campaign for a more protracted period, circumstances on the ground meant that they struggled to inflict decisive casualties on the British. London clearly took a view that the major threat to its authority lay in Belfast and that the countryside could be contained before being crushed. As a result, the British Army acted evasively in rural areas and adopted a lower profile than in the cities.

Rural IRA units gradually acquired the ability to destroy British Army road vehicles and in some areas it became unusual to see motorised military patrols. To counter this disadvantage, the British used its locally recruited part-time regiment, the UDR, supported by an RUC Reserve to gather intelligence and act as a lightly armed counter-insurgent militia. Strenuous efforts have been made over the years to portray the two forces as well-meaning part-timers doing their best to protect society, insinuating that any attack on their members was motivated purely by sectarianism.

Lost amid this tendentious propaganda is the reality. Both the UDR and the RUC Reserve were recruited locally and had, therefore, a comprehensive and detailed knowledge of their areas of operation. As local men, they were able to distinguish between various accents that are so distinctive to a Northern Irish ear, but would not resonate with regular soldiers reared in Britain. A County Derry accent would go unnoticed, for example, if questioned in South Tyrone by Londoners, but would immediately draw the suspicion of a Dungannon UDR patrol. As local men with roots for many generations in an area, some UDR members were even able to recognise young Republicans by family resemblance to older relatives. They had, too, the ability to differentiate between families sharing similar names, an invaluable asset to the authorities in parts of the pre-postcode Six Counties where locals used ancient patronymics to identify each other.[12] In closely mixed rural areas, members of the UDR or RUC Reserve were intimately familiar with the rhythm and pattern of life in their district and could recognise instantly if something was out of place.

Whether on or off duty, these men acted not only as the eyes and ears of the regular army but actively supported it logistically and militarily. That they had dual military and civilian roles added to the danger they posed to the IRA. Employed as school bus-drivers, postmen, refuse collectors and every other position in the workforce, they had a perfect 'cover' for travelling covertly through Republican districts, not only to observe but often to monitor. A dustman may appear a harmless worker until he sifts through the bin for information – a routine practice by every intelligence agency.

The Provisional IRA would have been incredibly naive, not to say extraordinarily stupid, had it failed to recognise the threat these forces posed. Unsurprisingly, therefore, the Provisional IRA responded by proactively targeting UDR members and RUC Reservists, whether in or out of uniform. The Provisional IRA was determined not to repeat the errors of past campaigns (in particular, that of Operation Harvest) and allow themselves to be defeated by a local militia. To this extent, they succeeded in breaking the unquestioned and unchallenged supremacy of the armed 'night watchman' of the old Orange state. In time, this was to have an impact similar to that of the Belfast Brigade breaking the siege on its own community.

Taken together, the Provisional IRA campaign in urban centres and rural areas had not just forced Britain to prorogue Stormont but had also undermined Orange supremacy. The problem faced by the Provisional IRA, however, was that while it had broken the siege, it would find it more difficult to follow up with a successful debouchment. At grass-roots level, a large number of IRA activists believed that their war could be won by undermining the British people's desire to remain in Northern Ireland. This they thought would be achieved by 'sending enough soldiers home in coffins'. In a theoretical sense, this might have been possible. At about the same time, a high casualty level among troops in Vietnam (forcing the drafting of reluctant civilians) had, after all, caused the Americans to rethink their support for war in South Asia. But the IRA did not have the capacity to inflict the scale of death on the British Army that would impact to a similar degree on the British public. The war was doomed to becoming a slow grind.

10
The War in England

Peter was from a Unionist background but from early adolescence had never felt comfortable within that world, a world which by 1967 was beginning to unravel, if only, at first, at the edges. Although not widely recognised, and very rarely commented on, it is a fact that many other families from the Unionist tradition had sons and daughters, children of the post-Second World War era like Peter, who also were critical of the whole entity of the Northern Ireland state. They had never experienced religious discrimination themselves, of course, but had witnessed it while with Catholic friends, or at a distance, walking in Catholic areas, especially in cities such as Derry where the discrimination against Catholics was especially conspicuous.

Derry was a city in which a clear Catholic majority was excluded from power and where working-class Catholics were crowded into poorly maintained and cramped houses in the Bogside district, many dating from the nineteenth century. More immediately evident was the behaviour of the RUC at public events, or even worse, the day-to-day behaviour of the B Specials. Peter knew from family experience the contempt for Catholics expressed by this force, a mixture of the patrician and what he later would come to recognise as racist. Seeing the behaviour of the RUC and the attitudes of some of their elders more generally made many young liberal Protestants of his generation acutely aware of the perversity of the state and the society in which they were living.

To the extent that at the early stage of the civil rights struggle Peter and some of his friends articulated Irish Republican sentiment and outlook, these were very often uncultivated and by and large found expression in the uncomplicated idea that Ireland should be independent in its entirety from Britain. For the most part, this came second to what was also a somewhat inchoate notion of socialism. While in many respects this was mirrored in the perspectives held by many young Catholics, the profound difference in their respective social, political and economic experiences quickly propelled many young Protestants of this generation in a different direction from their Catholic friends. While Peter and his immediate milieu could make sense of the movement for civil rights, they could not connect this immediately with another wave of struggle in which 'the Brits had to be driven off our streets.'

However, their antipathy to Unionist rule combined with a strong sense of social fairness that would see many playing an important role in the early civil rights movement and mass organisations such as Peoples' Democracy. Yet it was not obviously clear to them what driving the Brits off the streets had to do with socialism, civil rights, or a romantic notion of 'Ireland her own'. From time to time, Peter recognised that there certainly was a connection but the culture and the structure of the sectarian state would ensure that connections would have to be, initially at any rate, 'theoretical'. What tended to happen was that two parallel views took hold – for a vague notion of 'socialism' and against British state repression in the Six Counties. The obvious link between the two would take time to develop in his and his friends' minds.

Ironically, it was initially by going beyond the straightforward 'Brits Out' line that Peter and his peers were able to make the links between the commitment to socialism and the fact that it was Britain on the streets of Derry, Belfast and elsewhere in the North that blocked broad working-class change. The British Army supporting the Orange state – and then proceeding to continue the work itself – was deepening and recasting sectarianism in the North. This was how they would come to understand the role of British imperialism in the north of Ireland. He realised that the divisions created by the Orange state were indeed real, practical divisions. How could working-class Protestants and Catholics make concrete, politically practical, solidarities? These divisions meant that however he and his friends might wish to be in solidarity with their Catholic counterparts, the reality, by 1969, of first RUC and then British state repression, made practical solidarity with the struggle on the streets and in rural areas, manifested in an immediate sense as opposition to overwhelming state repression, extremely limited. One thing for sure was that practical participation was a non-starter.

Increasingly, the struggles for a united Ireland, civil rights and 'against British imperialism' became less difficult to link, especially where the daily reality of the British state hit you, literally, full in the face. However, while Peter believed these could, should, be linked, the fight against British state strategy was made more difficult by the turn taken by those directly having to fight the British state. The turn away from mass community engagement effectively limited the scope for taking the struggle forward at that point across the sectarian divide. Yet how could it have been different – it was, in a sense, a kind of historic trap. And yet, whatever the arguments, if the British could not be confronted on the streets of Belfast and Derry and in the rural areas of the North, the chances of finally addressing the peculiarities of the northern state and British rule would be hopeless.

So in the misshapen world of Northern Irish society, Peter found it difficult to articulate his views in either Unionist or Nationalist areas. In the former, he would have been treated as a traitor while the latter would have suspected him of being an infiltrator or enemy agent. Deepening strong solidarities with Catholic friends in the North was becoming increasingly difficult, as his sister would find to her cost. In time, he found it easier to accept an opportunity for study in England where he immersed himself in socialist politics. The British left, as elsewhere, is and was divided on many issues, not least of which was the Irish question. Peter, nevertheless, aligned himself with the sections of the left that supported the Irish insurgency and campaigned vigorously for the 'Troops Out' movement.[1]

The initial period after the beginning for the insurgency seemed to be unproblematic and with even the increasingly marginalised British Communist Party critical of the role of the British state. This was not the same, needless to say, as solidarity with those fighting the British state. Between 1969 and 1974, the solidarity movement was clearer in showing solidarity with those actually fighting the British. Initially, this focused upon state repression and saw the formation of the Anti-Internment League, a broad movement of the far left and many within the British Labour Party. The objective was to end internment and push for thoroughgoing reforms of the state apparatus in the North.

As the insurgency took hold and the clear objectives of the British state became focused upon breaking opposition to its form of state-down 'reform', its view of the 'new' North would look much like the old one with perhaps the most egregious forms of repression concealed by caveats. In any event, it was what the British themselves were doing that was driving an agenda to which the solidarity movement in the UK would have to respond. The question was, simply, whether the movement in Britain would be one of solidarity (with those fighting the British state), or opposition (to the activities of the British state). While it might be obvious that these could not be separated, the fact that they were considered separately, said a great deal about the attitude of progressive movements in Britain in relation to Ireland down the decades. This was to be an important, never fully resolved distinction.

In the first instance, solidarity would be unquestioning as expressed, famously, in a solidarity demonstration in London, by John Lennon carrying a picture of his Bloody Sunday song under the headline 'For the IRA against British Imperialism'. For others, the line pursued would be summed up by the epithet 'Unconditional but Critical Support for the IRA'. But for others still, any overt or covert support, or reference to the IRA, would have to be expunged. By the mid-1970s, this would evolve so that those engaged in anti-state activity in Britain could describe themselves as giving unconditional but critical support to all those fighting British imperialism – supporters would not have to refer to the IRA in this broad-church understanding. It was a sign of the power of the British state – including the media – to intimidate that the 'IRA' began to recede as an organisation directly seen as central to those offering solidarity in Britain; nevertheless it reflected different views in the UK about what the war in the North was actually about. And yet, reasonable enough as this might be, many on the anti-imperialist left felt that it was first the Orange state and then the British who were, as they always had, setting the terms of debate. The key issue was solidarity with everyone fighting the British state and this might on occasion imply outright solidarity with the Provisional IRA, while at other times, more obviously with those in Catholic areas under direct attack by the state.

In Britain, while the solidarity movement never properly resolved this important tension between open 'solidarity' and 'opposition', the actions by the British state itself always undermined what were sometimes seen as doctrinal, at others reasonable, differences. This would happen on many occasions with perhaps the most significant being that of Bloody Sunday in 1972. Arguably, this was the high point of unity within the solidarity movement. However, despite the continuing sympathy shown by many others from a radical background, the pattern of struggle developed in such a way that it was difficult to read it as anything other than one between the British state and the IRA. Of course, this was how the media in Britain portrayed it and many in the North felt equally comfortable with this perspective. And so at times, the cause seemed hopeless, as IRA bombing in England created an anti-Irish hysteria among the general population, allowing the police to use heavy-handed tactics. As many Irish people in Britain were to discover, British police used these tactics, not just to deal with Republicans, but to intimidate political activists supporting demands for a change in British policy in Ireland.

What continued to cause surprise during the years of IRA activity was that in spite of the frenzy caused by bombs in England and ongoing attacks on British soldiers in Ireland, there remained a strong, well-organised public opposition in Britain to the government's Irish policy. On occasion, there were thousands of participants in protest marches and many of those involved were neither Irish born nor of Irish descent. Many of the most active protesters were left-wing, British working-class people who recognised the need to rein in the British establishment. If the solidarity demonstrated after Bloody Sunday was the high point in Britain, other moments reinforced this reality of working-class solidarity for those suffering British state repression in the North – although it also would reveal how limited this solidarity might be. Solidarity might be evident on particular occasions, but it would find little expression in the halls of what was supposed to be working-class power such as the TUC or Labour Party head office.[2] This was to be demonstrated nowhere more tragically than in 1980 and 1981 during the hunger strikes.[3]

Figure 10.1   John Lennon carries poster at 'Bloody Sunday' demo (© Red Mole).

From an IRA viewpoint, a long drawn-out war of attrition posed major hazards. Given the relative size and strength of the antagonists in the struggle, it was virtually impossible for the IRA to win a military victory in such an uneven engagement. Britain had a history of fighting colonial wars and, while seemingly losing out in many of these campaigns, had mastered the technique of drawing an opponent into a protracted conflict. To many in the IRA, it appeared that Britain's purpose in dragging out an extended engagement was to allow London to influence the eventual outcome in its favour.

Britain had fought a holding operation during the 1950s in what London described as the 'Malayan Emergency'. The Communist Party of Malaya, composed largely of ethnic Chinese, had launched an armed campaign to liberate the country from British imperial rule. With the country producing a significant proportion of the world's rubber supply, London decided that it would not allow Malaya to fall outside its sphere of influence. Fighting a war far from home and in a climate hostile to imperialism, the British opted for a limited objective. Their war aim was to contain insurrection (partly through the use of exacerbating ethnic tensions) and eventually to ensure a transfer of power to a regime favourably disposed to Britain and international capital.

Many of those leading the IRA in the early 1970s were of a generation well acquainted with the events of the 1950s. Moreover, as insurrectionary Irish Republicans, they had what amounted to a professional interest in London's approach to colonial uprisings. Recognising the hazard of protracted war as a distinct possibility, leading members of the organisation sought a means of delivering a decisive blow or series of blows that would hasten the end of the conflict.

Public positions notwithstanding, senior Provo strategists and their middle-level management were always aware of the enormity of the task they faced. As with any such conflict, it was important for the IRA never to indicate weakness and to demonstrate a willingness and capacity to continue fighting indefinitely. All but a tiny minority of the leadership was, nevertheless, aware that given time Britain would almost certainly gain the upper hand militarily. IRA resources were finite and, given its support base, puny in comparison to what Britain could draw on. By early 1973, with operations at an intense level in Ireland and fighting units stretched to their limit, it was decided to divert resources to England (and occasionally beyond) and attack the enemy on his home base.

Irish Republicans had been bombing England intermittently for over a century. The Irish Republican Brotherhood (IRB)[4] and its Fenian Dynamiters bombed London in the nineteenth century, a campaign that led directly to the formation by Scotland Yard of what was then known as the Special Irish Branch (now known simply as Special Branch). In the early twentieth century, Michael Collins ordered the burning of Liverpool docklands in 1921. Two decades later, the IRA launched a campaign exclusively directed at bombing England. The fact that almost every previous Irish Republican bombing campaign in England ended in failure had little impact on the Provisional IRA.

In spite of this, the underlying rationale for the Provisional IRA's English bombing campaign was not based on sentiment. Their worldview was forged in the very bitter and unforgiving environment of Northern Ireland, where there was little scope for emotion and no reward for heroic failure. Unlike the earlier 1950s campaign, where a majority of Republican activists were from south of the Border, most Provisional IRA were northern born and understood instinctively the implications of drawing their sword on the Six-County state. Above all else, they abhorred the idea of failure. Determined to prevent defeat and in order to compensate for shortage of resources, the Provisional IRA attacked England. The organisation viewed it as a potentially decisive theatre in its war with Britain. Many ordinary UK voters were indifferent or even hostile to retaining troops in Northern Ireland. The IRA believed that by hitting London, the extra pressure could persuade the British population to demand a troop withdrawal.

On the surface, the tactic appeared attractive politically and militarily to Republican activists and their supporters. England had much less security on the streets than Northern Ireland, and for

England to resort to Second World War security measures would have been intolerable for most people living there. Moreover, the Northern Ireland issue had quickly moved off centre stage as far as British news editors were concerned and it seemed to many Irish Republicans that only by detonating explosives in England would they keep the British population aware of what their government was doing across the Irish Sea. And finally, since the important decision makers lived in England, the IRA believed that it would require something happening in their own backyard to shake them out of their complacency.

Their strategic aim was twofold. In the first instance, it was to make the English population realise that a war with the IRA would not just be fought at a safe distance across the Irish Sea in Ireland which could be viewed comfortably on television. Many Republicans felt that if the English sent their soldiers to make war in Ireland, that the lRA should in return visit war on England. Secondly, the IRA realised that by striking England (and London in particular), they would garner much greater international coverage for their operations than if similar actions were taking place in Ireland. And such coverage was always important, since it kept the 'Irish question' alive in quarters that might otherwise have ignored it.

In early 1973, the IRA's Army Council sanctioned a Belfast Brigade request to bomb England.[5] Although still a very powerful insurrectionary force, the IRA in Belfast had suffered heavy losses. They knew that maintaining their 1972 level of operations was going to be difficult and saw an English bombing campaign as an option for taking pressure off their hard-pressed volunteers. One of their first attempts was to bomb the Old Bailey in London. The Active Service Unit succeeded in planting and detonating a bomb, but the operation ended with most of the team arrested.

The almost immediate capture of the ASU was viewed with concern by IRA leaders. There was always a risk of arrest connected with any operation, but on this occasion the fear was that the operation had been compromised before it started. IRA headquarters put a temporary halt on the English campaign and reviewed its options. The result of the review was that operations in England would thereafter be organised directly through IRA General Headquarters (GHQ) staff members. This strategy proved more effective and helped improve security for IRA operators in Britain, although it remained a high-risk zone of operation for the ASUs and all too often ended in their capture and imprisonment.

Although the IRA viewed the English campaign as something that, when successful, carried a significant pay-off, the organisation knew too that it came at a price. Campaigning in England was a costly and debilitating business. Operating in a hostile and alien environment meant that the personnel deployed had to be of an extremely high calibre. Only the best and most skilful operators could hope to survive the challenges of remaining effective and unobtrusive. For an army that depended heavily on the initiative and leadership skills of its middle-level personnel, the IRA's England campaign put a heavy strain on the organisation's materiel and manpower. GHQ had priority in requisitioning resources and on occasion almost emasculated some brigade areas by drawing on their best personnel for the English campaign.

These men and women had no natural support base in England. The environment was quite different to what IRA volunteers were familiar with at home. There were no safe districts and they enjoyed very limited sympathy. They had difficulty concealing their presence as their hard-to-disguise accents immediately drew attention wherever they went. There was, of course, a large Irish population in Britain but this community was kept under intense surveillance. Moreover, after many rounds of Irish rebellion, Special Branch had well-established covert intelligence 'assets' planted deep within the Irish community.

After the initial round of bombings, known Irish Republicans travelling to England had little chance of remaining undetected. The English police monitored all suspects and either captured them red-handed, or rendered them impotent through police proximity. With such a high level of security activity and scrutiny, the IRA found it best to use operatives with no known connection to the movement or its objectives. In itself, this frequently posed a difficulty since unknown personnel were also often inexperienced. Unknown but skilled operators were not only a rarity but were also a precious asset sorely missed by the organisation in Ireland.

Unlike their counterparts in Northern Ireland, British police had little difficulty obtaining a flow of intelligence on potential suspects from a largely cooperative population. With a large network of supporters in Ireland, even known figures could remain unobserved for months on end, surfacing only to carry out operations. It was much more difficult to do anything similar in Britain where police and public were actively watching for any suspicious activity and as often as not were being briefed by both police forces in Ireland on any suspected Republican sympathiser who had dropped from sight. There was too the danger of leaks from internal IRA sources of the names of those who had gone to England. As soon as British police knew who they were looking for, it was only a matter of time before that individual was unearthed and arrested.

In spite of great difficulty, the IRA continued to bomb England until the end of its war and at times did so with spectacular results. A British prime minister came within a few feet of being assassinated by a bomb in Brighton, the cabinet had a narrow escape when mortar shells fell in the garden of 10 Downing Street and the City of London's primacy as an international finance centre was put briefly in doubt when the Baltic Exchange was devastated by a massive explosion.

And yet with all of this, the British did not concede defeat. The IRA's English campaign certainly made a powerful point, reminding Britain that its war in Northern Ireland was not a cost-free exercise. Whether in the long run it was the best option for Republicans is another question. Might a different approach to a British working class battered and embittered by Thatcherism have paid higher dividends? Might it have been possible to create a firm political alliance with sections of Britain's alienated and marginalised population that would have put real pressure on Westminster? We cannot know.

Ultimately, the underpinning logic for an IRA bombing campaign in England is open to question. Even more than in Ireland, the IRA did not have the capacity to bludgeon the English into submission in Britain. The campaign had, therefore, to have the power to deliver an unexpected knockout blow (the 'puncher's chance' in boxing language) rather than grind the British economy and population into the earth. The 'puncher's chance' can be a dangerously seductive strategy and one that sometimes tempts the unfortunate further along the road than it is wise to go.

Arguably it might have been better to concentrate on building a broad political support base among the British working class and to make Ireland an integral part of the left's agenda in the UK. However, there is not a definitive answer to this question. There is at times an almost impermeable wall of uncritical popular support surrounding Britain's military, and circumstances are rarely conducive to creating a political campaign of support for those at war with 'Our Boys'.

11
Britain's Response

James sat upright on the bed as he heard his name called out. He recognised the voices of the detectives who had come to escort him to the interrogation rooms across the courtyard and he was frightened by what he now knew was awaiting him. Arrested five days earlier, he was being subjected to what was, by the mid to late 1970s, a well-practiced RUC regime of torturing prisoners in order to get confessions that would gain information and secure convictions.[1]

At this stage, James knew the process well. Uniformed police gaolers would hand him into the detectives' custody and he would be taken across the centre's courtyard. As soon as he entered the interrogation area, his torment would begin again. Two or three RUC detectives would invite him to sign a confession implicating himself in a series of IRA operations and also to tell them all he knew about the organisation. Refusing to do so would bring immediate pain, stress and humiliation. One policeman would hold him firmly in an arm lock while the other, holding James's free elbow would bend the wrist inward. The pressure would be held for long agonising periods until his wrists and hands and arms felt as if an electric current were attached to his fingertips.

After a time, the detectives would release his wrists and invite him to do 50 press-ups. Refusal meant an immediate resumption of the bent wrist abuse. It was only a temporary respite, because when he had completed the exercises on the floor he would be asked again about a confession. Once more he would say no and once again he would have his wrist bent only this time he was weaker and more exhausted. So intense was the pain that the previous day James had fainted several times while having his wrists bent.

Occasionally, his interrogators would introduce a slight variation to the floor exercises and make him do sit-ups or squats. On other occasions, they made him stand spread-eagled against the wall. The exercises, particularly standing against the wall, were humiliating and he knew it. He also knew he had a lot of information about the organisation that he could not afford to give the RUC and that he must hold out at all costs. If that meant accepting an amount of humiliation so that he could regain his composure, then so be it.

He knew there was a seven-day limit to the length of time he could be held in police custody. He understood too, that time was a very relative concept depending on how one experiences the period. He had never before felt five days pass so slowly. As he walked towards the euphemistically named 'Interview Room', he realised that he had another 48 hours to hold on.

James was worried approaching the room but his apprehension increased further still as he entered the chamber. Instead of the usual two or three detectives, there were at least six present. Some of them were huge men and instead of wearing suits and sports coats, these policemen were dressed like physical training instructors. Yet again he was asked to confess and again he refused to admit to having anything to confess. He was waiting for his wrists to be bent when instead, a tall policeman took him in a bear hug from behind and with his arms pinned to his sides, he was brought, still trussed, to the floor. Two other policemen immediately took hold of his feet and he was pinned, immobile on the ground. Still shocked by the suddenness of this development, he felt completely traumatised when another policeman placed a black, plastic bin-liner over his head and tightened it around his neck. He was smothering and the sensation was like nothing he had experienced before. In terror, he struggled with the strength of a drowning man. Surprised at the panic-induced power of the otherwise slightly built man, the RUC men temporarily lost their grip. James tore at the bin-liner and gasped for air. In the ensuing scramble to regain position and replace the bag on James' head, the policemen bruised and marked their victim.

While the interrogation session lasted for over an hour, the episodes with the bin-liner lasted only for minutes at a time and then for brief seconds in the position of outright suffocation. It was, nevertheless, so shocking that it took him years to make these rational calculations about time lines.

When the bin-liner treatment failed to extract a confession from James, the RUC's interrogation moved into 'warm down' mode. The rest of the day was filled with stress positions and exercises, but no additional physical torture. On the sixth day in custody, a senior RUC officer informed James that he was to be charged on the basis of a verbal statement that he had made. James looked up in surprise, since he had not made any such statement. The RUC man explained cynically, 'We have drawn up a statement for you and I will swear in court that you made it verbally. And who do you think the judge will believe … an officer in the Royal Ulster Constabulary or a dirty wee Provo like you?'

The Provisional IRA never believed that Britain was a neutral peacekeeper in the Northern Irish conflict, nor did its members accept that the British government stumbled aimlessly into the conflict at its beginning. Republicans believed Britain had a strategic interest in remaining in Ireland and that London weighed its response to all events in this light. This view runs contrary to the British government's publicly stated position that it did not have (nor has now) any interest in staying in Ireland and only does so at the request of the people of Northern Ireland. As a result, it is difficult finding written evidence to prove the Republican perception but it is possible nevertheless to study Britain's response to the IRA insurrection.

The British state has enormous resources (as does any state) exercising as it does control over military, policing, the judiciary and legislation. The state also manages social spending, allowing it to roll out services such as housing, health, transport and welfare.

During the Northern Irish conflict, London made no bones about using this power to support its policy. Community groups supportive of Republicans were denied access to funding available to others, housing estates were designed to facilitate British Army containment and cross-Border roads were left in disrepair to disrupt easy access by IRA supply chains. At a more mundane level, some elements of the British government apparently held the view that the conflict was due to the unemployed having too much spare time and funded a grandiose programme building sport and leisure complexes.

In spite of these odder initiatives, Britain's military machine engaged at a more serious level, albeit with some restrictions. Britain was bound by several constraints in its actions in Northern Ireland. The Six Counties were an integral part of the United Kingdom and successive British governments found it difficult to use the scale and type of force that most likely would have been deployed had the battle been fought in a remote theatre of war (as in Iraq or Afghanistan, for example). Northern Ireland is a small region close to London, making it difficult to prevent news of events reaching Britain. There was, too, the great number of Irish people living in Britain who had to be considered. This community was usually passive in the face of British state repression, but their acquiescence could not be counted on in the event of mass slaughter in Ireland. As mentioned earlier, internationally known pop star, Beatle John Lennon, marched in public with a poster condemning the British government after the Bloody Sunday killings. Finally, there was also that 'scourge' of every British government: the decent fair-minded section of the British public that looks behind tabloid press headlines.

Britain's government, nevertheless, had several advantages when dealing with the public's understanding of insurrection in Ireland, including its ability to influence or even control the media. Well-known journalist Peter Taylor, in an article for *Index on Censorship*, wrote in 1978:

> Nowhere, in the British context, has the relationship between state, broadcasting institutions and programme makers been more sensitive and uneasy than in matters concerning Northern Ireland. Conflict arises whenever broadcast journalism challenges the prevalent ideology embodied in government policy and reflected in the broadcasting institutions it has established. In principle, the broadcasting authorities should stand between the media and the state as benevolent umpires, charged with the task of defending each against the excesses of the other, guardians of

the public interest, upholders of a broadcasting service alleged to be the finest in the world. In practice, where Northern Ireland is concerned, they have become committed to a perspective of the conflict, which identifies the public interest increasingly with the government interest.[2]

There was then a similar outlook in the print media, which was (and is) still largely privately owned. Journalists working for these papers were (and are) not necessarily government stooges, but proprietors generally speaking expected that those they employed would subscribe to a broad consensus. Human rights activist and former prison chaplain, Monsignor Raymond Murray, writing for the Theatre Writers' Union conference on censorship in London on 28 January 1979, made the point:

> On the unjust killings of civilians they [the government] always got their story to the media – they were fired at first, the civilian was carrying a weapon, pointing a weapon, etc. The British media accepted the Army spokesmen – as did Radio Eireann often. The big lie was one of the most hurtful things to people who suffered and knew the truth. The British Army version was what the people in charge of the British media wanted themselves; so they would not seek out the truth.[3]

In his book *Low Intensity Operations*, Brigadier Frank Kitson, the British Army's senior counter-insurgency expert, had said explicitly that 'countering of the enemy's propaganda and putting across of the government's point of view, can be achieved either by direct action, as for example the provision of leaflets, or the setting up of an official wireless or television network, or by trying to inform and influence the existing news media.'[4]

As a consequence of relentless determination by the British establishment to impose an all-party consensus *vis-à-vis* Northern Ireland, almost all elements of the media accepted without question their government's definition of the issue. Britain's involvement in Northern Ireland, they maintained, was legitimate, proper, well intentioned and benevolent. Having accepted their government's characterisation of the problem and its causes, Britain's media thereafter confined itself to reporting the conflict in terms of British governments striving to contain 'violent and often fanatical terrorists'.

At its best, British media coverage never rose above exposing occasions when government agencies exceeded or broke their own rules. Rarely did the British media delve more deeply into whether its own government might be the guilty party in so far as it was committed to defending an undemocratic status quo in Northern Ireland. With the ability to create its own definition of the problem,[5] British governments ensured that its agents kept the media briefed in its way of thinking. Concepts such as 'peace-keeping', 'keeping warring factions apart', 'murder' and 'terrorism' were fed to the press and accepted almost without challenge. And while a section of the British people did not buy uncritically into this tendentious propagandising, a sufficient number did to allow British governments to roll out a series of 'low intensity operations'[6] for approximately a quarter of a century.

Between 1969 and 1972, Britain maintained the Stormont regime with the same Unionist party governing that had mismanaged the Six-County state for the previous half century. Although recognising that reform was necessary, Britain showed a clear preference in the early phase for deploying armed force rather than instigating sweeping change. During this period, London attempted to use its overwhelming military advantage to subdue opponents of the regime while trying to carry out 'running repairs' on the flawed state of Northern Ireland. When a bloody siege of the Lower Falls in Belfast, shooting dead rioters who held petrol bombs, internment without trial and the Bloody Sunday massacre failed to suppress the movement for radical change, British strategy changed.

Stormont was prorogued and replaced by direct rule from Westminster. British military strategy adjusted subtly thereafter to supporting the new, emerging policy of power-sharing within a Northern Ireland still embedded within the United Kingdom. Since a *sine qua non* for any such arrangement was to have willing participants, it was necessary to make this option politically feasible for compliant Nationalists in the SDLP (incidentally, Dublin governments also enthusiastically supported this strategy[7]).

Britain responded, therefore, by gradually turning towards reinforcing what it liked to call 'the civil power' as a means of providing a transition towards the form of governing arrangement it sought. This second phase of the Troubles was characterised by London masking the role of its military force behind a screen of what it described as 'restoring normality'. Instead of using its armed forces to bluntly crush opposition by *force majeure*, Britain began the more complicated (and long-term) process of using its military muscle to bring about its desired political outcome. In other countries, this had been termed 'use of the deep state'.[8]

Use of internment without trial had proven difficult to justify internationally and was, therefore, phased out and replaced by what appeared on the surface to be due legal process. The caveat was that instead of a normal court system, the British government introduced extraordinary measures to deal with the situation. Trial by jury was suspended in Northern Ireland and replaced with non-jury Diplock courts.[9] Rules of evidence were inverted under this system and seven-day detention orders were provided for.

Unlike elsewhere in the United Kingdom, a defendant in a Diplock courtroom had to prove that he or she did not make an alleged confession voluntarily. And contrary to the British norm elsewhere, an uncorroborated but contested confession was always deemed sufficient to secure a conviction on even the most serious charge in a Diplock court. This aspect of the special legislation provided an incentive for police interrogators to torture suspects during the time they were held in custody; abuse of people detained in police centres was widespread and systematic.[10] In time, the judicial system in Northern Ireland became a risible perversion of what British justice was supposed to be. Courts sat, with the judiciary providing a thin veneer of respectability, not to uphold the law, but to convict and sentence.

In the early phase of the conflict, while Britain sought to deal with the Northern Ireland issue by military suppression alone, captured combatants were treated as such and given *de facto* prisoner-of-war status. With the changing strategy, new designations were deemed vital. Those convicted in Diplock courts were not to be recognised as having any political status and, after the altogether arbitrary date of 1 March 1976, were to be treated as ordinary criminals. An entirely new prison, called the Maze Cellular, had been built to deal with this transformation.

Policing was supposed to have primacy over the military and every effort was made to convince the outside world that Northern Ireland was in effect a security problem best dealt with by normal law-and-order methods. The fact that the police force was armed with plastic bullets, pistols, rifles and armoured vehicles meant that the RUC was much more than an 'ordinary bunch of local coppers'. The fact that they also required the support of between 8,000 and 10,000 locally recruited militia of the UDR[11] (later to become the RIR[12]) and roughly the same number of regular army personnel meant that Northern Ireland could hardly be described as a normally managed and policed society. Nevertheless, Britain steadfastly refused to describe the situation as a war or even as an insurrection.

The outward signs of the new strategy were not obvious at first and most people on the streets of Northern Ireland, including some in the IRA, believed that little had changed. What was to take time to become clear was the extent of the undercover activities of the British state as it set about implementing its decisions and as British intelligence extensively engaged in manipulating the situation in favour of Westminster's preferred option. By the very nature of undercover practices, it is impossible to detail what exactly the British did in those years but we do know nevertheless that there is a lot that confirms what went on in those years. Broadly speaking, the intelligence agencies recruited two types of agent. In the first instance, British intelligence wanted people who could reveal the whereabouts of war materiels and to keep them briefed on operations planned by insurgent (and counter-insurgency) organisations. Equally, and no less important from their point of view, they wanted to recruit people who would influence the decision-making process within the different political constituencies and not just within the Republican movement.

A more controversial and still officially suppressed aspect of the British response was its clandestine operations and manipulation of unofficial supporters. The *sine qua non* for a continued IRA campaign was support from a significant section of the civilian population. The obvious corollary of this was that when the larger, conventional force was unable to engage the guerrilla, it would be tempted to seek to weaken him by attacking his most vulnerable sector – the guerrilla's civilian supporters. This method of countering irregular or guerrilla warfare is as old as human conflict: ancient Rome applied it mercilessly, Napoleon resorted to this method, as did the US Army when fighting Native Americans. Many examples exist of civilian populations being punished in the twentieth century. The tactic is as central to conventional military thinking as that of a boxing coach encouraging his charges to hit an opponent's ribs in order to 'bring down the head'.

Britain and its military encountered some difficulty adopting this tactic directly in Northern Ireland. As part of the United Kingdom, an official policy of systematic reprisals against the region's Catholic population would have been impossible to conceal and politically out of the question. Fortunately, from a British military point of view, their political dilemma was resolved as Loyalist death squads filled the void. It is unlikely that official documents will ever be forthcoming to establish conclusively that Her Majesty's Government's military and intelligence services remotely controlled the death squads. What can be said is that an outside observer would find it difficult to accept that the British military refused to employ a tactic it had used in Malaya, Kenya, Cyprus, Aden and elsewhere. The policy of 'outsourcing' operations that would be difficult to defend in the House of Commons is of course neither new nor unheard of since. The existence of 'extraordinary rendition' to have suspects tortured and killed by others is evidence of that.

There is little doubt but that the campaign by Loyalist death squads played a part in undermining support for the IRA struggle in Republican areas. For a period in the early 1970s, the IRA had adopted a policy of counter-reprisal. By the early 1980s, this was discontinued. As time went by, Republican supporters grew increasingly disheartened with the impact of incessant Loyalist killings. By the second half of the 1980s and into the early 1990s, it appeared obvious that the IRA was unable to defend its supporters. At the time, Sinn Féin regularly demanded that its elected representatives be permitted to carry weapons for their personal protection, but failed to extend the call to include all vulnerable members of the community. This was an obvious method of protection and would have revived the broad-based citizens' defence committees that had sprung up everywhere in the early 1970s. However, the IRA had become so rigidly hierarchical by the mid-1980s that it could not contemplate placing that much trust in the mass of the people, who remained powerless in the face of a debilitating assault.

Ultimately the British state recognised that it could not simply do what it wished in Northern Ireland nor could it summarily end the insurrection. London was prepared, therefore, for a long, drawn-out war of attrition. Through the second phase of the conflict (post-internment, pre-hunger strike), Britain used its power in an attempt to undermine the insurgents by confining as many activists as possible to prison. The objective was to entomb the IRA physically as well as politically and with the organisation's capacity thus downgraded, the so-called 'moderate' SDLP would fill the vacuum and again enter a power-sharing administration.

The hunger strikes of 1980–81 derailed this plan. Not only did the strikes make compromise difficult for both the SDLP and the Ulster Unionist Party, but it demonstrated that the insurgents had a bedrock of support that could not easily be eroded. It was clear that the IRA would have to be involved in any future settlement. It would appear that the British introduced a third phase, which involved creating conditions that would encourage a significant section of the IRA to engage within Northern Ireland's parliamentary political process. This phase was no less controversial than earlier periods. It seems that 'guiding' the IRA towards parliament involved what was to become known as the 'shoot to kill' strategy. As ever, incorporating repression was central to plan.

12
Reviewing Strategy in the Mid-1970s

Danny's mother Susie brought the note to Tony personally. She had been to the jail that morning to visit him and after discretely passing the tiny note to her, he advised her to be extremely careful and give the message to no one other than Tony. In case a reply was needed, Tony opened and read the tiny communication in Susie's presence. Danny did not need an answer to his note, but Tony needed to find an answer to the information sent by his friend.

Danny had been arrested two weeks earlier and this was the first chance he had to send word out to his comrades of what happened during the police interrogation and to brief them on the extent of police intelligence. So good was the RUC information, it seemed to him, that on one occasion, police interrogators felt sufficiently confident to show one of his captured comrades a series of photos taken surreptitiously of a group of IRA personnel at a training session in a sympathiser's house.

Returning to his old unit in mid-1975 after a brief spell in prison, Tony found that a lot had changed with the ceasefire. There had been a dramatic increase in recruits from areas that had not previously been noted for their ardour. In one small town where he had known little comfort in the past, it now appeared entire families had joined since the cessation of offensive operations. Elsewhere, he found that men who had quietly drifted away from the movement before the ceasefire were now back and apparently occupying positions of considerable influence.

IRA meetings that had previously attracted four or five hard-working individuals now looked more like small political demonstrations – on occasion, up to twenty volunteers were present. Incredibly too, the IRA was organising training camps in rural parts of the Six Counties. These camps were ostensibly secret, but it appeared to Tony that a lot of people seemed to know of their existence. To an extent it looked to him like the worst option to have taken. An insurrectionary organisation cannot have its structures partly secret and partly public at the same time. By lowering its guard, the organisation was inviting penetration, yet by not taking the opportunity to build a popular defence force to thwart the upsurge in Loyalist death squads, the IRA was removing itself from the supply of dedicated recruits it would need in time of conflict.

Most worrying was the absence of direction. There was no sign that the British government had any intention of withdrawing its forces, yet the IRA leadership appeared to be dithering about what to do. To be fair to GHQ, its officers were not pretending that they had won any concessions, but they were unconvincing when explaining how they intended to move the situation forward. He also had a feeling that the conflict was in danger of sliding into the worst type of sectarian encounter as Unionist gunmen increased attacks on Catholics.

It was obvious to him that the British were trying to prolong the ceasefire, but the IRA had no alternative strategy other than to return to the type of conflict they had fought before the fighting stopped. This they did gradually and without making any announcement as in time the ceasefire petered out.

A few more months after the resumption of armed activities, many of his worst fears were confirmed. Most of the new recruits had returned to being passive, and worse, the RUC were making devastating raids on whole IRA units. In some districts, entire units were being rounded up in a single swoop. It was clear too that the RUC was determined to secure convictions by any means necessary. Without internment, they were now forcing confessions from men and cared little how they did so. Worse still, the RUC was acting on better intelligence.

Tony had little doubt that wide-ranging remedial action was necessary, but wasn't sure exactly what should be done. His closest confidants were insisting that they had to increase the level of activity but the question was how? Early in 1976, he was called to a meeting in the west of Ireland where leading members of the organisation talked of establishing a Northern Command in order to streamline operational delivery. It sounded to him as something worth trying.

By the early mid-1970s, it had become clear to senior IRA members that in light of a high level of attrition, a readjustment had to be made. The IRA Army Council, therefore, accepted an opportunity in late 1974 to call a temporary ceasefire that lasted into mid-autumn 1975. They did so knowing that the Belfast Brigade was in a parlous position and other units in rural parts of the Six Counties were suffering from a debilitating shortage of equipment. Both the British and the IRA used this interval to review their positions and prepare for the next round.

There was a realisation at the time within IRA circles that granting a ceasefire was a risky option. Several older veterans of the 1956–62 campaign even mentioned the Kenya uprising when General China (Waruhiu Itote) of the Land and Freedom Army arranged a temporary cessation of hostilities between his people and the British. Negotiations at the time in Kenya came to nothing. During the three-month lull in fighting the Special Branch in Nairobi gathered extensive intelligence about the group that supplied food, money, volunteers and ammunition to the fighters in the forests. When the 'China Peace Overture', as it was called, failed, the British swept in and arrested more than a thousand suspects in three days.

In spite of such anxieties, the IRA called a ceasefire and opened covert negotiations. As the British government drew the IRA into a round of surreptitious talks, London, it seemed clear, had developed a dual 'either/or' strategy that it intended using to deal with the Irish situation. In the first instance:

(a) The IRA would be invited to end its campaign and acquiesce with London's plan for a shared administration in a Northern Ireland firmly embedded within the United Kingdom but in return would gain admittance into the local political establishment.

Should the IRA fail to accept the offer:

(b) Britain would use its considerable political and media influence to designate the IRA campaign as a criminal terrorist enterprise, transfer as much responsibility for military operations as possible to local Unionist militias (normalisation or Ulsterisation) and settle back for a long war of attrition at the end of which the IRA would either be annihilated, rendered impotent (and thus irrelevant) or exhausted and thus eventually agree to option A.

Republicans, initially, did not match the British with anything like such a well-developed plan of counter-action. The IRA leadership had a relatively uncomplicated view of the state of affairs. They would use the break to rearm, retrain, recruit and prepare for a return to war if their demand for a British declaration of intent to withdraw from Ireland was not met. By early summer 1975, the IRA Army Council had recognised that nothing was coming from London that would meet their demands and ordered units to drift back into action. This was to happen with no announcement or declaration that the ceasefire was ended.

With no remnant of a ceasefire apparent by late 1975 and the IRA clearly unwilling to accept a return to a Stormont regime, the British authorities launched Plan B. In a very short few months, the IRA learned that its preparations for a return to war were inadequate. The ceasefire had engendered a taste for peace in many, including IRA supporters, and this desire was increased by the fall-out from a relentless sectarian war being waged by Loyalist death squads.

Implementation of London's decision to transfer a major portion of responsibility for combating the insurrection to locally recruited forces (a policy known to some as 'Ulsterisation'[1]) caused Loyalists to intensify this onslaught. The British government argued that its Ulsterisation policy was an essential step in its plan to restore Northern Ireland to 'normality' and hence, its subsequent determination to increase the RUC role and that of the UDR acting as a support to what was described as the 'civil authorities'.

It is difficult to accept that Britain was unaware of the consequences arising from placing locally recruited militias (Protestant and Unionist for the most part) in direct conflict with the IRA. Unless the IRA abandoned its campaign, it was inevitable that as the two sides came into conflict, the struggle would assume a sectarian dimension. As history records, this happened and many RUC and UDR members died, often while off duty. Whatever rationale the IRA offered for the imperative of acting as it did, many Protestant people viewed this campaign as a sectarian assault on their community. This anger in turn lent a semblance of justification from a Unionist point of view to a largely indiscriminate killing campaign waged on Catholics.

Some within the IRA leadership initially viewed this intensified Loyalist onslaught as an attempt by a current within Unionism to prevent Britain disengaging from Ireland. Other Republicans argued there was a much more sinister explanation. They insisted that what was happening was the action of Kitson-esque pseudo-gangs murdering civilians in order to undermine support for the continuation of a Republican armed campaign.[2] In either case, the killings tested Republican morale.

Internally, the IRA was experiencing difficulties. Many of those recruited during the ceasefire lacked the appetite for combat and with the resumption of hostilities, retired as quickly as they had joined. Worse from an IRA point of view, the 'Trucealeers' had inflicted considerable damage on the IRA. With little intention of getting involved in armed conflict, they often broke the basic rules of underground organisation and flaunted their membership in public, frequently compromising the security of previously unidentified sympathisers. As a consequence, the RUC was able to make devastating raids on the IRA infrastructure in the months immediately after the ceasefire's end. Reeling under the impact of multiple arrests and vigorous implementation of the 'Ulsterisation' policy with its emphasis on the primacy of the RUC and attempted criminalisation of Republicanism, the IRA belatedly began to consider an adjustment to its strategy. Unlike the British, the IRA did not have a contingency plan. It took some time for one to emerge and then only after considerable debate.

Having originally developed as a military response to Northern Irish Catholic vulnerabilities and needs, it was hardly surprising that the first attempt by the IRA to analyse its predicament centred on tactical requirements rather than on strategic political initiatives.

Problems were seen as lying within the organisation's military structures and practice. A high-profile group of former internees from Belfast offered an analysis of the problem that was critical of the ceasefire and argued for a fundamental restructuring of the IRA. To streamline the day-to-day management of the Republican army, it was necessary, they said, to have a more responsive local command structure in the form of a Northern Command. Moreover, it was important for reasons of internal security to reorganise units into self-contained cells that would undergo more intensive training in armed combat, counter-interrogation methods and political education.

More significantly, they argued for, and persuaded the IRA to accept, what was described as a 'Long War' strategy. These men pointed out that the movement had declared 1972 and then 1973 as the 'Year of Victory'. When this claim failed to materialise, they said, volunteers and supporters grew disillusioned, as British governments were quick to point out the IRA's inability to deliver. The concept behind the Long War strategy was that the organisation would resolve to pursue its armed campaign for whatever length of time it took to force the British government to declare its intention to withdraw from Ireland. It was equally important in this scenario that the British government would be convinced that armed Irish Republicanism was not a passing phase, but something that would stubbornly fight until satisfied.

In the clamour for answers to the post-ceasefire onslaught from the British, the IRA was persuaded to accept the formula. Those who proposed it have always insisted that this reorganisation saved the IRA from destruction. Such claims were hard to prove then and impossible to corroborate with the passing of time. The IRA recovered, albeit slowly, from the hiatus of 1974–75 not just because of restructuring but also due to the input of groups of dedicated volunteers who were for the most part operating as they had at the beginning of the campaign.

The major difference, and its benefit is questionable, was the ever-present scrutiny of the IRA's newly created Northern Command officers as they set about implementing the policy of building a cell system. This system often appeared better in theory than it proved in practice. Insurrectionary cells are only as secure as their component parts are impervious to outside identification and penetration, something that rarely if ever happened in the IRA. Moreover, a cell is always vulnerable when making contact with others outside its own membership.

In another sense, the reform package changed relationships within the organisation. Unlike the previous regime, where IRA GHQ staff was a southern-based entity that occasionally met a limited number of staff officers from the combat units on an infrequent basis, Northern Command penetrated every crevice of the IRA. In an effort to better coordinate the activities of various poorly coordinated rural units, Northern Command began regularly to visit country areas that had previously remained isolated from IRA officialdom. This certainly raised morale and created a greater sense of coherence, but it also facilitated the work of those agents inside the organisation intent on doing damage to the IRA.

The greatest threat to a cell system, of course, is when someone from Headquarters (particularly if they have responsibility for coordinating or scrutinising activities) is working for the opposition, and it is now recognised that this did happen. It is likely that other, well-placed Crown agents will have their identities revealed in the course of time but it is now widely accepted that at least two leading members of the movement – Freddie Scappaticci and Denis Donaldson – were carrying out this role for British intelligence.

Scappaticci and Donaldson undoubtedly inflicted considerable damage on the IRA and Sinn Féin, and they were certainly not on their own in performing their roles as informants and agents of influence. Britain's intelligence-gathering agencies have centuries of experience in managing and collating information and have long honed their skills in Ireland. They had a presence in both jurisdictions on the island before the 'Troubles' and would merely have increased and expanded their activities as soon as the Northern Irish conflict began to escalate in the late 1960s. According to the IRA's own accounts, its Belfast Brigade discovered that British intelligence had acquired a well-placed informant on its staff as early as the first half of the 1970s. It is well known that the Crown's recruitment process did not stop then and that British intelligence and the RUC Special Branch continued to obtain other sources.

To what extent the presence of enemy agents within the movement affected the outcome of events has long been a subject of intense debate. Due to the emotional impact that the existence of suspected or actual treachery has on people, it has been difficult making a balanced assessment of this issue. There is little doubt that many IRA operations were compromised by information being leaked to British authorities. High-profile incidents such as the ambushing of IRA ASUs at Loughgall in Co. Armagh and Gibraltar,[3] or the loss of large amounts of munitions such as the capture by Gardai in the

Republic of Ireland of a hundred rifles and four machine-guns near Five Fingers Strand in Donegal on 23 November 1987, were most certainly the result of informers. What is more difficult to assess was the impact agents of influence had on the direction of the movement.

To a degree, information leakage is a constant factor in every insurrection and must be taken into account by any group determined to succeed. There is no method that can be employed to prevent an opponent subverting some insurgent fighters apart from ensuring that the guerrilla soldier is kept out of the enemy's hands. The decision by the IRA towards the end of the 1970s (and persisted with thereafter) to encourage the bulk of its members to remain in their own homes and depend on counter-interrogation techniques to combat having its men subverted,[4] granted their opponents an enormous advantage in terms of access to active volunteers.

This strategic mistake was the result, though, of other calculations that in practice viewed armed struggle as providing leverage alongside a conventional parliamentary political strategy. Under this scenario, the armed wing could not be allowed to assume an identity of its own and was thus prevented from 'going to the mountains'. In light of this, it can be said that a strategic error at leadership level allowed British intelligence to inflict more damage on the IRA than might otherwise have been the case. Ultimately, though, it must be admitted that agents of influence can only take people where they want to go.

However, it is undeniable that the reorganisation into a cell system was accompanied by a brief but spectacular upsurge of activity towards the end of the decade. On 27 August 1979, the IRA delivered its largest single blow against the British Army when 18 British soldiers were killed in a double explosion near Warrenpoint, Co. Down. On the very same day in Mullaghmore, Co. Sligo, the IRA assassinated a close relative of Queen Elizabeth II, Lord Louis Mountbatten.

From an IRA point of view, it proved virtually impossible to maintain this level of action in the months that followed. In spite of Herculean efforts by its volunteers, the IRA was finding it increasingly difficult to prosecute its campaign against the British government. As the 1970s gave way to the 1980s, with Margaret Thatcher in power in London, there appeared little prospect for immediate advancement. Yet when the incredible impact of the hunger strikes washed across the country, fresh opportunities opened up. Another adjustment to strategy became possible and, in light of the circumstances, was clearly needed.

13
The Gradual Adoption of Parliamentarianism

Even with the obvious emotional appeal of a hunger strike, Catherine was astonished at the response. Having worked for over ten years with the Sinn Féin party, she was aware of the difficulty of attracting support in the South. This was different though, and the streets were filled with people angry with the British government and anxious to do what they could to save the men in the H-Blocks.

What really surprised her was the willingness of those protesting to engage openly with the authorities. Unlike so often in the past, on this occasion a Republican protest was out in the open. A caravan had been placed in the town centre and she and other party members maintained a regular office schedule offering news and information on the prison crisis to the public and simultaneously using their base as a convenient location from which to organise the daily round of protest actions.

It was obvious too that a very different calibre of person was being attracted into the movement as a consequence of the broadening of the support base. She was concerned that the new recruits might have a different set of priorities than those held by her and the men she had known who were now in prison. Her doubts were assuaged however, by reassurances from senior members of the party who reminded her of how they had managed the meeting arranged to establish the broad-based Anti H-Block Committee in her area and elsewhere, and installed steering groups controlled by the IRA. It seemed a reasonable answer and with the pressure on to help the campaign to find an acceptable resolution to the hunger strikes, there was little time to spare for philosophical musings about issues that might never arise.

Any lingering worries she had dissipated after the first hunger striker died. The urgency of the situation precluded any doubts and every hand was not just welcome but badly needed. There soon grew a sense of desperation as more men died and it began to seem that the only means of exerting pressure on the British through the Irish government was to undermine Fianna Fáil. Making the movement less exclusive seemed to be a necessary step to take.

With the passing of time and with the hunger strike ended, Catherine began to feel that this tactic was more and more dubious. Her doubts appeared to have been confirmed during a subsequent general election campaign when the local party mandarins set out new rules for canvassing. Among the revised regulations was a diktat that all members of the party calling upon voters must wear 'approved dress'. The decision that irked most, however, was when an ex-prisoner and highly respected volunteer was ordered not to canvass in his hometown and environs, but was instead dispatched to the far end of the constituency. The rationale, ostensibly, was that this man was too closely identified with the armed campaign and the movement's demand for an end to Partition. It seemed that he was something of an embarrassment to the party's local bureaucracy as it tried to distance itself from the IRA's war in the North. She observed later that these mandarins had no inhibitions about flaunting themselves at the same volunteer's funeral when his death at the hands of the SAS provoked an outpouring of emotion among the local youth, as his remains were taken home for burial.

Figure 13.1   A crowd march in support of hunger strikers, 1981 (© Belfast Exposed).

Whatever verdict history will render on IRA restructuring of the late 1970s, it became clear to the organisation early in the 1980s that the 'spike' in operations in 1979, when the IRA assassinated Lord Mountbatten and killed 18 British soldiers on the same day, could not easily be maintained. Moreover, realists knew that it would be virtually impossible to exceed this high level of activity. Some argued that better equipment would allow for an increase in the level of operations and at one level, this was undoubtedly true. On another level, it was an illusion.

When the organisation managed to secure large quantities of modern and effective weapons and explosives from Libya in the mid-1980s, the theory of an improved arsenal was tested with disappointing results. Even with vastly superior materiel than

Figure 13.2 Demonstration in support of hunger strikers, 1981 (the author's name can be seen on one of the taxis) (© Pacemaker Press).

previously available, the IRA would have needed access to safe areas south of the border and greatly increased numbers of recruits, if it was to achieve any measure of success. To do so required a more favourable political environment for Republicans than was then the case. In the course of time, the Libyan shipments were not used to pursue military objectives but as bargaining chips in a political negotiation.

No matter how the IRA looked at the situation it was obvious that, while they had the ability to disrupt almost any political settlement designed to address the Northern Irish Troubles, Republicans were unable to impose their own will on the area. The balance of forces ranged against them augured badly for a favourable outcome politically; furthermore, this in itself denied the organisation the conditions necessary to allow it to access the manpower needed to mount a more intense military campaign.

By the end of the 1970s, the IRA was finding it more difficult to win supporters in the Republic of Ireland. There remained, of course, the old and long-term support base concentrated along the Border and in a few of the rural counties further south. These people and areas made a remarkable contribution to the IRA campaign in terms of providing training grounds and logistical back-up. In spite of constant Gardai surveillance and harassment, they remained incredibly steadfast over the decades. What they did not have, though, was the weight of numbers to force Dublin authorities to alter its drive to crush the IRA.

Insurrectionary Irish Republicanism was strong enough to worry the Republic's governments, but not large enough to have decisive political clout in parliament or in the community. Dublin cabinets were frightened by the spectre of northern Republicanism but only to the extent that they attacked it at every opportunity. After ten years of bitter conflict in the North, Southern Ireland wanted the IRA war to end rather than the IRA to win. Any lingering doubt about the southerners' views were dispelled in 1981 when, at the height of the long and agonising hunger strike in the H-Blocks, only two IRA candidates were elected to the Republic's parliament. If the IRA message was to resonate in any meaningful way in the Republic, it was going to require more than repeating tired slogans of the past.

North of the Border, the situation was different but still not satisfactory. Republicans had a much stronger base but were in direct competition with the Social Democratic & Labour Party (SDLP), which was supported by both the British and Irish governments, who viewed the party as a counterweight to the Provisional IRA. In fact, it is likely that the SDLP enjoyed more than mere British goodwill. There is evidence that cultivating a malleable party (the so-called moderates) among the ranks of the disenchanted has long been a key plank in British counter-insurgency strategy. Indeed, British government operatives currently working in Afghanistan speak with remarkable frankness about their plans to identify and negotiate with what they describe as the 'moderate wing of the Taliban'.[1]

Nor indeed was the work of British intelligence confined to compliant Social Democrats. In an article about former MI6 man Alastair Crooke in the *Financial Times*, a former high-ranking member of the Secret Intelligence Service is reported as saying that their strategy was to build discreet long-term relationships with so-called 'reasonable people' within radical movements and then, over a long period, use those relationships to separate moderates from extremists and 'thus influence the situation'.[2]

With the SDLP still the dominant electoral force within the Catholic community, it was possible for the British government to argue that the IRA was a minority group of 'terrorists' without meaningful support. This meant that London felt free to overlook Republican demands and deal exclusively with them through security measures. Moreover, for as long as the IRA's political wing, Sinn Féin, remained outside normal political circles, the SDLP was accumulating additional influence if only by default and at the expense of Republicans.

Beyond the Catholic community, the Unionist population was not happy in spite of having the unqualified support of the British government with all its resources. Unlike the 1920s, the Unionist community was under physical pressure from the IRA campaign of the 1970s and 1980s. London had placed a major part of the responsibility for defending Unionism's vision of Ulster on their own shoulders and while they enjoyed a distinct advantage in terms of arms, finance and the fallback support of regular British Army troops, Unionists were not able to defeat the IRA as it had at the start of the twentieth century. Caught in the paradox of being unable to win and never likely to lose, Unionism was incapable of offering any imaginative or creative initiative to resolve the situation.

A further difficulty from an overall strategic point of view was the ongoing inability of the IRA to influence a significant section of British public opinion. Chauvinistic Irish Nationalists may not have viewed this as surprising, but there were a range of other complex historical factors that had to be taken into account. With a huge number of people of Irish birth or descent living in England, there was a potentially large number of people willing to support a demand for improved democracy in Ireland. Moreover, Britain had a large and well-established democratic, working-class tradition, which was not always a tame tool in the hands of the establishment. Taking these factors together, there were grounds for believing in the possibility of developing a significant radical opposition to British government policy on Ireland.

As noted above, the Troops Out Movement did develop, and on occasion attracted significant support, but never to the extent that it could influence a British election or even get a toehold in any of the three main political parties, including beyond the fringes of the Labour Party. At the end of the day, the British establishment was able to portray those campaigning for British withdrawal from Ireland as IRA supporters or duped liberals, misguided at best and sinister at worst. Living in Britain and supporting insurrectionary Irish Republicanism was not an easy option and to do so over a period required courage. In spite of their best efforts, these courageous people were not able to transform their campaign into a wider struggle for democratic reform in the UK, in spite of the fact that most of those engaged were involved in other progressive movements.

Further afield, the Irish Republican cause was finding it increasingly difficult to cope with the aggressive propaganda offensive combined with diplomatic initiatives being employed by London and Dublin.

While there remained a core of Irish Republican activists in the US, they were having little success in influencing the US State Department towards demanding a British withdrawal from Ireland. It was possible to gain some traction with issues relating to human rights and equality issues in Ireland, but on every constitutional issue, the US authorities (for a variety of reasons) supported the British and Irish government line on Ireland. The US offered help and assistance to the SDLP for its 'unity by consent' analysis, a position that Republicans saw as tantamount to 'first surrender and thereafter appeal to Unionism to behave better'. Without an alternative strategy to challenge this position, it appeared little could be done to alter the situation in the US.

As the 1970s ended, IRA realists were forced to accept that the political landscape both at home and abroad offered little prospects for Republican success in the short term. There did not appear to be any significant power base anywhere with sufficient influence or strength capable of assisting the IRA to achieve its objective. The movement could endeavour to be optimistic, but that was not enough. The deliberations that had taken place in the aftermath of the 1975 ceasefire were still germane but this time it was not possible to argue merely for a reorganisation of the IRA. Other steps had to be taken if the Republican struggle was not to grind painfully to inevitable decline and defeat. The question was not whether something had to change, but what and how.

Having already carried out an organisational restructuring, the IRA had few options left. Traditionally, the organisation had a troubled relationship with conventional electoral politics. There was a widely held belief that electioneering and the prospect of elective office was merely the thin end of a wedge that would inevitably lead to abandoning insurrection and with it, the political programme that uncompromising Republicans saw as the *sine qua non* of their cause.

Nor was this a mere academic argument. Many in the organisation had very clear memories of the process that led to the split with the Official IRA in 1969. There was a widely held view among even those who had not been part of the movement at that time, that the Official IRA emphasis on electoral politics had diluted that organisation's radical instincts and gradually lured them into a position of ineffective reformism on both sides of the Border. Older Provisional IRA members could also quote a number of groups that had started out claiming that they would enter the political arena in order to promote the Republican objective, only for them to either become embedded within the system or even worse – as in the case of Fianna Fáil – to actually reinforce that very system by repression of the IRA.

The opponents of parliamentary engagement had a powerful argument on their side in both terms of history and logic. Nobody could quote an instance in Irish history when a party had entered an existing parliament and changed it. Moreover, with scepticism about parliamentary politics so deeply engrained in the IRA, there was a fear that this form of political engagement would lead to an end to the struggle and that the years of sacrifice would have been for nothing.

Another realistic option for the IRA would have been to engage in an escalating round of social agitation designed to undermine the grip of the establishment in both North and South. There was clear precedent for this form of action by Republicans. While not directing the civil rights movement of the late 1960s, Republicans had played a valuable role in the campaign during the period immediately before the outbreak of insurrection. Republicans had inspired and participated in the annuities protest of the 1930s and indeed during the various stages of the Land War in the final decades of the nineteenth century. Moreover, the bulk of the Republican movement of the 1980s would have required little encouragement, since they were well used to unconventional means of protest and agitation and had little if any respect for the establishment or its rules.

Working against the option of social agitation and building a mass movement was the Republican leadership's fear of any course of action that threatened its ability to control every aspect of any such programme. Social agitation and a mass social movement by their nature unleash the popular will and invariably throw up their own leaders and spokespersons. Even those who hanker after a mass popular movement and those who work for years to bring it about are apt to see it slip from their control; often as it appears that their labours have just begun to bear fruit. Veteran leftists such as Communist Party member Betty Sinclair, who had played a leading role in hunger marches during the 1930s, campaigned against fascism in the 1940s and opposed Stormont's sectarianism through the 1950s and 1960s, found herself and her party colleagues (and their analysis and advise) marginalised as the civil rights movement that they had worked so long to build began to develop momentum. Moreover, the IRA leadership was aware that it too had benefited from the preparatory work of others when stepping in to fill a space created by the mass civil rights movement in the early 1970s.

The other alternative to electoral politics or the building of a mass movement was to remain 'as you were' and hope, *à la* Micawber, for something to turn up. Whatever attraction the policy of inertia might have had for some, it was in reality not an option at all.

The circumstances in which these options were reviewed are important to consider. As a consequence of the Labour government's drive to crush the IRA after the 1975 ceasefire, the authorities in Northern Ireland had, as part of the attempt to portray Republican insurrection as a criminal enterprise, removed political recognition for captured Republicans. In protest, Provisional IRA (and INLA) prisoners refused to wear prison-issue uniforms or carry out prison work. This led to a long, drawn-out and bitter struggle between prisoners and the authorities, with prisoners being forced to live in their cells, wrapped only in a blanket, where, in order to escalate their protest, they smeared excrement on the cell walls. With no obvious end to the protest in sight, prisoners went on hunger strike, first in late 1980 and then again in 1981, when ten of their number died.

In 1979, the IRA had, by its own standards, a successful year militarily. A large number of operations had been carried out and by any yardstick the armed wing of Irish Republicanism was visible and potent with lethal attacks delivered on high-profile targets. Elsewhere, however, the outlook was not giving the organisation much ground for optimism. Pope John Paul VI had visited Ireland and his condemnation of the IRA provided British Prime Minister Margaret Thatcher with a propaganda windfall. Worse still from the organisation's point of view was the Pope's refusal to mention the IRA prison protest in the H-Blocks. The movement risked the danger of finding itself politically isolated within a gradually diminishing archipelago of Provo strongholds in the Six Counties.

Significantly, however, the long year of hunger strikes that began in October 1980, lasting until 3 October 1981, created conditions that allowed the movement to break out of this threatening position. Support for imprisoned Republican prisoners produced one of the most intense periods of political protest and activity in twentieth-century Ireland. Many people who had political or moral reservations about the nature and validity of the IRA's armed campaign were, nevertheless, opposed to mistreatment of prisoners and the Thatcher government's crude and disingenuous attempt to brand them as non-political. This was the first upsurge of a mass movement since British paratroopers effectively drove the civil rights movement off the streets in January 1972 by killing 14 civilians on Bloody Sunday in Derry.[3]

The Republican leadership recognised the power of mass popular actions but instead of creating a broad revolutionary movement from what they had helped create, opted instead for a centrist parliamentary path. Seeing the emotional support generated by the prison issue and realising that it would be necessary to involve as many as possible in the campaign for political status, the Republican leadership issued an open invitation to all people interested in helping, to join the struggle and endeavour to save hunger strikers' lives. Coming as they did from a world of underground conspiracy and militarism, the IRA leadership was unwilling, however, to risk allowing a mass movement to find its own way. The Army Council sought to ensure that the campaign did not take an unexpected turn or create parallel structures to the Republican movement. The IRA therefore briefed its members and trusted supporters to make sure that the Anti H-Block committees being set up throughout Ireland were firmly, if discretely, kept in Provo hands. The strategy was successful from a Provisional IRA leadership point of view, leading eventually to the basis for the nascent New Sinn Féin. The IRA leadership's reluctance to trust the popular movement was, however, to create a support base that was confined in its ambition to that of the Republican leadership and that eventually was to prove quite modest.

Yet in spite of difficulties that were eventually to emerge, huge numbers of previously uninvolved persons joined the campaign. Over the course of the struggle, tens of thousands took part in protest and political activity. For some, this was often almost continuous activity for a whole year and with many of the most enthusiastic being in their late teens or early twenties, it was also, for most of them, their first taste of political activity. The hunger strike movement poured onto the streets in a torrent of action. With daily protest events and three major electoral engagements during the period, a new generation was awakening to the value and practice of mass action. The input of energy astonished onlookers and proved electrifying for those who were part of the struggle. In Republican areas of the Six Counties, young capable people were emerging to lead the Anti H-Block campaign. More significant still was the emergence of another group of equally young and dynamic Anti H-Block supporters in many urban centres in the Republic. As the hunger strikes ended and the Anti H-Block movement began to wind down, Republicans were assessing the situation and examining the failures and achievements of the period and asking whether it was possible to maintain this impressive and powerful machine.

Two aspects of the campaign had been most obvious. In the first instance, there was a mass movement of (and literally on) the streets demanding political change. In the second instance, the movement had participated in a number of massive electoral political campaigns that had seen Republicans win seats in the British House of Commons for IRA hunger striker Bobby Sands and for two IRA prisoners (one of whom was hunger striker Kieran Docherty) in the Republic's general election of the same year. Even those hostile to the hunger strikers and to the mass movement generated by the strike were prepared to admit that the spectacle of thousands of mostly young people, engaging in widespread street protest or working frantically during elections for pro-hunger strike candidates was impressive, not to mention daunting for their opponents.

What was of still greater importance was the broad-based nature of the mass movement. Not confined to the usual hard-line Republican constituency, the Anti H-Block campaign drew a broad cross-section of left-wing and working-class people behind its cause. Very few radical elements of Irish society remained outside the movement and for a period a real opportunity existed to forge a new and dynamic anti-establishment mass movement. Fear of losing control, and a limited understanding of the nature and power of a mass mobilisation of people, led the IRA leadership to impose its authority on the movement with unfortunate consequences. The left was not prepared to subject itself to the IRA's centrist economic policies nor were many in the Republic anxious to vote for a Nationalistic Sinn Féin agenda that they found difficulty identifying with.

The months after the end of the hunger strikes were, therefore, a crucial period in the course of the Provisional IRA struggle. It was a time when the mass movement initiative that had presented itself in 1968–69 only to be crushed in 1972, re-emerged. The IRA had an opportunity to enhance this momentum but backed off from doing so. Just as they had withdrawn arms training from non-members after the early 1970s, the Republican leadership again proved reluctant to put its faith in the people. The emphasis was to be put on a parliamentary electoral strategy with an elastically adjustable social democratic agenda. A rigid hierarchical party structure that grew out of the IRA was put in charge of the party. It was the type of party machine that the Provisional leadership understood and wanted, partly because they could grasp its remit but, more importantly, because they could control it.

Elsewhere in Ireland at the time, the Republic's economy was in decline and its workers were bearing an unfair and disproportionate share of the tax burden. There was widespread discontent with the situation and on occasion, over 100,000 people marched in protest against the tax regime and against the flagrant avoidance of taxation by the better-off. As the southern economy faltered and the tax regime drew more and more criticism from working people, the old curse of emigration began to become increasingly obvious, as ever-growing numbers of people (a majority of whom were young) left the country to seek work abroad.

Economic ineptitude and turmoil were causing instability in the South with a series of general elections that usually proved inconclusive in terms of delivering an overall majority to any party or a clear-cut recovery policy. The late 1970s and early 1980s were the time when neo-liberal economics were being imposed across many developed countries. The Irish ruling class was also anxious to employ these measures. After the sight of thousands of young people on the streets supporting members of an insurrectionary movement in the early 1980s, coupled with Ireland's history of direct action, the Irish bourgeoisie was reluctant to take on the working class with the same type of head-on challenge that was used in the UK and the US.

A different approach was deemed necessary and a form of Irish corporatism was introduced. In a short time, this arrangement became known as 'Social Partnership'. The Irish trade union movement had developed into a very centrist organisation by the mid-1970s and either failed to recognise or was unwilling to resist the pitfalls inherent in this arrangement. The Irish Congress of Trade Unions (ICTU) proved to be a 'soft touch' in the negotiations and in return for being allowed to win a set pay-increment for its existing membership, meekly allowed itself to be used as a crucial pillar of the deal. The absence of any concrete guarantees embedding social wage factors into Irish society meant that when an economic downturn inevitably occurred, the Irish working class would have few built-in protections, such as a universal National Health Service or even secure accommodation.

It was against this backdrop that the Provisional IRA leadership began to consider how best to preserve the momentum generated by the hunger strike period. Whichever path they opted for required significant change to the outlook and culture of the movement. To choose conventional electoral politics inevitably meant the end to armed insurrection. Only in a time of revolutionary upheaval such as in 1918, when Sinn Féin won 73 out of 105 available seats, does a party come from relative obscurity to win a parliamentary majority. Moreover, when a political earthquake of this nature takes place, it rarely happens as a result of conventional political engagements at constituency level. On the contrary, it is almost always the result of revolutionary upheaval and the creation of a new assembly challenging the authority of the status quo – as happened with the creation of soviets in Revolutionary Russia or more pertinently, when Irish Republicans established an Irish parliament (or Dáil) in 1919 in defiance of the ruling British administration of the time.

Progress in a parliamentary environment is slow and painstaking and more often than not involves making frequent adjustments to the party programme. Parliament, moreover, demands unavoidable and non-negotiable adherence to certain rules, such as recognition of the institutions of state. There is too the dilemma of how and when to enter into coalition and/or agreements in order to make political advances when in order to do so involves adjusting to the programme of the other partner in the arrangement.

There were many in the Republican movement who knew what was involved in accepting the parliamentary path and were more than anxious to follow it no matter what. There was an even larger group in the movement who believed assurances from prominent members of their leadership that it would be possible to participate in conventional parliamentary politics while engaging in an armed insurrection. There was also the traditionalist group who were prepared to remain wedded to the old methods come what may, and there was a small minority who argued for a very different course – that of a left-wing mass movement built from the experience and remaining momentum of the Anti H-Block movement. Because of the IRA's clandestine and hierarchical structures, these issues were never properly debated with a frank and open analysis.

14
Options and Opportunities

They were therefore reduced to moving within strictly parliamentary limits. And it took that peculiar malady which since 1848 has raged all over the Continent, parliamentary cretinism, which holds those infected by it fast in an imaginary world and robs them of all sense, all memory, all understanding of the rude external world - it took this parliamentary cretinism for those who had destroyed all the conditions of parliamentary power with their own hands, and were bound to destroy them in their struggle with the other classes, still to regard their parliamentary victories as victories.

The Eighteenth Brumaire of Louis Bonaparte, Karl Marx, Chapter 6[1]

'We've been shafted,' Paddy said to Jim, 'somebody has talked the old idiot into abandoning everything he has preached all his life.'

The pair had just left the local, pre-convention meeting that had been convened to decide whether or not to have the IRA support a motion to end abstentionism at the upcoming Sinn Féin Ard Fheis.[2] The two men were members of a particularly busy ASU, based just over the border in the Republic and were not happy to have the movement commit itself to a parliamentary path.

From their point of view, the ending of abstentionism (Sinn Féin's policy of refusing to take seats the party might win in any parliament) was not the end of the world in itself, but the circumstances around how it would happen were important. If the resolution to accept seats in the Dublin parliament was accepted as things then stood, they feared that the movement would, in time, fall under the influence of career-minded individuals. They felt that the organisation had not produced a political party with the same uncompromising determination as its army. They argued that once ambitious politicians gained the upper hand they would do any deal and accept any compromise in order to gain and retain office.

Their problem was how to prevent the motion being accepted. From their point of view, the movement included three distinct constituencies: militants such as themselves, mandarins who saw the party as an opportunity for personal political advancement and, worst of all in the boys' opinion, the 'long-rifles'. 'Long-rifle' was a term of abuse for men who had left the North on the run and thereafter refused to cross back into the Six Counties to fight. The term was a reference to these men's penchant for claiming to be able to inflict damage on the Crown from great distances inside the Republic.

Due to a policy decision in the late 1970s to arrange for a 'permanent and stable leadership', a disproportionate number of the despised long-rifles emerged in the Provisional middle management, especially along the southern Border counties. The individuals making up this contingent acquired disproportionate influence due to their longevity in the organisation. In practice, the decision to create a permanent and stable leadership meant creating an IRA bureaucracy and, as often happens, bureaucrats are easily convinced that maintaining the institution is more important than achieving the objectives for which the organisation was created.

The ASU members knew that the mandarins and long-rifles would vote for whatever promised the easier lifestyle. They also realised with alarm that their own influence in the organisation, even at local level, was limited. Too late they had come to recognise that front-line fighting men may achieve a certain status, but that those who remain safely back at base assiduously courting the rank and file have an enormous advantage in a debate about tactics and strategy.

The IRA was hierarchical, but not to the point of inviting a split in an organisation that had a long history of such. The IRA leadership changed policy not by fiat but by a more subtle approach. Careful pre-meeting preparation was used to ensure that any opposition to leadership proposals was overwhelmed by an infusion of prominent and senior 'on-message' spokespersons.

To counter this stratagem, the two ASU men had pinned their hopes on allying with a well-known veteran of the IRA's 1956–62 campaign, a man who, 16 years earlier, had split from his comrades in the Official IRA on the issue of abstentionism. Having assured them of his support right up to the meeting, they believed they had a reasonable chance of carrying the day. However, when the veteran had his 'Pauline moment' just before rising to address the gathering, Paddy and Jim knew they had lost and, believing that opposition was futile, decided instead to concentrate on strengthening their military unit.

When the IRA's political wing Sinn Féin voted to end its abstentionist[3] policy in 1986 and take any seats it would win in the Dublin parliament (or northern assembly if established), the motion was presented as an 'either or' option. Delegates were effectively asked to consider whether the movement should continue to isolate itself from the mainstream of Irish political life or, on the contrary, engage in as many aspects of conventional, parliamentary politics as possible. With high-profile members of the movement, such as Gerry Adams and Martin McGuinness, actively promoting the option of entering parliament as the only viable means of broadening the struggle, a majority of party members agreed to the proposal.

To an outsider from the left, the debate may well have appeared odd. Many delegates were not arguing about what impact the decision might have on movement policy, but whether it would lead to an ending of the armed insurrection. Ruairi O'Bradaigh and Dave O'Connell, prominent opponents of the proposal, argued that entering parliament without a clear majority (enabling that majority to make whatever changes it wished) would inevitably lead to the armed campaign being sidelined and thereafter ended. Gerry Adams and Martin McGuinness, leading supporters of the proposal, insisted that they were as committed to insurrection as everybody else and promised that the armed struggle would not be endangered by entering parliament.

Time was of course to prove the critics of Adams and McGuinness right in respect of the physical force campaign. Within seven years of the decision to end abstentionism, the insurrection was brought to a close. By the time the Provisional IRA ceasefire was announced in 1993, though, the argument about insurrection had become academic. Many of those who proclaimed it to be their primary concern were quite content to accept its end. Gerry Adams and Martin McGuinness were mistaken in 1986 when they promised that the war would continue unabated, but they clearly understood the extent of exhaustion within the Republican community and knew how anxious most were to lay down their arms.

Due to the nature of the Republican movement, the outcome of the debate that took place at the Sinn Féin conference had been decided well in advance. The IRA and Sinn Féin are separate organisations with separate constitutions and capable in theory of acting independently of each other. In practice, the relationship was different and more complex. The Sinn Féin party that voted to end abstentionism in 1986 had grown out of the trauma of 1969. And while the small group of people who had split away from the Dublin-led movement in January 1970 to form Provisional Sinn Féin believed in a traditional Republican orthodoxy, a considerable number of those that joined in the years thereafter were in reality supporters of Provisional IRA fighters rather than Republican ideologues, a situation that was ultimately to leave the party floundering for want of a political lodestar when Partition ceased to be an issue two decades later.

For the duration of the insurrection, those people were committed to the armed struggle and to backing those who carried it out. During the 1970s, Sinn Féin acted as the IRA's civilian support base rather than as a separate political party. The IRA did not strictly speaking tell Sinn Féin what to do, but it did not have to, since Sinn Féin members tended to understand their role as one of doing whatever their 'army' saw as necessary. Unlike a Marxist-Leninist uprising where the party controls the gun, Irish Republicanism had created a situation where the army had overwhelming influence over the party. What this meant in practice at the time of the debate over abstentionism was that whosoever controlled the IRA was going to have their way at the annual conference.

By 1986, the IRA was firmly in the hands of former internees from Belfast who had been advocating entry into parliament since the late 1970s; their only major concern on the day was to avoid a damaging split. The IRA decision-making process is, by its very nature, inimical to democracy. As an army with a militaristic outlook and culture, the IRA operates along strictly hierarchical lines with its leadership not only having enormous power but also enjoying the type of authority that comes only to those who are in command of people who agree to be led and instructed.

When the Army Council and GHQ Staff of the IRA decided to adopt a parliamentary path, it was a relatively straightforward matter of placing people loyal to the Army Council and GHQ Staff in positions of influence throughout the command chain. An internal schism in late 1984 and early 1985 had led to the dismissal of an influential group of IRA activists centred on the well-respected Ivor Bell.[4] He and his supporters were critical of the drive towards electoralism and their removal had purged the most competent and best-organised opponents of parliamentarianism. And with the right people in place, the leadership began its work of persuading the rank and file of the benefits of its chosen path. There was no open discussion about alternative options and the ramifications of proceeding with an electoralist strategy; most volunteers were prepared to accept recommendation made by the leadership and endorsed their decision to enter parliament.

It would be wrong, nevertheless, to suggest outright duplicity on the leadership's part. Discussion within the IRA was not the open and transparent debate one might find in an academic environment. There was no attempt made to research and outline any alternative to stagnation on one hand or parliament on the other. Influential critics of the new strategy such as O'Bradaigh and O'Connell were not given equal access to the rank and file in order to present their case. What discussion took place focused almost entirely on whether parliament could be used to hasten the end of Partition and whether participation in elected assemblies would inevitably lead to an ending of the insurrection.

Within a decade, it had became clear that those who had warned that participating in parliament would end armed struggle were correct. However, it also became clear that the vast majority of the membership remained content to accept the outcome. This fact alone must indicate that most members of the organisation were content to be persuaded of the merits of the parliamentary option if that meant an end to the armed conflict.

Amidst the controversy about whether ending abstentionism would lead to an end to armed struggle, many questions and options were overlooked or not even recognised. In the first place, the bulk of those participating in the 1986 *Ard Fheis* debate did not consider the most likely outcome of entering and working in any parliament under circumstances other than winning a landslide majority. In reality, Sinn Féin would have to embark on a campaign of gaining influence with other parties and interests already in the system. What other use could the party make of its seats apart from the publicity value that would soon wear off, as the novelty of their presence faded? Because unless Sinn Féin could persuade Fianna Fáil, the Irish Labour Party and Fine Gael to undergo an astonishing transformation and lend their support to the IRA's armed campaign, the party would have to make a series of compromises that would allow for common ground with the others to emerge.

Sinn Féin could expect a greater portion of seats in a northern assembly but then that would in turn involve doing a deal with the SDLP and more significantly with hard-line Unionism. Any deal likely to appease Unionism and the SDLP would surely involve not just recognition of Partition but acceptance of a very conservative social and economic status quo and one that would be in keeping with the broad outline of policy pertaining in the UK overall. Most small, minority groups in a parliament quickly lose their identity through irrelevant obscurity or through entering into some form of arrangement with a larger party that requires a dilution of their original manifesto.

A rare few manage to do something constructive with their time in parliament either by using their platform to harass and harangue their opponents at every opportunity or some other form of activity. People like the Socialist Party TD Joe Higgins relentlessly exposed the skulduggery and rascality of the Republic's governing coalition and its leaders by raising relevant issues during debates in the Dáil. Others, such as the late Frank McGuire MP for Fermanagh/South Tyrone, used their position to visit places, such as the Long Kesh H-Blocks, that would have been out of bounds to non-elected persons. Then there was Bernadette McAliskey MP, who used her seat to highlight physically an outrage, as she did at the time of Bloody Sunday when she punched the Home Secretary in the House of Commons. What all these have in common is that they never sought to gain influence or power by currying favour or entering into arrangements with the conservative establishment.

By entering the parliamentary process without any similarly clear social or economic policy, Sinn Féin was hoping to find common ground with the powerbrokers. South of the Border, it was patently obvious that the two largest parties in the state – Fianna Fáil and Fine Gael – were never going to accept any form of left-wing agenda and, in spite of its name and origins, the Irish Labour Party was lukewarm about socialism. Nor, since they were committed to the maintenance and protection of the southern state, were the established parties there ever going to endorse any form of militant, much less military, campaign to remove Partition, especially as this would most likely involve civil disturbance in the Republic.

Moreover, in terms of realpolitik, the established political parties would only permit Sinn Féin access to any of the avenues of publicity or influence if the party agreed to accept the rules as defined by the establishment. They were certainly not going to permit a small parvenu to gain a significant toehold at their expense by playing a mixed game of Armalites and ballot boxes. To feature on television and radio, to be interviewed by the national newspapers and invited to the high-profile events, Sinn Féin had to agree to a set of rules that all the others played by, and that meant an end to arms and an acceptance of all the conventions of parliamentary behaviour – not to mention all existing constitutional arrangements.

Unlike the ANC with its control of South Africa's trade unions and a well-organised mass social movement of street protest, the Provisionals had placed themselves in a position where they had only two avenues of struggle: the option of armed insurrection, or in its absence, parliamentary politics. In time and as the physical force campaign became increasingly impossible to sustain, the IRA was forced into relying more and more on its parliamentary wing. Eventually, this was to crystallise into a situation where the movement only had its parliamentary wing. Sinn Féin soon discovered that on many issues it had little power to alter the outcome of events and, fearing being reduced to utter impotency, found itself having to cling to its seats in Stormont and Leinster House (the Dublin parliament) at all costs.

In time, this was to force Sinn Féin to abandon any pretext of being a socialist party. The arguments used were remarkably similar to those employed by New Labour in Britain. Making Sinn Féin 'electable' was the mantra and the party's left-leaning members were told that they had to be patient. They were told that the leadership, which alone it was said had a grasp of the big picture, was making minor tactical adjustments in order to take greater strides forward in the future. Eventually, with the party's public line having less socialist content, people with a less socialist outlook were able to gain increasing influence.

The IRA has always been vulnerable to this type of ideological erosion. During the period when fighting an insurrection was a priority, the movement recruited people who would fight. Little emphasis was placed on political education and, while the average volunteer was working class and not hostile to a socialist agenda, few had given much time to studying the debilitating impact of centre-right social democracy. There was moreover, an understandable but mistaken view in some Republican quarters that because people had once borne arms against an imperialist state, that alone was enough to ensure their ongoing revolutionary zeal.

The Republican leadership promised its support base that it would be possible to bamboozle the opposition and 'walk both sides of the road'. They said that they would talk peace but quietly would remain ready to resume hostilities if necessary. They promised that the movement would remain committed to revolution in spite of its public commitment to new and exclusively democratic and peaceful methods. This sounded attractive to a number of old and tired Provisional IRA men, but it never had a chance of working in practice.

Governments in Britain and the Republic knew very well that the Provisional IRA was as capable of misleading them as any other political opponent. They knew exactly how to deal with this strategy by revealing in detail whenever the IRA deviated from its commitment to purely parliamentary practice. British and Irish government agents had the IRA too heavily penetrated by the early 1990s for the Provisional IRA to be able to bluff on matters of strategy. It was possible, admittedly, for the organisation to get away with one-off, albeit occasionally spectacular, operations but was not able to do so constantly.

It was impossible for the IRA to avoid surveillance on each and every occasion, and when IRA operations went wrong, as they did, the twin-track policy fell apart, with crushing consequences for the political party. Moreover, while the organisation could hope (in theory at any rate) to evade attention with a limited number of operations, it could never hope to retain an overall operational capacity without it coming to the attention of the enemy agents within its ranks. In short, Sinn Féin had to stick to its promises if it wished to retain the goodwill of the establishment and stay in the game.

Closing the insurrectionary option forced Sinn Féin and the IRA to find another avenue. Without a policy of mass action and social activism, the organisation had no option but to build its strategy around parliamentary engagement. With a minority of elected members in the northern and southern assemblies, the organisation was forced to make its pitch for the lowest possible common denominator that would allow it to appeal to other interests and parties. In practice, this meant creating a pan-Nationalist consensus on both sides of the border, a policy that depended on winning support from the conservative sections of society that had no interest in removing Partition if by doing so it upset the state's equilibrium. These parties were, moreover, fundamentally opposed to socialist transformation of society and most were staunch advocates of neo-liberalism. They had, after all, chosen economic corporatism and were committed supporters of US foreign policy and admirers of its 'Chicago School' of economic management.

The Provisional IRA was moving away from the radical anti-establishment world out of which they had arisen. They were moving away from the type of confrontational, participatory politics that a small group of their members had advocated from inside the northern prison and that would very likely have created a new wave of socially transforming politics and of a fundamentally different nature.

15
The Road Less Travelled …
The Left Alternative

Harry's cell was the first to be served the evening meal and in spite of a long week listening to a medley of bloodcurdling Orange songs being played over and over again by the trustees on their record player, he was completely thunderstruck with the spectacle. The 'Fear-Romhar' (Fatty), wearing a makeshift Orange sash, was sitting on an upturned bin, pretending to play a flute as the trustees pushed him along on the food trolley. Republicans in the H-Blocks did not celebrate the Twelfth of July but the occasion was not going by unmarked.

Trustees, supervised by prison officers, were used to delivering food around the cells on a small, wheeled float. It was usually a sullen ritual with plastic plates of HMP Maze fare being set over thresholds and doors being immediately slammed shut thereafter. Today it was different. The class officer, known to the Blanketmen in H3 as the 'Fear-Romhar', had decided to introduce some excitement to the wing he was charged with supervising.

It was all a flagrant violation of prison rules. Prison officers were supposed to be non-partisan and were certainly not allowed to parade around a wing pretending to lead an Orange band. These were the H-Blocks, though, and the authorities in HMP Maze were concentrating on crushing the Blanket protest with very little heed paid to what their own employees did.

In many ways, the Blanket protest epitomised the very nature and depth of alienation that existed in Northern Irish society. Moreover, it illustrated the length Britain was prepared to go in order to impose its will. When 'Special Category Status' was abolished in 1976, captured Republican fighters found that they were in a bind. To accept the designation of criminals meant not just demeaning themselves within the prison environment, but to acquiesce in Britain's new strategy of deeming the Irish conflict a non-political and criminal enterprise. Yet how could people in jail prevent the authorities doing with them as they wished?

Prison protests are often short and, more often than not, ineffective. By the very nature of such institutions, all power lies with the jailer and protest is therefore nigh on futile. Prisoners realise very quickly that beating the system is not an easy option and in most cases, they come to terms with reality and make the best of their lot. That Republicans refused to take what many would have seen as the realistic option and adjust to their circumstances was an indication of their profound alienation from the state and all its organs. That they received such huge support from their communities for their efforts highlighted not only that they were not viewed as criminals by the Catholic community, but that that same community was also deeply at odds with the ruling authority.

It was this dogged refusal to accept the role of a mere criminal that had Harry standing, wrapped only in a coarse prison blanket, when the bizarre procession came to deliver his evening meal. Under different circumstances, he might even have enjoyed the spectacle but not this, with its deep and symbolic message. As an active IRA operator before his capture, he knew the commitment needed to fight and had it in plenty. Yet he never had any wish to humiliate his enemy and this was what he sometimes felt was the most obnoxious part of being in prison – how the authorities loved to demean prisoners.

As with others in the IRA, the people who had been at the centre of the battle for political status through the hunger strikes – the imprisoned IRA – had an opinion about how the movement should develop. Many of them had been very active when free, a considerable number had held senior positions in the movement and knew its strengths, weaknesses and needs well, and all were spending years incarcerated on behalf of the movement and its cause. Moreover, since they had had time aplenty to read, think, talk and reflect, they were well capable of participating in and contributing to policy decisions made by and impacting on the movement.

Amazingly, they were neither consulted nor canvassed for their opinions. This strange situation was due to an old IRA practice of relieving all its imprisoned personnel of their status and denying them any influence over events on the outside. In many cases, there was good reason for this custom. It was not possible for an organisation as prone to having its members arrested and jailed as the IRA, to have those in prison complicating day-to-day management of the organisation by sending messages and directives to those struggling to maintain a coherent structure on the outside.

Moreover, since prisoners were by definition removed from the field of conflict, they could not be depended upon to make an informed judgement about operational matters on the outside. Also, there is a degree of uncertainty mixed with half-truths circulating in an underground movement at the best of times, without having confusing or misinformed directives sprayed about by people looking on from afar. There was, also, the unspoken fear that giving prisoners a voice might tempt them to vote for surrender in the hope of gaining early release. A further anxiety was that prisoners might exert undue influence on their comrades outside the walls to attempt ill-conceived escapes.

However, in spite of all these well-grounded concerns, no such logic applied to debating matters of policy that did not directly impact on day-to-day administration of the organisation or would be likely to force the leadership into a precipitous plunge towards self-destruction. In reality, refusing to draw on the experience and knowledge of almost a thousand of the movement's most dedicated members at a crucial period in the insurrection indicated a determination to enforce the acceptance of a preset agenda rather than explore the available options.

Since the time of the hunger strike, a number of IRA prisoners (including the author) had been re-evaluating the progress of the struggle. They had grown alarmed at the evidence of a mass movement of people working tirelessly and heroically to support the hunger strikers and how this mass movement was eventually unable to influence the outcome. There was little doubt that northern working-class Republicans had made an incredible and Herculean effort to alter the tide in favour of those in prison and still it was not enough. No longer could anyone argue for a greater effort from that community. They had given everything in that phase of the insurrection. Mere effort was not enough and further exhortation to greater sacrifice was pointless. A new and more potent alignment of forces was necessary to break out of the encirclement in which northern Republicanism had found itself trapped.

Unlike those pushing for acceptance of a purely parliamentary strategy, this group of prisoners were firmly to the left of the movement and Marxist for the most part. They argued that it was imperative that the IRA put in place a strategy that would allow it to win significant support in the South and that its politics and strategy would also allow it to make a significant impact on a strategically important section of the British working-class and radical population.

They argued that to do so, the Republican movement in all its parts had to embed itself within the working class and become an organic part of that class's struggle for improvement in its conditions of life. Moreover, they stated that armed struggle had to be re-evaluated and seen as a tool rather than have it installed as a fetish, as was the case with many conservative Republicans who had grown so jaded in their convictions that they confused armed struggle with Republicanism and had come to see one as the keystone of the other.

This group of prisoners estimated that the starting-point for any new departure had to be the existence of a mass movement that had grown and developed through the hunger strike. They

Figure 15.1   Covers of Congress '86 (© Tommy McKearney).

argued that while many of those who had dedicated so much time to the prisoners' cause were not convinced socialists and certainly not Marxists, they were for the most part working-class people who could instinctively understand and empathise with a mass social movement. With energetic engagement and education, this constituency could be persuaded to support a campaign to improve conditions for working people.

These left-wing Republican prisoners argued that a series of measures would have to be enacted within the Republican movement in order to allow it to recalibrate its direction. It would be crucially important that all members of the organisation understood the necessity for change and that time be taken to develop a programme suited to the conditions in Ireland at the time. They reasoned that it would be futile attempting to introduce a strongly socialist policy, programme and process by stealth and that instead it should be done openly and honestly.

Claims that the Republican support base was not willing to accept a Marxist programme were challenged on the basis that only the party would be required to accept a scientific socialist programme. Moreover, an urban working class, and a less well-off rural constituency that was the heart of the Provisional IRA which had accepted the designation of rebel for so long, would not necessarily baulk at the suggestion of revolutionary politics. As further evidence of the fact that a frank espousal of a conventional orthodox socialist policy would not alienate its entire base was the fact that at that time the Workers Party was regularly winning significant support in Dublin while claiming (somewhat questionably perhaps) to be a Marxist-Leninist party.[1]

In terms of persuading a majority of the movement of the need and value of such a departure, they said that if the same energy and time was spent cultivating a socialist position as was spent pushing through the ending of abstentionism (which many Republicans instinctively feared) then the outcome could have been just as decisive in favour of socialism. Time, they said, was not the enemy. The Sinn Féin publicity machine was, after all, talking at that time of a long war. Why not, the imprisoned Leftists asked, a long struggle for socialism?

They had argued that conditions were suitable for a firm statement of intent from the movement, laying out its position as a party of the working people. The Provisional IRA had emerged from a mass movement of people demanding social and economic justice and had remained a predominantly working-class organisation. There should not be, these prisoners said, any great difficulty making the case among the movement's support base for a programme that would position itself unambiguously behind working people's issues and in a coherent and planned fashion, especially since Sinn Féin and the IRA had long stated that its primary aim was the establishment of a 32-county socialist republic.

The prisoners' group argued that building on the movement that already existed would entail an amount of political education, but that this would be of an explanatory nature rather than something requiring a change to the fundamental outlook of those participating. Their view was that Republicans had for too long taken a one-dimensional view of armed conflict. Too many Republicans saw physical force as the one and only method of struggle. This viewpoint had to be challenged, they said, and replaced with a broader view of the means for a revolutionary transformation of society. It would not be sufficient to merely proclaim support for socialist objectives, but it would be necessary to engage organically in social and economic movements of the working class.

As a first step, they suggested a determined and coordinated campaign to win influence within the trade union movement. While it would be possible to attempt a series of coups within the existing unions, the prisoners argued that that type of underhand tactic would merely alienate other trade unionists and weaken organised labour in the process. It would be much better to encourage the Republican support base to take out trade union membership if they were not already members and begin to work within the existing structures in order to gain influence through credibility. There had been trade unionists and trade union leaders present within the Anti H-Block committees, they pointed out, and therefore the world of organised labour was hardly alien territory to Republican grass-roots. While reactionary elements within the trade unions might attempt to stymie a concerted effort by Republicans to organise within the labour movement, it would not have been possible to prevent such a large number of people joining and influencing the union movement. With a principled and structured base built within organised labour, the prisoners argued that it would become possible not just to work for change in society on their own, but to begin the work of building a new left-of-centre consensus in Southern Ireland. This, they said, would challenge what was then and remains an historic anomaly in Irish politics in that a very considerable percentage of working-class people vote for the populist and right-wing Fianna Fáil party, not only in rural Ireland, but in urban centres as well.

This odd phenomenon has its roots in the Irish Civil War of the 1920s when the Irish Labour Party had, *de facto*, taken the side of big business and accepted the Treaty by agreeing to form a loyal opposition within the Free State parliament. Civil War feelings ran deep and took a long time to heal. The Labour Party remained fixated by its old ally throughout the decades that followed and re-entered the coalition with an ultra right-wing Fine Gael party in the early 1970s, ensuring that Republican Ireland would not forgive or forget. This did not mean, however, that all Labour Party voters or members were of the right. What it meant in practice was that the working-class vote was damagingly split and channelled ineffectively behind right-of-centre parties and policies. A new and dynamic socialist Republican movement could hope to overcome this rift in time by attracting working-class voters away from Fianna Fáil on the one hand, while strengthening the position of serious left-wingers within the Irish Labour Party on the other.

A structured left-wing party working to a serious and principled socialist agenda had an opportunity, too, to reason with working-class northern Unionists in a manner that the increasingly nationalistic Sinn Féin could never hope to do. None of the prisoners doubted for a moment that it would be easy to change the outlook of the Unionist working-class population, but a socialist programme would at least step out of the narrow world of '*Irish News* and Catholic Church republicanism' that the pan-Nationalist path of the Sinn Féin party was unavoidably taking. Outside Ireland, these prisoners suggested, a decidedly social mass movement with clear socialist aims in Ireland would be able to form a direct working relationship with constituencies in Britain feeling the impact of Thatcher's neo-liberal policies.

This group of prisoners who were eventually to leave the IRA and organise themselves as the League of Communist Republicans argued that neo-liberalism had a finite ability to attract the support of the working class. They said that sooner or later the crisis-prone nature of uncontrolled free markets would cause a disaster in the system, which would open the door for socialism. They insisted that a left-wing party that held firmly to a position through the years of capitalist advantage would emerge, having demonstrated the validity of its long-term analysis, and would be in a position to gain accordingly.

Twenty-two years after the 'Abstentionist' debate, the insurrection is over. Sinn Féin now holds 14 seats in the Dáil but has not managed to fundamentally challenge the status quo. North of the border, they are partners with the DUP in the administration of Northern Ireland, having accepted Partition and the implications involved in this, including adapting to the neo-liberal consensus that reigns in

Stormont. The small group of communist former prisoners have ceased organising themselves as a group, but many of them continue to argue for a mass working-class movement through realignment and reinvigoration of the left. It is hard now to fault their analysis of either the past or present.

16
Parliamentary Sinn Féin, 'Surrender and Re-grant'[1]

It was the sight of an unkempt official in civilian clothes standing beside the immigration officer and pointing in his direction that alerted Seamus to what was about to happen. Before reaching the immigration control desk, he knew that he would be asked to accompany the uniformed officer to the holding area. Three hours later, he was still sitting in Montreal Airport's secure-room and with every minute that passed, he knew that his chance of getting through to join his wife and children on holiday was fading fast. At least the Canadian authorities were treating him courteously, he thought. When he had tried visiting his brother's family in New York some years earlier, US immigration officials had acted with gratuitous boorishness when refusing him entry.

As the deadline for his connecting flight passed, the Canadian immigration official told him formally that he was to be deported. He knew that he had little option but to settle down and wait for his flight back to Ireland. As evening turned to night and passenger traffic through the airport began to slacken, the immigration official standing watch over him began to relax and eventually they started to talk.

'Who was that guy standing with you at the immigration control desk?' Seamus asked. 'You don't expect me to answer that', the official said, 'but I will tell you this, he is not employed by the Canadian government. We did not just pick you out of the queue at random, your passport tells us that you have a terrorist conviction in Ireland and when we see that, we have instructions to detain, question and deport.'

Seamus laughed and replied, 'As a matter of fact, when I was arrested the Irish Constitution claimed jurisdiction over the northern Six Counties, so I could even claim that I was merely trying to enforce my own government's constitution.'

The Canadian official was nonplussed. He obviously knew nothing about Articles Two and Three of De Valera's 1937 Constitution, but picked up on Seamus' surprisingly good-humoured attitude and joined in the banter. 'You're obviously not a very important Irish terrorist', he said 'or you would have got through. Look at the list of your buddies who were invited to the White House for St Patrick's Day.'

Seamus was left alone for a few minutes to reflect on the conversation. His Irish passport had identified him as a terrorist to the Canadian authorities, so in spite of all their ballyhoo about helping to find a settlement, Dublin still looked on the northern insurrection as a subversive episode that they had helped quell. That the British government shared this view did not surprise him, and if Ireland

and Britain was taking that position, it was obvious that others such as the US and Canada would do the same.

He also began to think about what the Canadian had said as a joke. The IRA leadership had accepted US and Canadian politicians and civil servants as honest brokers during the course of the Irish peace negotiations, yet both governments continued to view the IRA as a terrorist organisation. If the IRA believed it had no option but to continue with a process overseen by elements hostile to Irish Republicans, why on earth did it at least not ask Sinn Féin's leadership to stay away from White House parties until all its supporters were allowed to visit the US? The Fureys won't play gigs that don't allow Travellers to attend,[2] so why do Gerry Adams and Martin McGuinness go partying where Republican ex-prisoners are banned?

When the IRA announced that it was calling a ceasefire in August 1994, its leadership had already been in secret negotiation with the British and Irish authorities for a number of years. The Republican movement had not been able to reach a deal that would bring an end to Partition, the union with Britain, or indeed very much else. The only concession the two governments had agreed to up front was to allow the IRA's political wing Sinn Féin to enter into the political system in return for a definitive end to the IRA insurrection.

In doing so, the two governments were not only recognising reality but were at the same time employing a sophisticated counter-insurgency strategy. By the mid-1980s, the British government's intelligence agencies had heavily penetrated the IRA. To have reached such a position was advantageous to the British but one that, from their point of view, had to be managed with some skill. The British were also aware that while the IRA was vulnerable, it still retained the support of a significant section of the Catholic population in the Six Counties.

The British state held such a strong position *vis-à-vis* the IRA that they could have demolished the organisation as it was then structured had it been willing to accept the consequences. Freddie Scappaticci, head of IRA internal security, was a British agent and had had access to the organisation's secrets and layout.[3] His information alone was sufficient to lay bare the organisation's structures and membership. Denis Donaldson, a member of Gerry Adam's 'kitchen cabinet', had assisted him in his espionage efforts. Moreover, with the reorganisation of the movement in the aftermath of the 1975 ceasefire, which ensured that the bulk of IRA members lived in their own homes, it would have been a relatively straightforward matter to arrest a critical mass of the movement in one swoop.

To do so, however, would have risked further alienating the Catholic community. More dangerous still, from London's point of view, was the real possibility that such an action could very well have cleared the field for a new, younger and more militant organisation. A new grouping with a clear field would undoubtedly have been harder to infiltrate. And it might possibly have developed political strategies that Britain would have found much more difficult to cope with than the mellow social democratic programme of the then-existing Republican movement.

Britain knew that it had a window of opportunity in Ireland with the Republican leadership then in place, but it had to act while it had the space. After more than twenty years of insurrection and turmoil in Northern Ireland, the governing authorities in London and Dublin recognised that the IRA and its supporters could not be transformed into a conventional parliamentary organisation overnight. Moreover, it was also accepted that moving too fast could risk splitting the Republican organisation. For the two governments' objective to be achieved, they needed the vast majority of IRA supporters to come to terms and accept a new dispensation that under other circumstances would have been inconceivable.

With Britain taking the lead, a careful and cautious political minuet that came to be known as the 'Peace Process' was organised. The objective, undoubtedly, was to embed Sinn Féin and the vast majority of its support base deeply and inextricably within the then-existing constitutional framework. Any settlement would need to contain sufficient reform of the Northern Ireland state and administration, for which Sinn Féin could claim credit. From this point of view, it was important that the entire chain of insurrection was contained and thereafter transformed into a conventional parliamentary organisation and that this process should not be confined to the Republican leadership.

Both governments knew that a return to Unionist majority rule was not a viable option, since Republicans could not be persuaded to accept it; for their own reasons, neither state was prepared to tolerate any form of all-Ireland arrangement, even in the unlikely event that Unionists could be tempted to consider such a possibility. The plan was to return to a new version of the 1970s 'power-sharing' administration. This course of action was complicated by the fact that the two governments knew that on this occasion they needed to gain endorsement from a majority of the Unionist and Republican constituencies for the renewed effort to have any real chance of success. The absence of any significant grouping from the political settlement, the governments recognised, was bound to undermine its chances of survival.

By the nature of Northern Irish politics, this was a tall order, since any concession to Republicans, no matter how minor, would be interpreted by Unionists as betrayal. Unionism itself was in the throes of a struggle for supremacy between the middle-class Ulster Unionist Party and Ian Paisley's populist Democratic Unionist Party. This battle ensured that little room existed within Unionist ranks for the pragmatic assessment of a situation where, in reality, its old enemy Sinn Féin was coming round to accepting Partition and the Union as legitimate.

London and Dublin had two major factors in their favour. All parties to the Northern Irish conflict, with the exception of the British government, were traumatised and exhausted by the years of struggle. An entire generation had lived without normal electoral politics in Northern Ireland and, after 20 years of direct rule from London, there existed a widespread appetite in many quarters for a more responsive local administration.

The *sine qua non* to the process was that the IRA would declare a ceasefire. This occurred in August 1994, when Sinn Féin supporters celebrated in the streets of Belfast as if they had won a war. The IRA had not won the war outright and, as a consequence, was unable to impose its terms and conditions on the settlement. It became imperative, therefore, for those who wished to influence events to gain representation at whatever conference would be organised. To do so, the IRA had to secure seats in the upcoming elections. The IRA and its political party, Sinn Féin, understood the need for favourable media coverage and immediately demanded an end to the broadcasting ban on interviews with its members and travel restrictions on its spokespersons. These (retractable) privileges were soon granted and the IRA's public face, Sinn Féin, was seen and heard on all major networks. The novelty value of interviewing members of an organisation that had been banned from the airwaves for decades ensured intense media interest.

To the surprise and indeed dismay of those hostile to Sinn Féin and the IRA, Republican spokespersons were found to be articulate, intelligent and well-briefed in media techniques. They performed well on television and radio and when the Dublin government arranged visas to the US for leading members of the organisation, they added to their profile as capable politicians and even as potential statesmen.

In return for ending the armed insurrection, Sinn Féin was given an opportunity to present itself as a conventional political party and, perhaps more important, as a party that could help deliver an end to the long years of conflict in Northern Ireland. The party revelled in its new position and, just as important for organisational purposes, exploited skilfully the new-found freedom from police harassment. With fresh faces and a young and energetic party membership used to self-discipline and aggressive in party promotion, it was little surprise that before long they began to make serious inroads into the electoral support base of their rivals for the Catholic vote, the SDLP. With the signing of the Good Friday Agreement in 1998, it appeared that Sinn Féin had indeed managed to deliver a permanent peace and their prestige was even further enhanced. As the party's stock rose, they overtook the pedantic SDLP as the major Catholic party in Northern Ireland.

Not surprisingly, Sinn Féin was unable to make as favourable an impression on the Unionist population as they did on Catholics. Having ruled the Six Counties for 50 years with absolute authority, and then having been subjected to a 20-year-long insurrection, Unionists were not easily placated. Nor were they ready to accept that they would have to share the administration of Northern Ireland with people they viewed as murderous rebels and gunmen, people to be punished rather than appeased.

Nevertheless, there was a realisation within the Unionist population that the IRA was offering a ceasefire and that was something they were reluctant to reject out of hand. In spite of the enormous support that the British government had given to Unionism during the insurrection, Unionism too was weary of the conflict. The IRA had inflicted a heavy toll on the Crown's locally recruited forces and the bombing campaign had undermined the area's prosperity. A further factor impinging on the Unionist outlook related to the outward migration of bright young Unionists. After having monitored and manipulated population levels so assiduously when ruling from Stormont, Unionism was acutely aware of the migratory patterns of the region's inhabitants. Whereas in the pre-insurrection days, the greater number of people emigrating from Northern Ireland was Catholic, the trend had been reversed during the conflict. Exacerbating this problem from a Unionist point of view was that the pattern was most discernable among students who had attended university in Britain and did not return after graduation. More worrying still was the knowledge that many

Figure 16.1   Children in Belfast celebrate the end of the IRA campaign in 1994 (© Belfast Exposed).

middle-class Unionist parents were content to have their offspring remain permanently 'out of and away from the Troubles'.

Unionists were, as a result, faced with a dilemma in so far as they too desired an end to the conflict, but were reluctant to make the type of concessions necessary to bring it about. Their response was to meet all proposals for a resolution of the conflict with a set of preconditions that Republicans would find difficult to accept. A list was drawn up, including demands for a definitive statement from the IRA that the insurrection was over, the organisation was committed to non-violent means, the IRA's weapons would be surrendered to the British authorities, and that Republicans would give total and unconditional support to policing in Northern Ireland. On one occasion, Ian Paisley went so far as to demand that the IRA return money it had taken in bank raids.

Echoing the callous arrogance of Terrence O'Neill's gaucherie in the 1960s, when describing Catholic behaviour if given a job, David Trimble described this process as 'house training' for Republicans. Creating still more problems was the fact that the rivalry between the two main Unionist groups resulted in both parties finding themselves in a competition to determine which of them would appear to be taking the firmest line against the Provisional IRA. And all the while, neither the UUP nor the DUP was prepared to risk taking responsibility for conclusively wrecking the prospects of a settlement.

There was, at the same time, awareness within Unionist leading counsels that London wanted an end to the conflict and was anxious, with the Provisional IRA in compromise mode, that the opportunity should not be missed. Unionism knew that it could not risk provoking British governing circles into losing patience and imposing its own settlement. More astute and thoughtful Unionist strategists and thinkers believed that the Anglo-Irish Agreement of November 1985, which gave Dublin a measure of input into Northern Irish affairs, came about as a result of the then Ulster Unionist Party leader James Molyneaux failing to engage sufficiently with the existing political current. Neither the UUP nor DUP leaderships had any intention of allowing their parties to be similarly wrong-footed again.

What emerged was a political game of bluff and counter-bluff between Republicans and both major Unionist parties. How much did Sinn Féin want entry into an administration, and to what lengths was Unionism prepared to go to keep them out? In short, it was the type of bargaining and negotiating and politico-diplomatic horse-trading that the British government understood and played with such consummate skill. It was also not only a process that drew Sinn Féin deeper into the milieu of parliamentary and constitutional politics, but into the politics of the existing constitutional arrangement as well.

The Republican leadership was faced with something of a dilemma in this situation. They wanted to bring the IRA campaign to an end, but were wary of the consequences of saying so frankly and unequivocally to its grass-roots. The culture of armed resistance, not to mention the rank and file's commitment to the cause, their dead comrades and the years in struggle, made it difficult for many volunteers to admit, even to themselves, that the war was finally over without a clear-cut victory. It was difficult for the IRA high command to admit frankly to its volunteers that they, the leadership, had decided finally to abandon armed struggle in favour of a strategy that the IRA had decried for decades. They were unwilling to acknowledge that a new era had arrived that would involve an acceptance of Partition and the Union and an irreversible break with armed insurrection.

In order to allow the IRA grass-roots to come to terms with the new dispensation, the leadership found it necessary to sanction a certain number of military operations and retained the arsenal and structures of an army in waiting. This allowed IRA volunteers to believe that they were pursuing the twin strategy of the Armalite and the ballot box when, in reality, no such option was available and the endgame was always going to be the same. IRA leaders told Republican volunteers at ground level that the ceasefire arrangement was a tactical manoeuvre that could be reversed at any time. The British government understood that these reassurances were necessary in order to prevent a split within IRA ranks, but also recognised that sooner or later, it was important to remove the organisation's capacity for insurrection.

A well-known personality from the civil rights era once described the process as similar to that of boiling a frog. If the frog is placed in a saucepan of hot water, it will jump out immediately. If, on the other hand, it is placed in a pot of cold water slowly heated until boiling, the frog, not noticing the gradual rise in temperature, will eventually be boiled. So too with the IRA: by incrementally reducing its capacity to fight, the situation almost imperceptibly became irreversible.

In the early days of the ceasefire, the IRA's grass-roots was allowed to believe that it could continue with a limited number of operations, especially finance raids, for which it would simply deny responsibility. This proved to be a disastrous miscalculation. A post-office robbery carried out in November 1994 resulted in the death of Frank Kerr, a worker in a sorting office. This led to the subsequent arrest of several IRA personnel who, to the embarrassment of the organisation, demanded recognition as political prisoners. The IRA was forced to admit that some of its members had been responsible, though it claimed the Army Council had not sanctioned the killing. Two years later, on 6 June 1996, during an attempted robbery, at another post office in Adair, Co. Limerick, Garda Gerry McCabe was shot dead and once again IRA personnel were arrested and convicted of the shooting.

As a result, IRA bona fides were questioned. How could the governments in London and Dublin, Unionists and others asked, deal with a group that appeared to be so disingenuous about its relationship with arms? How could the Sinn Féin Party expect Unionism to enter into meaningful negotiations with it when there was clear evidence that the IRA ceasefire was only partial? These breaches of the ceasefire continued with a regularity that was at times, difficult to understand. IRA members were arrested in Florida attempting to buy guns and ship them back to Ireland.[4] Prominent and well-known members of the Republican movement – Niall Connolly, James Monaghan and Martin McCauley – were arrested and detained in Colombia in August 2001, after having been in contact with the revolutionary underground FARC movement. The Colombian arrests demonstrated just how fragile was Sinn Féin's confidence in managing the situation when the party attempted to deny knowing the three men, a lie that was easily exposed by the publication of photos of former IRA prisoner James Monaghan at Sinn Féin *ard-fheiseanna*.

Each time the IRA was caught trying to duck under the ceasefire stipulations, Sinn Féin paid a political price. At best, the connection proved a political embarrassment, as Sinn Féin tried to insist to other parties and to the media that they were serious about a settlement. At worst, such as, for example, after a group of Republicans were caught by the Police Service of Northern Ireland (PSNI) in the act of kidnapping Irish Republican Socialist Party (IRSP) member Bobby Tohill from a Belfast pub in 2004, it led to the collapse of the political institutions. As a consequence of these actions, the IRA was eventually forced to make a choice. It could retain its capacity for conducting armed insurrection and in so doing inflict terminal damage on Sinn Féin's prospects of taking part in a devolved administration in Stormont. Or, it could dismantle its military machine and allow the political institutions to get up and running. The Provisional IRA eventually chose the latter option.

For years, the IRA had insisted that it would only negotiate while continuing to fight. Therefore, when the organisation declared what was, in effect, an unconditional ceasefire in 1994, the organisation was indicating that it was not going into talks from a position of strength. Moreover, as random IRA operations continued to bedevil the political wing's progress, greater restrictions were placed on local units' ability to act, in case they damaged the 'Process'. Slowly and surely, the movement came round to accept that it would have to abandon its relationship with its long tradition of physical-force Republicanism. After an extensive period when the armed wing of Republicanism led its political party, the roles were reversed.

As a first step, the Provisional IRA had to issue a statement that their war was definitively over and that they would henceforward adhere to purely democratic and peaceful means. This was in some ways a meaningless statement, since no Army Council or GHQ staff can hope to bind the hands of future generations. What it did do though was to publicly humiliate the organisation by forcing it effectively to say 'please' and then 'pretty please'.

Next, the IRA had to undergo the indignity of decommissioning its arms. This caused enormous difficulty to an organisation that saw itself at one time as being part of the international movement for national liberation and the last line of defence for its own support base. The trauma was so great within the movement that many of its members went into denial. In County Fermanagh, the local commander attempted to spread the egregious story that decommissioning had never taken place. He told his astonished listeners that the head of the supervisory body had been compromised by IRA intelligence and forced to make a bogus report confirming the destruction of materiel. This unfortunate Provisional was obviously blind to the fact that, as we now know, Britain, with its high-ranking agents in the IRA, had no need to rely on a couple of clergymen or a Canadian general to confirm decommissioning.

Finally, the Provisional IRA had to give its public support to policing. This was brought about by having the Sinn Féin leadership tour the country, convening meetings in order to convince its membership of the value of supporting Northern Ireland's police force. The party did not distinguish between different forms of policing and refused to differentiate between the type that helps old ladies and gentlemen across the road and the kind that defends the state or arrests trade unionists for unofficial picketing.

Having accepted this raft of changes, the insurrectionary period of the Provisional IRA was finally at an end. Sinn Féin, the parliamentary organisation, had emerged to replace the army that had challenged the state. As Bernadette McAliskey said at the time, the process had a familiar ring to it. She said that it was reminiscent of the Tudor policy of 'surrender and re-grant'[5] in sixteenth-century Ireland, when English power was being imposed across the entire island. The Provisional IRA leadership had achieved a certain status by surrendering its old programme and being allocated a place within the British system in Ireland. The era of New Sinn Féin was firmly established.

17
From Armalites to Populist Conformity

Jack was a loyal party member and a volunteer, but he was more than a little unsure about the deal. I wonder, he asked himself, if we were still in our teens would we have accepted the Good Friday Agreement? He was not fooled by the bland assurances being bandied about by the leadership. The cavalcade through West Belfast when the ceasefire had been announced was an embarrassment, he had thought; we haven't got the socialist republic after all. He was a realist, nevertheless, and understood better than some of the others that the decision to end the campaign was the only option left. To persist with a war that the IRA wasn't going to win would only turn a tragic situation into a disaster.

Jack was aware that since the early 1980s the IRA had been struggling to maintain a certain level of operations. He also knew that it was becoming more and more difficult to recruit new and dynamic members into the organisation. Too many of the volunteers were of the original 1970s intake, well known to the RUC and closely monitored. It was inevitable, he reasoned, that a small population in a small geographical area would eventually succumb to the relentless pressure that the British state could bring to bear on it. He knew people who were unyielding in their loyalty to the movement but who were quietly telling him that they could not continue indefinitely with the war.

The rate of attrition among both Republican volunteers and the civilian support base was becoming increasingly debilitating towards the end of the 1980s. Too often, the British Army had been able to anticipate operations and either capture entire ASUs or worse, slaughter them. Loyalist death squads were acting with impunity and inflicting serious damage on Republican communities as the IRA's defence strategy appeared to have collapsed. If there were readily available alternative strategies in the field of physical force, Jack could not see them nor had he heard anyone else articulate a viable option.

Calling off the campaign was difficult to accept and left him with a sense of disappointment. Yet, a good retreat is always better than a calamitous stand, he thought, so let's get on with what has to be done next. The seemingly endless round of 'seeking clarification' and negotiating that preceded the Good Friday Agreement appeared to him not to be well handled. He feared that on occasions the organisation had actually underestimated the strength of its hand and surrendered too much too early. Things like the release of prisoners and quashing of all convictions handed down by no-jury Diplock Courts should have been conditions for a ceasefire rather than bargaining chips at discussions about the formation of devolved government.

Sinn Féin was so anxious to get into an administration that it argued over the make-up of the administration and failed to secure tax and spending powers for the new executive. With little say over the shaping of the Six County economy, the party would have to acquiesce in the delivery of whatever London insisted upon and this would in time drag Sinn Féin into endorsing the centre-right economic policies of New Labour and its successors.

The Good Friday Agreement of 1998 was not in itself a magic formula that delivered peace to Northern Ireland. Nor was it, as Seamus Mallon of the SDLP, described it, 'Sunningdale for slow learners'. The Agreement came about partly as a result of protracted negotiations behind closed doors, but more precisely as a result of the exhaustion of the Northern Irish population. The deal followed in outline a proposed settlement insisted upon by Britain in 1973, but differing significantly in that the British government was intent that, on this occasion, the IRA and its support base plus the overwhelming majority of Unionists would be involved as an integral part of the deal.

Having seen the earlier attempt fall because of opposition from both militant Republicans and hard-line Unionists, Britain was determined not to repeat the experience. With a ceasefire in place and both Sinn Féin and the DUP participating in the negotiations, the key elements of an arrangement that would hold were in place. This was a crucial difference from what Seamus Mallon thought was an identical arrangement in 1973. Deals are made between people; the details of what is agreed are merely conditions and there is good reason to believe that the key components for a Good Friday Agreement-style compromise were not present in 1973 within either the Provisional IRA or hard-line Unionism.

Almost five years elapsed between the IRA's first ceasefire and signing of the Good Friday Agreement. The period had allowed Northern Ireland's population an opportunity to savour a prolonged spell of civic peace and for Sinn Féin to permit its members and supporters to come to terms with the shape and style of the new era. During the interval between ceasefire and Agreement signing, the broadcast and print media frequently featured Sinn Féin party leaders and spokespersons and their profile consequently rose to unprecedented heights. In the process, the party had grown to understand the power of appearance. In an era of brief but powerful photo opportunities and reputation-making or breaking soundbites, it was no longer advisable or suitable for the party's representatives to wear shabby clothes or speak off the cuff. Before long, the party management was well known for the sharpness of its dress and the monotonous uniformity of its press releases and interviews.

The latter point was of particular significance. No Sinn Féin official ever gave a personal on-the-record opinion on any issue. Even for grassroots-level issues, party head office was consulted and an all-enveloping standardization pervaded the movement. This attitude was, to a certain extent, understandable. The party could ill afford to have a mischievous media canvassing differing opinions and writing them up as if there was 'another split in the ranks'. The result had, nevertheless, a stultifying effect on the movement as party members were unable to air their doubts in public or offer alternative options to what was emanating from head office without running the risk of being accused of damaging the movement and even the entire cause. Party discipline was impressive but came at a cost to the organisation's overall health. With none able to challenge the party leadership line, blunders remained uncorrected.

While debate was contained, the party was nevertheless energetically expanding its influence in sectors that had been previously off limits. Without having to defend an armed campaign or suffer the resulting ostracism, the party began to find that many previously hostile bodies were now prepared to engage with the party. The SDLP recognised the threat to its position but realised that to refuse Sinn Féin's elected representatives a share of local government committees would not only alienate potential voters but could also be interpreted as harmful to the cessation of hostilities that they had for so long demanded. Even certain Unionists at local-government level began to accept that Sinn Féin was 'here to stay' and that they had to reach some type of accommodation with the party's elected representative, if only informally and out of sight of the cameras.

A significant change also occurred at civil-service level where officials who had previously been unhelpful and even hostile became amenable to elected Sinn Féin representatives. Whether they were receiving specific orders from the Northern Ireland Office or just picking up the vibes from on high is unclear; but it gave the Republican party an amount of influence to which it previously could only aspire. The result was a growing realisation within the party that electoral, parliamentary politics was a game Sinn Féin could play well. More insidious, many representatives developed a taste for the relaxed and safe pleasures of electoral office and this soon replaced the old will to battle the establishment.

By the time the Good Friday Agreement was signed, many in the Provisional IRA were content to accept the unverifiable assurances from its leadership that it had negotiated a deal that could lead to an end to Partition by the centenary celebrations of the 1916 Easter rising. The Republican leadership was helped greatly by the hysterical reaction of the DUP who, for its own tactical reasons, was insisting that the Agreement was a betrayal of the Union. In contrast, it was Ulster Unionist Party leader David Trimble who described the situation most accurately. He reminded everybody that accepting the constitutional status quo could only be changed by a majority vote in the Six Counties, meant the Good Friday Agreement in reality had secured the future of Northern Ireland within the United Kingdom.

Public ambiguity surrounded the actual meaning of the deal as claim and counter-claim was made about its implications. Typically, minor details were seized upon by vested interests to deflect examination from the real essence of the deal. A clause, for example, that would provide for early prisoner releases was used to raise temperatures and sidetrack Unionist focus. This obfuscation was facilitated by conducting all negotiations behind closed doors and therefore ensuring that the Agreement was clouded in mystery until finally being revealed as a lengthy document parsed in difficult to read and, for many, almost incomprehensible legalese. A situation was created where the peace process and the political process were presented as being inextricably intertwined, making it impossible to critique the latter without being accused of trying to undermine the former.

All those bound into the Agreement by having supported its finalisation were obliged to carry out its implementation. They could and did insist that their own particular party's interpretation was the accurate one and that it was their political opponents who were breaking the spirit or letter of the deal. None could, however, renege on the basis of the deal. The Good Friday Agreement was in essence a simple piece of work dependent on a two-way pact that allowed each side to gain a little and both to concede on previously dearly held principles.

Sinn Féin and the IRA had to end armed insurrection and forever forgo any capacity to use force against the state. This was to be accompanied by an acceptance of the permanence of Partition and the Union for as long as a majority in the Six Counties wished them to remain in place. This meant in practice acceptance of what Dublin and the SDLP had long described as 'unity by consent'. Moreover, under the terms of the Good Friday Agreement, Sinn Féin was obliged to use its influence to support the institutions of the state through acceptance of Westminster legislation, the judicial process and policing. That Sinn Féin had accepted an arrangement based on an internal Northern Irish settlement was a stunning compromise. That this was accompanied by another raft of concessions such as arms decommissioning and support for policing was an astonishing ideological somersault by Irish Republicans. In a different context, this u-turn would be comparable only to Hamas accepting the state of Israel and renouncing the 'right of return'.

In return for Republican acceptance of Northern Ireland's legitimacy, Unionism was forced to admit the political representatives of the one-time insurrectionary, albeit retired, Irish Republican Army into the administration of the northern state. Unionism was expected to sit and share office with people who were not just suspected of having played a major part in the insurgency, but in many cases had actually been convicted in the courts of doing so and who were making no secret of their IRA past. Deputy First Minister Martin McGuinness, Minister for Regional Development Conor Murphy, Junior Minister Gerry Kelly, have all been imprisoned for IRA-related activities, while Martina Anderson and Alex Maskey represent the party as members of the Policing Board. A total of 11 of Sinn Féin's 27 MLAs have served time for IRA-related activities.

This was an enormous retreat for a constituency that had insisted on its right to rule without hindrance from the minority Catholic population and to do so with impunity. It was to take ten years before the greater majority of the Unionist population was able to come to terms with the deal. Middle-class Ulster Unionists under the leadership of David Trimble moved first when, with the SDLP's Seamus Mallon as his deputy, an administration was formed that included former IRA leader Martin McGuinness as minister of education in the Assembly's executive.

While the two middle-class parties were in charge, there remained a possibility that the arrangement might be disrupted by those not at the heart of the arrangement. When the two parties representing a majority of the working-class electorate, if not working-class politics, eventually won the larger number of seats in the Assembly, they both felt secure enough within their own constituencies to share the executive. At that stage, with the one-time irreconcilables in office together, the Good Friday Agreement was solidly embedded. With Sinn Féin and the DUP endorsing and actually operating the tenets of the Good Friday Agreement, two major and historic factors came into play in Northern Ireland. It meant, in practice, the end of the national question as a significant issue for most of the island's population and at the same time, the end of the Orange state as it had existed for decades.

When the Agreement was endorsed by an overwhelming majority of the Irish electorate on both sides of the border at two referendums run simultaneously, the people of Ireland had made it clear that they no longer regarded Partition or the Union with Britain as matters of immense national importance. They had stated clearly that they were content to accept the principle of unity by consent and to underline this fact, they endorsed the Dublin government's decision to abolish Articles 2 and 3 from the 1937 constitution that defined the national territory of Ireland as incorporating all 32 counties and their territorial waters.

Sinn Féin campaigned energetically on both sides of the border during the referenda for a yes vote while claiming that support for the Agreement would hasten the day of Irish unity. This was bending the truth, since the Agreement was explicit in stating that the constitutional position of Northern Ireland within the United Kingdom would remain secure for so long as a majority wished it to be the case. It would be a mistake, however, to take this to indicate that Sinn Féin supporters were unaware of the real import of the deal. In the ten years that have elapsed since the Agreement was concluded, the exact working of the arrangement has become abundantly clear and there is no significant erosion of the party's electoral performance as a result.

Irish unity remains an aspiration for many – but only an aspiration, a pleasant thought, but not something in which most people are prepared to invest time or energy. Certainly it is not something many see as worth spilling the amount of blood, sweat and tears that would be involved in doing so without Unionist consent. There remains a small coterie of die-hard Republicans still committed to the Republican Nationalist vision of forcibly uniting Ireland, but with miniscule support they are an anachronistic irrelevance. Real material conditions are what make a cause vibrant and lend it sufficient support to have an impact on the body politic. Support for the Provisional IRA insurrection aimed at breaking the link with Britain and creating a 32-County socialist republic was not grounded in a romantic Nationalist dream. It grew from an initial desire to smash the Stormont-governed Orange state and as such had a real strategic logic, since ending Partition by necessity meant ending the northern regime.

The Good Friday Agreement had clearly not removed Partition, but its full implementation would frustrate Protestant supremacists and prevent a return to Orange domination. A raft of legislation had been passed over the years that made it more difficult to discriminate in employment. Structures were put in place such as the Northern Ireland Housing Executive and fair employment legislation that made it harder to skew the fair allocation of housing and work. And when Unionism, ranging from the liberal professional classes to the Paisleyite enragés, had joined a shared administration with the representatives of the IRA, they were acknowledging that the ancien régime was dead and that any attempt to resuscitate it would flounder under the scrutiny of the Assembly's Nationalist members. Moreover, no measurable element within Unionism appears anxious or willing to reject devolution, implying that they know and accept the ramifications of the Agreement and are willing, albeit with the usual raucous and bad-tempered behaviour in the Assembly, to keep it in place.

The Good Friday Agreement has resolved the constitutional issue in Northern Ireland in favour of Unionism and the British government while at the same time abolishing the discriminatory relationships that the Six-County state was meant to deliver as a means of its survival as a distinct entity. Something that has not changed, though, is the sectarian division of the Northern Irish working class, the real reason for discrimination in the first place. The Orange state may have been brought to an end, but in its place is a sectarian entity. This outcome has benefited a significant section of a Catholic middle class, born out of the ashes of the Orange state. The success of this, new, Catholic middle class has been created by neo-liberalism, which has provided material support to the new sectarian state, a state which gives employment to approximately 30 per cent of the economically active population in the Six Counties.

Moreover, the deep sectarian divisions in Northern Irish society were actually reinforced by one of the key elements of the settlement. In order to prevent a return to one-party rule, the British government had included a provision that position and influence in the executive would be allocated according to the d'Hondt system of governing.[1] In February 2010, in the *Irish Times*, former Taoiseach John Bruton described this system:

Each decision must, at minimum, have 40 per cent support of representatives who have registered themselves formally as 'Unionist' and also 60 per cent of those registered as 'nationalist' or vice versa. Representatives of parties who decline to register as either 'Unionist' or 'nationalist' may vote, but their votes do not count when it comes to deciding if cross-community consent has been obtained. Thus the votes of members of the Assembly who do not register in one of the two ancient camps are worth less than the votes of those who do.[2]

There is in practice, therefore, a major obstacle placed in the way of any party or group that wishes to campaign, for example, on the basis of a non-sectarian, class-based, socialist programme. A system that was devised in order to overcome the old and divisive Orange state has done so at the cost of embedding communal sectarianism, one of the most pernicious by-products of the ancien régime. If ever the Marxist dialectic of one contradiction giving way to a fresh contradiction was evident in any situation, it is surely visible in the Good Friday Agreement.

Having adopted a policy that relegated its campaign for a united Ireland to the status of window-dressing, Sinn Féin was forced to search for a new motor to keep its engine turning over. The party had committed to the concept, policy and practice of pan-Nationalism before and after the Agreement in order to gain the leverage necessary to stay within the process. As a consequence, the party found itself moving further to the right in order to retain its new-found associates among conservative Nationalism at home and right-wing politicians abroad, in particular in the US. Sinn Féin could not hope to keep Fianna Fáil and the Irish establishment in its corner if it pursued a consistently left-wing policy. Nor could it be sure of capturing the all-important middle ground in the North from the SDLP if it appeared too radical. Sinn Féin had long practised a populist policy in regard to many issues. Its stand on abortion typified this, when it regularly assured the handful of feminists in its ranks that it supported a woman's right to choose but ensured that no such policy would ever appear on its election manifestos.

The old dilemma for reformed insurgents had resurfaced for Sinn Féin. A group enters parliament intent on making change and finds it difficult to do so without making compromises within the confines of institutions designed to produce glacial progress. When coupled with Sinn Féin's need to show results as early as possible, this ensured a slide into right-of-centre social democracy of the Blairite mould.

Sinn Féin's two ministers in the first Northern Ireland Executive, Martin McGuinness and Barbara de Brun, both introduced measures to bring private finance initiatives into health and education. They offered pusillanimous apologies for doing so but nevertheless went ahead with the measures.[3] Gerry Adams, in a speech to the Dublin Chamber of Commerce in April 2004, reassured the city's business class that Sinn Féin was not as socialist as its opponents claimed. In response to a question from the floor, he said that while his party was officially opposed to public-private partnerships, 'Martin McGuinness, as minister of education, faced with the reality that he would either have no schools or an involvement in a qualified way with private finance, went for it. So I suppose that you could argue that that is the emergence of pragmatic politics.'[4]

In short, the party found itself on a course which involved further and deeper immersion in a centre-right consensus, that is, a consensus that has grown around high-flying British and Irish civil servants and the governing bureaucracy over many generations, while managing capitalism on behalf of the ruling class.

18
General Election Upset in the South

All was not well in the party locally. A young 'rascal' who had only recently joined the organisation (and that was only after the ceasefire was well embedded) had insulted Barney. After three decades in the movement and having spent a period in prison during the 1980s, Barney believed that he should be consulted on all arrangements for the annual Easter commemoration. He had, after all, organised the event in this locality for years and had been doing it when this young upstart was still only a child. More to the point, he had done it when this young 'blow-in' had been working in the 'States' well before the movement took the decision to call a ceasefire.

Now that the movement was in election mode, it seemingly needed 'new blood' and the polished, college-educated, thirty-something with the posh sentences was being favoured by the party hierarchy in head office. The head office boys in Belfast decided that 'The Graduate', as Barney called him, would front up the annual Easter commemoration in order to lift his profile and enhance his prospects at the upcoming local government elections.

Barney ground his teeth as 'The Graduate' worked the crowd in the graveyard after the commemoration. He had obviously learned the names of important, well-connected local Republicans and without a trace of embarrassment spoke to them about 'the Army' and 'the Campaign' and 'Gear' (IRA slang for weapons) as if he was an IRA veteran. Amazingly, in Barney's opinion, these long-serving IRA men seemed to bask in 'The Graduate's' flattery and revel in his banter.

Not for Barney though. After two decades acting as master of ceremonies at the local Easter commemoration, he had been demoted to the role of carrying a wreath in the parade. It was a petty issue and Barney knew it. What made it so intolerable, though, was the fact that 'The Graduate's' parents had been Fine Gael supporters until recently and the flashy young candidate appeared as comfortable with establishment figures in the local golf club as he now seemed to be in this Republican gathering.

Barney was still smarting a few days later when he spotted 'The Graduate' in a local coffee shop having a cappuccino with two members of the town's chamber of commerce. The sight of a member of the party sitting with prosperous businessmen further upset Barney but also gave him an idea. He contacted a friend who worked for a local radio station and briefed him about the trio in the coffee shop.

Two days later, 'The Graduate' was invited to the radio station for a live pre-election interview. Hungry for coverage he hurried off to the studio with a sheaf of statistics on local roads that needed mending, amenities that required building and school roofs that were at risk of leaking. He was doing nicely and growing in confidence when the interviewer began to ask him about Sinn Féin's macroeconomic policies. A more experienced politician, realising that this was not an area with which he was familiar, would have deflected the question, referred the interviewer to some obscure party pamphlet and moved on to another topic. 'The Graduate', however, felt secure talking with what he regarded as a country DJ and began to mention the need to attract foreign investment, to make the economy competitive and to encourage entrepreneurship.

'That doesn't sound like a socialist agenda to me', said the interviewer, 'and Sinn Féin says it is a socialist party.' 'The Graduate' felt the first twinge of panic. A little confused, he replied that yes indeed, the party was in favour of socialism but it was the type of socialism that supported business.

Barney was listening intently and with a degree of malicious satisfaction. '"The Graduate" my arse', he whispered, '"The Gobshite", more like it.'

Sinn Féin was on a roll. The 2007 Northern Ireland Assembly elections had been a resounding success for the party with a return of 28 seats and 26.2 per cent of the vote against 16 seats and a 15.2 per cent vote share for its SDLP nemesis. Better than that, the party had managed to carry off the difficult feat of keeping its support base pacified, while decommissioning the bulk of its arsenal and publicly committing its organisation to full and unambiguous support for policing in Northern Ireland. Best of all, as far as the party was concerned, was the restoration of an administration-sharing executive in Stormont with Sinn Féin at its core and Martin McGuinness acting as Deputy First Minister along with First Minister, the DUP leader Ian Paisley.

The executive has little real power. It cannot raise taxes, take control of security, or influence foreign policy. Westminster decides the size of its annual budget almost as parents supply dinner money to their school kids. Central government in London also determines the nature of the society over which the local assembly is allowed to administer. Westminster tolerates no challenge to the free market by Stormont – and in fairness to the Stormontites, none is considered. In reality, the Northern Ireland Assembly has about the same relationship with the House of Commons in London as the management of Tesco in Belfast has with its head office in the UK.

What the assembly does provide, though, are opportunities for politicians, who might otherwise find themselves overlooked, to strike a pose on a local stage. The Stormont building itself is a truly breathtaking example of the grand delusions of Unionism at the zenith of its arrogance and affords a suitably theatrical backdrop for the parochial dramas that it often stages. With 108 Members

of the Legislative Assembly (usually referred to as MLAs)[1] for a
population of 1.7 million people, the building is occupied by, per
capita, the greatest number of elected representatives of any area
in the British Isles or western Europe. Unkind critics might describe
this as 'jobs for the boys and girls'. Astute observers would say
exactly the same. Something not to be overlooked either is the
nomenclature where heads of departments are known as ministers,
a not insignificant concession for members of a body with greatly
curtailed powers. And the system does not stop at that: there are
speakers of the house, heads of committees and a seemingly endless
line of advisers and personal assistants.

Surrounded by the grandeur of Stormont and with the congratu-
lations of British government officials ringing in its ears for having
'brought peace' – if not a 32-county republic – to Ireland, it was
not surprising that Sinn Féin would feel that there was no citadel it
could not storm. So when the Republic's Taoiseach, Bertie Ahern,
called a general election in 2007, Sinn Féin welcomed the challenge
as an opportunity to make further advances.

President of Sinn Féin Gerry Adams departed from his usual
cautious reticence and made several optimistic predictions. His
party would be the story of the election, he told reporters, and on
another occasion asserted that after the final count, political party
leaders would be contacting him to discuss terms for Sinn Féin
support in the new Dáil. In private, the party was no less confident.
They had grown used to electoral success in the North and were
sure of a similar result in the Republic. Already holding five seats
in the southern parliament, the party's inner circle was convinced
that they would gain at least a further three seats and possibly six
if all went well. So certain was the leadership of its tactical sense
that it had backed its own judgement in a winnable seat in Dublin
Central to deselect a long-standing, popular but rough-hewn local
and replace him with a photogenic outsider. The result when it was
delivered was a major setback for the party. Worse still from the
party's point of view has been its failure to accurately diagnose the
reason for its failure.

Sinn Féin viewed the southern election as part of a grander
strategy where the party would couple its power base in the North
with a matching set-up in the South. The reasoning was that in the
event of Sinn Féin gaining a place in government in the Republic,
through coalition at first if necessary, the party could claim to have
brought about a loose form of unified administration across both
jurisdictions on the island. With the kudos derived from having

accomplished this 'historic task', Sinn Féin believed that it could look forward thereafter to embedding itself permanently in power. When its representation in the Dáil increased from one in 1997 to five in 2002, this course appeared to Sinn Féin to be a realistic option and there was talk within the organisation of a post-Good Friday Agreement electoral peace dividend. With a political philosophy that had grown more populist and ever less socialist over the years, the leadership and party opinion formers had apparently also failed to properly analyse the party's appeal.

Sinn Féin won elections, some of its mentors thought, because people liked its style of presentation and admired it for bringing peace to the North. Moreover, the profile of the party leader was in itself a vote winner, the rank and file was constantly told. Party advisers seemed to be imbued with North American theories of election winning and made the mistake of believing that appearance counts for everything and substance is only a useful accessory. The southern electorate did not agree. Sinn Féin had in reality two groups supporting it in the Republic. One was the old Republican base along the Border (and in one or two other rural parts such as Kerry). In these areas, the IRA campaign and its causes were well appreciated and understood if only for the reason that the Border communities were neighbours and often related through marriage and trade. Drawn largely from a set geographic location, this cohort was not likely to expand to any measurable extent.

The other base of Sinn Féin support was amongst the urbanised working class and especially where there were high levels of unemployment. Sinn Féin could realistically expect to make significant progress in these constituencies. For historic reasons, Ireland has never had a powerful social democratic party, as has been the norm in most other western European countries. The Irish Labour Party had aligned itself with the upper bourgeoisie during Ireland's Civil War in the 1920s and had participated in a rabidly anti-Republican coalition during the early 1970s. As a consequence of a series of such poorly judged decisions, the social democratic constituency had been shared for many years with the populist Fianna Fáil party.

In the 1960s, however, as Fianna Fáil grew more closely identified with the expanding class of entrepreneurs, Ireland's growing urban wage-earning population began to search tentatively for an alternative on the left. For a time it appeared that the Labour Party might fill the role, but these hopes were dashed by the abysmally authoritarian performance of that party when it joined the ultra right-wing coalition led by Liam Cosgrove in the early 1970s. As a result of the Labour Party's turn to the right in the 1970s, many working-class voters in the larger urban centres transferred their allegiance to the more radical Workers Party in the 1980s. In a strange case of *déjà vu*, the Workers Party succumbed to almost the exact same fate as the Labour Party in the 1990s, as it too abandoned its early radical political programme after losing any faith it had in socialism following the USSR's collapse and the fall of the Berlin Wall. With the demise of the Workers Party, the path was again open for a party of the left to articulate and promote the cause of the less well-off.

For a time, it seemed as if Sinn Féin had the potential to fill that niche, if not 'on the streets' and in mass movements, then maybe at least in conventional bourgeois democratic terms. With the ceasefire of 1993, working people were no longer afraid that the party would bring the 'Northern Troubles' to the South. The organisation did, however, retain a sufficiently anti-establishment mantle coupled with its left-wing rhetoric to convince many working-class people that Sinn Féin was indeed a left-wing party worthy of their vote. Sinn Féin, moreover, had inherited a network of grass-roots activists from the period of the IRA's armed campaign.

Some were former IRA personnel who had transferred their energies to party work, while others were long-time Sinn Féin party workers who had worked assiduously to build community support for the Provisional IRA through the years of insurrection. With their imbibed discipline and keen motivation, they had the makings of a formidable political machine. When the party captured a seat for the Dublin constituency in the European Parliament in 2001 and two Dáil seats in the capital in 2002, it looked very much like the beginning of a new chapter in the story of the rise of Sinn Féin in the Republic.

In spite of this progress, the party leadership, which was still Belfast-based, decided to retain its vice-like grip on the organisation. Throughout the Republic, Sinn Féin was managed and supervised by cadres of people who were uncritically loyal to the leadership. There was too, a very noticeable number of northerners inserted into organisational roles in the South in what many local party activists felt was simply a mechanism for ensuring control from Belfast. The leadership also rigorously controlled the selection of candidates to stand for the party at election time. While this is not unique to Sinn Féin, it added to the simmering discontent that was being felt in some quarters about the party's retreat from what were considered to be core principles.

In many ways, it was the selection issue that brought to a head the party's problems in Dublin. Nicky Keogh had been the local candidate in one of the city's working-class constituencies for a number of years. A former IRA prisoner and a diligent, hard-working community activist, he had painstakingly built up a solid base of support among the less well-off working and unemployed people in the area and had come within a handful of votes of taking a seat at the 2002 general election. The party's head office decided, however, that the more photogenic and middle-class Mary Lou McDonald would make a better candidate and imposed her on the local party organisation. While there was no immediate spate of resignations, there was a groundswell of unease with what many saw as a desire for embourgeoisement and an obsession with image. In time this, coupled with the series of u-turns made by Sinn Féin, led to a number of influential activists departing the organisation and in time establishing a new socialist Republican party, éirígí (Irish Gaelic for 'Rise up').

Nor did the impact of this unease stop at that. Many of those who were unwilling to leave Sinn Féin were nevertheless sufficiently disenchanted with its practices that they became passive members, contributing little to the party's activities. No political party can afford to lose substantial numbers of workers, but for one at a critical stage of its development, such a loss can be debilitating. Sinn Féin was at such a stage. With five Dáil seats and an ostensibly perfect political climate around it, the party had either to gain extra seats and grow into a serious contender for power, or falter and stumble into the also-ran category that spells slow extinction for all who occupy the slot.

With a diminished number of activists in key Dublin constituencies, the party had to work harder to retain its momentum going into the 2007 general election. It was, nevertheless, confident of its own ability and electoral skills; with the re-establishment of the Northern Ireland Assembly, it was thought that the resulting good coverage would lift the party above any local difficulties. The party was in fact over-confident and made further mistakes.

An electorate is composed of too many variables for any one event to determine the outcome of an election. There are, however, Richard Nixon-type moments when a significant mistake is made. One such incident occurred during the run-up to voting, when the Sinn Féin president's advisers allowed him to participate in a television debate with experienced southern Irish politicians. There were several southern-based Sinn Féin candidates, familiar with issues in the Republic and who would have performed competently, yet the party was trying to gain from the Adams presence. The gambit backfired as his unfamiliarity with the southern Irish administrative system was ruthlessly exposed on national television. The mishap inflicted significant damage on both Adams and Sinn Féin at a crucial time in the campaign.

Worse was the *faux pas* made by the candidate for Dublin central, Mary Lou McDonald, when without the endorsement of an *ard fheis* or special delegate conference, she said that in the event of being invited to join a coalition, the party would be willing to abandon its long-standing position on raising the Republic's very low rate of corporation tax. Her arbitrary statement was neither refuted by others in the party leadership nor was there a murmur of public dissent from within the organisation. Working-class people were left to conclude that it was party policy and if policy could be changed so arbitrarily, how trustworthy was the party?

Many working people saw it as evidence of yet one more untrustworthy party that would break its promises as and when it thought it expedient to do so. In many ways, this was the most damaging blunder of all. The party had lost its way and was struggling to find a niche. If Sinn Féin was not a party of the left, then what was it? By its acceptance of the Good Friday Agreement, it was telling the world that the national question had been satisfactorily addressed. National unity was still to be achieved but the Agreement would take care of that, Sinn Féin told anyone who cared to listen. In the absence of a national question, working-class voters, looking for a left alternative, saw little point in choosing a party so anxious to participate in a coalition with Fianna Fáil.

Sinn Féin had failed to read the signs and was clearly surprised at the rejection inflicted on it by the electorate. Sean Crowe lost his Dáil seat in Dublin, while Aengus O'Snodaigh barely managed to retain his position, gaining election without reaching the quota. Worst of all however, was the dismal performance of Mary Lou McDonald in Dublin North Central, where to the palpable shock and dismay of the party leadership, she finished well down the field. Her humiliation was complete when the successful independent candidate Tony Gregory told RTÉ that if Sinn Féin had not parachuted an outsider into the constituency and stayed with the local man Keogh, the seat would have gone to the party.

Nor had Sinn Féin much ground for optimism elsewhere in the country. It did manage to hold on to its three seats in rural Ireland, but this was little comfort when the wreckage was surveyed. Hopes for breakthroughs in Donegal, Sligo-Leitrim, Meath, Wexford and Cork were dashed. Sinn Féin appeared to be mesmerised by the setback, as its parliamentary leader Caoimhin O'Caoláin inexplicably offered to enter into a coalition government with the Fine Gael party. The leader of the one-time party of the Blueshirts, Enda Kenny, was not the least coy when he summarily dismissed the hapless O'Caoláin's overture.

In the aftermath of bitter disappointment in 2007, there was a real possibility that Sinn Féin would lose credibility with the Republic's electorate and slide into irreversible decline south of the Border. With only four deputies in the Dublin parliament, the party had difficulty making its voice heard in the chamber. When in 2008, they decided to vote for a bankers' bailout, at the beginning of the greatest economic crisis to affect Ireland in over half a century, it seemed that Sinn Féin was doomed to flounder aimlessly.

The depth of the crisis and an inspired (and ultimately successful) decision to challenge the government's refusal to hold a by-election in a Donegal constituency helped revive the party's fortunes at the 2011 general election, when Sinn Féin emerged with 14 seats. During its campaign, that never mentioned the questions of Irish unity or the union with Great Britain, Sinn Féin successfully tapped into widespread anger with the Irish banking sector and the Fianna Fáil government's determination to make taxpayers repay debts that had been incurred by private domestic banks with foreign banks. With the ultra-cautious and conservative Irish Labour Party determined to maintain its options of entering into a coalition with the right-wing Fine Gael, and therefore refusing to contemplate any debt default, Sinn Féin was able to run a forceful 'burn the bondholders' campaign.

Whether the policy was merely a development of the old Dean Swift's suggestion to 'burn everything British except their coal', or something more sophisticated is difficult to determine, since the party remains without power to implement its call. What was significant, however, was the very obvious lurch leftwards by Sinn Féin during the 2011 general election campaign. It is still unclear whether this is a decisive move by Sinn Féin towards adopting a coherent socialist programme, or whether it was a clever piece of electioneering. Whichever explanation proves accurate, it lends a certain weight to the long-standing claim made by other left

Republicans that sustainable progress is best made by pursuing working-class issues and abandoning centrism.

Nevertheless, people close to the party are now reporting that in the aftermath of the Irish general election, a debate is taking place within Sinn Féin around the question of whether to concentrate on a left-wing strategy, or whether to move on to the space formerly occupied by Fianna Fáil. That the question is being asked is, in itself, indicative of an absence of a firm socialist ideology in the movement and that ultimately, the party may well find the lure of sharing office (perhaps with a revamped Fianna Fáil) too tempting to resist, regardless of the compromise required to do so, as it has done north of the Border.

The latest general election campaign in the Republic has again demonstrated that there was little interest south of the Border in northern politics. Sinn Féin did not try to piggyback on its northern image and, if anything, found it convenient to ignore its record of implementing British government-ordained budget cutbacks in the Stormont Executive. To an extent it can also be said that the Provo journey had reached its end. The political movement that had arisen out of the maelstrom of northern politics was going to achieve no higher plateau than representation in partitioned parliaments. More profoundly perhaps, the stalling of northern Republicanism has meant too, the end for insurrectionary Irish Republicanism in its national democratic phase. A new leitmotiv for social change will have to be found or henceforth, opportunistic social democracy will be the only method for changing Irish society.

19
The End of a Journey

Throughout the preceding chapters, this book has argued strongly that the Provisional IRA campaign grew out of the daily experiences of Northern Ireland's Catholic working-class and less well-off rural population. The Provisionals' demand for British withdrawal and an end to Partition addressed a concrete need to end misrule and denial of rights as much as answering an old aspiration for Irish independence.

The mass civil rights movement was organised around a demand for democratic rights, which did not directly raise the constitutional issue. It was only when this movement was curtailed by lethal force that the IRA insurrection began and even then it was some time before frustration at Westminster's partisanship caused Republicans to call for British withdrawal. When the Provisional IRA insisted in the post-Bloody Sunday period that only an end to British rule would satisfy its members, it was at least as much a condemnation of London mismanagement as an expression of the desire for self-determination.

The nature of the capitalist state in Northern Ireland was that in its Orange period, it was forged upon an indissoluble set of social, economic and political relationships between a dominant Protestant civil society and the latter's openly celebrated repressive apparatuses. Together, this peculiar state-society configuration ranged from an exclusive Protestant housing policy, a gerrymandered political society, and economic discrimination against a Catholic minority. While the early movement for civil rights could engender a degree of cross-sectarian support, the nature of the Orange state and Northern Irish society effectively excluded the scope for the further development of a secularised opposition with the potential to affirm a progressive liberal, let alone a democratic socialist, agenda for change. While one should never exclude the possibility that a British withdrawal might have been brought closer by the insurgency, given what has transpired, it is reasonable to argue that until the repressive apparatuses of Stormont were reined in (and in many instances broken), further progress proved untenable.

The insurgency, beginning in 1968 with mass, initially cross-sectarian (if not class-based) civil protest and then mass civil disobedience, quickly developed into a broad-based, armed insurrection by one section of the population but was soon transformed into a war of limited social insurgency against the Orange and British states. The armed insurgency was successful in so far as it made transparent the nature and purpose of the Orange state's repressive and oppressive political life. But it did more than simply show to the world the nature of Orange repression, since at the very least it successfully, and this is important to remember, broke the foundations of Orange state sectarianism – anti-Catholic discrimination in housing, welfare, the economy and politics. This was a transformative war.

If the swearing-in of the Northern Ireland Assembly on 8 May 2007 'parked' the national question (for the time being at least), the same arrangement also sent another vehicle of history to the breaker's yard. The unwritten 'Protestant Social Contract' was finally rendered defunct. For over two centuries after the Act of Union between Britain and Ireland,[1] a majority of Ulster's Protestant working-class and rural poor refrained from asserting their social and political autonomy. They gave allegiance to the ruling business and aristocratic elite in return for preferential treatment *vis-à-vis* their Catholic neighbours, a concession granted in order to silence the Presbyterian-inspired demand for democracy that caused insurrection at the close of the eighteenth century.

For years, this gave Unionism the appearance of being an unassailable, cross-class monolith. In practice, this was more illusion that reality. Tensions always existed within the wider Protestant community and nobody personified this better than Ian Paisley and his Democratic Unionist Party (DUP). Their dislike for Republicans was almost matched by their distaste for big-house, big-business Unionism. This aversion was nurtured and exacerbated over the years by having to tolerate the leadership of a smug ruling élite, in order to maintain Unionism's 'social contract'. The DUP deal with Sinn Féin is more easily understood, therefore, if viewed as the acquisition of pole position by replacing an overbearing senior partner with a detested junior partner.

Ian Paisley and the DUP's elevation have come at a price however. Had he managed to capture Stormont from Terrence O'Neill 40 years earlier, it would have meant a change of leadership within an unchanged regime. That he was obliged to take office in tandem with an aggressively Nationalist party ensures not only the end of

Unionism's social contract, but also means tacit acceptance that there will be no return to a Protestant parliament for a Protestant people. This fundamental change to the Six Counties – final acceptance that the Orange state is no more – has relegated the urgency of the national question in the minds of many who formerly fought so energetically for Irish unity. However, as the Orange state was being buried, it was, by degrees, giving way to the sectarian state, codified in the 1998 Belfast Agreement and consummated on 8 May 2007 in the marriage of convenience between Sinn Féin and the DUP.

When long-time antagonists Ian Paisley and Martin McGuinness agreed to share office as First and Deputy First Minister respectively in a Stormont regime, one of the longer-running political conflicts in western Europe – the Irish national question – was apparently laid to rest. Difficult though it was for some to accept, it was clear that no significant section of Irish society was prepared at that time to contest in any determined fashion the constitutional arrangements on the island. Irish people had voted in huge numbers for the Good Friday Agreement in 1998 and have stayed loyal to its promoters at each election since. There remains, of course, a widely shared but not intensely sought-after aspiration that the Six Counties might one day come under Dublin's jurisdiction. For the vast majority, though, it is a distant aspiration that fails to motivate anything other than occasional nostalgia. At the moment, removal of Partition engenders no great passion among the population at large.

Small pockets of 'physical-force' Republicans remain irreconcilable, and their dejection is understandable. Many have participated in a protracted, gruelling and costly struggle with the British state in order to break the Union. Their leaders and supporters told them for years that the objective was worth their endurance. They were and remain angry and bewildered as former comrades give *de facto* recognition to London's authority and have enthusiastically entered into an arrangement with the DUP to administer the Northern Irish state within the United Kingdom.

Yet no matter how peeved the unreconstructed 'physical-force' Republican constituency may be, its influence is minimal. Just how inconsequential they are as a body was starkly illustrated during the 2007 Assembly elections in Northern Ireland when its candidates received approximately 1 per cent of the total vote. Nor, in spite of occasional attempts to re-ignite insurrection, has anything happened to suggest that this derisive vote was an aberration or that it might improve to any meaningful extent in the future.

Single-issue Republicanism focusing exclusively on a unitary Irish state has shrivelled because it had finally accomplished as much as it was able to achieve. The reality is that only a handful of people within Republican ranks promoted a semi-spiritual and Nationalistic vision of the 'Irish Republic'. Insurrectionary Irish Republicanism has always drawn its real dynamic from the socioeconomic conditions in which the population live and the struggle to improve their circumstances and bring about a more agreeable form of governance for supporters and advocates. History and the conditions which shaped it, meant that armed, insurrectionary Republicanism offered a vehicle capable of removing an unpopular ruling order – usually London-based or sustained – and thereafter replacing it with a more tolerable or responsive authority.

This was the case in the last quarter of the twentieth century when many Northern Irish Republicans took up arms against the British state. Just as earlier generations had found it appropriate to use political violence to shift the British government positions on issues such as Catholic emancipation, poor relief, land reform and of course, self-determination, Northern Irish Republicans resorted to arms after the attacks on Catholic areas in 1969, in order to remove a stubborn impasse. After decades of waiting in vain for London to correct the discriminatory allocation of housing, biased employment practices, contempt for Nationalist cultural mores and exclusion from participation in the administration of the area (and having seen a peaceful civil rights movement swept physically and bloodily from the streets), many Northern Irish Catholics adopted the tactic of insurrection. The logic was simple. At first, it was a gut reaction seeking protection from bloody onslaught. Thereafter, and as London veered towards protecting its own interests rather than clearing up the mess for which it was responsible, armed Republicanism strove to remove Britain and replace its rule with something more equitable and tolerable.

Irish establishment figures and commentators have often contended that a bottomless chasm existed between constitutional Nationalism and 'physical-force' Republicanism. At leadership level or in public discourse, this distinction may have had a certain resonance. Among the people, though, the boundaries have not always been so clear. Large sections of the population have pragmatically shifted their loyalties effortlessly from one to the other and back, as prevailing conditions seemed to require. While some may view this as the electorate's capriciousness, it is just as reasonable to view it as the exercising of pragmatic political choices and hence the phenomenon of what has been described as the dramatic rise in Sinn Féin's electoral fortunes over the past 15 years in Northern Ireland.[2] In the 1998 Northern Ireland Assembly elections, Sinn Féin secured 17.63 per cent of the vote against 21.97 per cent won by its rival for the Catholic vote, the SDLP. By the 2003 Assembly elections, this had changed. Sinn Féin won 23.5 per cent of the vote against the SDLP's 17 per cent, while by 2007 Sinn Féin's dominance was more pronounced when the party captured 28 per cent of the vote against 15.2 per cent for the SDLP. Considering that in 1982 – the year after the hunger strikes – the Republican party could only garner 10.2 per cent of the vote, Sinn Féin's progress has been remarkable.

Yet Sinn Féin is not being rewarded simply for its constituency work rate or its slick publicity machine. Its success is also down to it having convinced the Nationalist electorate that it accomplished a task many of them viewed as paramount – better, fairer, more inclusive governance. How they did it is of less importance to those who felt mistreated for years.

The Orange state was not overturned in one swift movement. It took several decades before it was dismantled. Housing discrimination, which was an area of intense controversy for decades, was addressed by the Housing Executive Act (Northern Ireland) 1971 and public housing today is provided by the Northern Ireland Housing Executive. There is general agreement that this body is neutral and professional and has removed one source of grievance. Discrimination in employment is not a thing of the past but, due to legislation, it is much more difficult to practice in larger businesses and in the public sector. Indeed, a significant corollary of the curtailment of anti-Catholic bias in the public sector has been the striking increase in the number of Catholics in middle and senior management positions. This in turn has led to a dramatic expansion of a new Catholic middle class, people who often hold more conservative attitudes than did their parents. In spite of remaining discrepancies in employment rates between Catholic and Protestant, many in Northern Ireland now believe that the greater difficulty with employment is not so much discrimination as a general absence of jobs. There is also equality and human rights legislation in place that, while often inadequate, at least offers a process for redressing many of the problems endemic under the pre-1973 Stormont regime. (There is one notable exception in terms of equality legislation and this relates to economic inequality.)

When these reforms were sealed with the access to administrative power via the Good Friday Agreement, it signalled a very definite end of an era in Northern Ireland. Insurrectionary Republicanism had advanced the political agenda to a stage that parliamentary practice failed to match. Northern Catholics now have opportunities to participate in local political, social and economic life to an extent that earlier generations could only have dreamt of. Republicans may have failed to break the Union but they certainly smashed the one-party state of James Craig, Basil Brooke and the Ulster Workers Council.

Having broken the old Orange state and replaced it with an administration that not only includes members of the Catholic population but also former senior members of the IRA, the question must now be asked whether Republicanism has reached the limit of its radical potential in Ireland.

20
A New Republic and a Relevant Republicanism

We develop new principles for the world out of the world's own principles. We do not say to the world: Cease your struggles, they are foolish; we will give you the true slogan of struggle. We merely show the world what it is really fighting for, and consciousness is something that it has to acquire, even if it does not want to.

Letters from the Deutsch-Französische Jahrbücher,
Marx to Ruge, Kreuznach, September 1843[1]

As the Provisional IRA military machine has passed into history and the political party that it generated has drifted into centrism, those continuing to advocate radical Irish Republicanism must now review the philosophy's ideological foundations, its practices and its relevance in modern Irish society. This is especially so when other issues exercise the minds of people to a greater extent than the continuation of Partition or the Union. Unemployment, poverty, access to housing, hospitals, education and protection for citizens are of more immediate concern to a majority of the island's population than is the question of Irish unity.

In common with other parts of the world, Ireland, north and south, is experiencing the devastating impact of a global economic recession. There is no immediate sign of the downturn ending or of how far the economy (both in the North and South) must fall before the recession ends. What is emerging though is evidence of just how shallow was the level of prosperity that the country thought it had achieved. The almost endless series of revelations about incompetence and corruption among the ruling elite has surely placed doubt in people's minds about their rulers' ability to continue to manage. Eventually, there must come a time when working people begin to realise not only the uselessness of the current ruling clique but that the political and economic system in place was and is fundamentally flawed and defective.

This situation asks fundamental questions about how society is organised and how wealth and power is distributed. These are questions that require answers different to those currently provided by the parties in power (or in opposition) either side of the Border. There is clearly not just a need to end corruption in political and business life, but to put measures in place to create sustainable, long-term prosperity. This will only come about through a radical transformation of the social and economic system in both the northern and southern states, and their replacement with a republic in which the means of production, distribution and exchange are used to promote the well-being of people rather than make a few wealthy. Radical Republicans have, therefore, to adapt to conditions prevailing in the twenty-first century and work to bring about a new and different republic – one that is not merely independent but a republic that is also socialist.

Radical Irish Republicanism has always contained an important if not vital transformative ingredient that places it in an ideal position to play a pivotal role in creating a new society. Not only has Republicanism in Ireland developed from the existing socioeconomic conditions but it also, always, outlined answers in the context of changing rather than reforming the state. Fenian involvement in the agrarian campaigns of the late nineteenth century impacted on the Home Rule movement and ensured that it could not simply become a 'dainty deal' between the British and Irish elite. At Easter 1916, the Irish Republican Brotherhood and Irish Citizen Army uprising prevented John Redmond's party finding an Irish settlement within the British Empire. In a later era, Provisional IRA tenacity was a crucial element in undermining the Orange state. In this late neo-liberal period, Irish Republicanism, which for long struggled against Protestant sectarian (Orange) domination, needs also to resist the City of London and the philosophy that it epitomises. Radical Republicans will, undoubtedly, continue to struggle for an independent republic, but with the knowledge that its realisation addresses real and relevant issues.

A one-plank Republican platform confined to breaking the Union and ending Partition is not capable of mobilising sufficient support to bring about the type of fundamental change required. Recognising this fact is central to any recalibration of radical Republican ideology. With the ending of the Orange state and the establishment of a shared administration in Stormont, a significant majority in both parts of the island indicated that they are prepared to tolerate the parameters of the Six and Twenty-six County states. Far fewer Northern Irish Catholics now see an urgent need to change current constitutional arrangements than at the beginning of the 1970s and for half a century before. Unsurprisingly, therefore, an even smaller number of people in the Republic feel they need support a campaign to reunite Ireland politically. Radical Republicanism cannot survive in any meaningful sense if it insists on confining its programme to achieving something that is not deemed a pressing necessity by more than a small minority. Nor is it realistic to argue that a significantly large section of society can be persuaded of the need for the political unification of Ireland in the abstract. History demonstrates that people demand fundamental constitutional change in order to address their immediate social and economic needs rather than (simply) to satisfy some elusive aspiration.

None of the above means that Partition and the union with Britain are not matters of profound importance. The sectarian divisions characteristic of the current political dispensation are facilitated by, if not actually an inevitable result of, political isolation within a confined entity arising from an isolated and divided state on the edge of the United Kingdom. Unionists may argue that total integration within the United Kingdom might, in theory, address this issue. But this would only happen at the cost of retaining the social and economic structures that London demands, including in the current period, free-market neo-liberalism. It is logical, therefore, to argue that ending the current constitutional position of Northern Ireland within the United Kingdom would be a positive step towards ending sectarianism and replacing it with more normal class politics – a vital step towards building a socialist republic. In many ways, this brings us to the heart of the immediate task facing radical Republicans – the need to win working-class support for a socialist republic and recognising that this also means engaging positively with that section of the working class that is Protestant.

Partition defined the social, political and economic parameters of Ulster Unionism's sectarian Orange state. The mass mobilisations beginning in the late 1960s were a response to the variant forms of repression inherent in the working of that state and its civil society and the consequent British intervention. Before the insurgency got into full swing, many felt that the only way to end repression was to reform the Northern Ireland state. However, as time went on, it was Stormont itself and then Britain's role (in other words, imperialism) in Ireland that was seen as the problem.

Partition, which was not perceived in the early civil rights era to be the central issue, came to be seen (by Republicans at least) as the central obstacle to social, political and economic progress. By arguing that the current sectarian state arose out of the ashes of the old sectarian Orange state, we are pointing up the limited nature of reform in the North. Nevertheless, the material basis for the old Stormont-governed Orange state is gone and there is, now, no economic benefit in being a Protestant working-class person in post-Good Friday Agreement Northern Ireland. The new sectarian state, while obviously building on the social divisions driven in the first instance largely by religious or supposed religious affiliation, depends on recognition of 'equivalence' rather than on recognition of religious dominance. So for us, the issue becomes whether the struggle against Partition as such is the only basis on which to forge a united working class prepared to struggle for a socialist republic (in the current period). The argument here is that this struggle, though important, is not the only basis on which to create working-class solidarities. The Orange state made such unity impossible, but while its eradication has left a sectarian state in its place, this is not, at the level of state institutions, based on the privileging of one section of the working class over another. Partition remains a problem for sure, but a different problem from the one that existed between 1920 and 1998. 'Partition' became part of the agenda for those in revolt against the state and its society but what this struggle showed, paradoxically, or counter-intuitively, was that reform was possible, but only by insurgent and revolutionary means. But like all states of revolution, one inherits much from the past and while the insurgency ended Orange supremacy at the level of the institutions of state, it could not, reflecting the society out of which the struggle was borne, destroy sectarianism *per se*. In fact, sectarianism has deepened, becoming institutionalised within the state and civil society more broadly to such an extent that it is inscribed in the 1998 institutional settlement.

What is of equal relevance now is that, as a consequence of a monumental upheaval within the global economy, Ireland north and south is in a defining period. Both jurisdictions are experiencing crisis, albeit, not as yet manifested in anything approaching political upheaval. In the northern jurisdiction, there is a constitutional inability to bring redress to the region's problems coupled with a political hysteresis arising from sectarian community politics. South of the Border, the state has the constitutional wherewithal to correct its plight but is blighted by decades of a style of governance that has embedded rapacious crony capitalism as the only form of administration that most people know or can even conceptualise.

The northern state, and hence its people, suffer from the very deal that delivered the peace in two very crucial respects. In the first instance, as mentioned above, in order to find a formula for ending the insurgency and to prevent a return to one-party rule, Britain created a political system that involves the process of sectarian designation in the Northern Ireland Assembly. Parties are obliged to designate as either Nationalist or Unionist (or lose influence) and thus find themselves competing to represent either the Nationalist or Unionist section of society. This in turn has led both main parties, Sinn Féin and the DUP, often to define their programmes in terms of identity rather than economics. Sinn Féin emphasises its commitment to the Irish language and Gaelic football, while the DUP demonstrates its loyalty to Britain's royalty and armed forces. The result of this is that neither party feels it can afford to alienate any substantial section of its communal support base – which would almost certainly happen if a socialist and/or non-sectarian programme were to be adopted.

The second factor is that due to a perennial fear among Unionists about erosion of their position within the UK, the Good Friday Agreement did not grant fiscal powers to the Northern Ireland Assembly. The coalition of parties that make up the Northern Ireland Assembly's Executive do not have tax-generating powers and as such are unable to make the type of intervention that would improve their constituents' living conditions. The impotence embedded within Northern Ireland's political institutions lies at the heart of the area's difficulties. Contrary to talk of power sharing, the administration is almost powerless. It cannot take fiscal and monetary decisions of any import and it has no role in foreign or security issues. Moreover, deprived of an opposition by its establishing mandate, it is systemically incapable of generating vital alternative political and economic strategies.

Although different in many crucial respects, the Republic also suffers from systemic failures. For more than ten years, the ruling Fianna Fáil party told the people that it had discovered a new and better way of managing an economy. Reality was, of course, more prosaic. 'Celtic Tiger' prosperity was built on treacherous foundations. The Republic attracted industries that were too often assembly-line plants that sought to locate in areas without strong organised labour traditions. These companies were only ever going to stay for so long as the costs of production in Ireland were lower than elsewhere. They never promised to build indigenous capacity nor had they any commitment to the Irish economy. Ireland's corporatist partnership of government, business and the Irish Congress of Trade Unions (ICTU) was content, nevertheless, to gather the benefits of a temporary boom and displayed little ability to provide for the future.

With increasing employment and tax revenue, the state created and encouraged a dearth of economic regulation that caused amazement even among Wall Street cynics.[2] When the euro became common currency within several EU states including Ireland, Dublin-based financial institutions began borrowing money at European interest rates and loaned it with heedless abandon to speculators in the construction industry. For almost a decade, Ireland Inc. took on the semblance of a nineteenth-century Californian gold-rush town. During this period, Ireland appeared to some as evidence of an economic miracle. All the same, most elements of an unsustainable speculative bubble were present. The state's budget was balanced largely by having a nearly fully employed youthful population (with the corollary of less spending required on social provision) and tax revenue from the construction and property industries, with no provision made for a turndown in the sector. There was, moreover, no concern at government level for the implications of diverting so much national wealth into domestic, non-profit-making property at home and abroad. While this was happening, the ICTU was in a supine state, as it tolerated an arrangement that saw one section of the workforce prosper financially while others stood still and all the while no long-term irreversible powers and benefits were being transferred to the working class.

The decade of economic prosperity has ended in the Republic and in its wake many citizens are again experiencing real hardship, unemployment,[3] despair,[4] and the return of emigration. There was, and still exists, a nefarious system of cronyism in the Republic of Ireland where a complex arrangement of privilege and favour ensured that people of influence in all walks of life remain tied into current power structures. Trade unionists, prominent businesspeople, retired members of the Dáil and media personalities were appointed to state bodies, semi-state bodies and private companies in a manner that reinforces the received wisdom of the governing consensus while effectively hindering the introduction of the type of radical measures necessary to bring about recovery.

In spite of this social and economic turmoil, the fractured nature of radical Republicanism, reflected in a somewhat unsettled prospectus, makes a progressive path, or set of progressive paths, difficult to gauge. Different and discordant messages are emanating from its very disparate ranks. Unsurprisingly, after the tumult of the past decades, there is little or no consensus among the diverse constituency of Republicans outside 'establishment Republicanism'. Some are unwilling or unable to recognise the profound changes brought about by a post-Good Friday Agreement Ireland and believe they can return to the ways of the early 1970s. Blindly disregarding the almost total absence of popular support for armed insurrection, they continue to make a fetish of the use of arms. Without a relevant analysis and no policy apart from repeating mantras about 'betrayal' and the 'right of the Irish people', they are doomed to obscurity through becoming an historical irrelevance. In the meantime, though, they are creating one of the great paradoxes in contemporary Northern Ireland. With a resumption of armed struggle deeply unpopular among a majority of Republicans, advocates of physical force are in practise, diverting attention from the failures of Sinn Féin to make meaningful progress through its engagement in the assembly and in the context of economic catastrophe for tens of thousands of working people as neo-liberalism runs aground. They clearly feed off increasing discontent but their solutions are of a different order and for a different time and place. Mass protest and social insurrection cannot be reduced to a fetish of armed struggle.

Non-establishment Republicanism is, though, a wider constituency than that encompassed by devotees of armed conflict. Several well-known figures, such as former MLAs Davy Hyland, Geraldine Dougan and Pat McNamee, have grown disenchanted with Sinn Féin policy over the last decade and have left the party. A large number of local government representatives, including prominent Dubliner councillors Christy Burke and Louise Minihan, have also resigned from the party in recent years. In some areas, groups of former party activists have resigned from Sinn Féin, some to form programmed political organisations such as the socialist Republican party éirígí, while the 1916 societies in Tyrone and Fermanagh, for example, have opted for a more flexible approach to policy.

There are, of course, significant numbers of people who view themselves as non-establishment Republicans and who were not part of the Provisional movement. For example, members and ex-members of the Irish Republican Socialist Party, activists from the Official wing of Republicanism and individuals who for different reasons have not affiliated to any organised group are still politically active.

It would be unrealistic to believe that all of those mentioned above could or would come together. There have been bitter hostilities between some of them in the past and ideological differences persist. At the same time, it would be a mistake to think that a radical

Republican alternative can only emerge from those who have been part of long-standing movements and tendencies. There is, after all, a generational aspect to politics. The Provisionals, the Officials and IRSPs have all had their era, none are now centre stage, nor will they return. The drifting away from Sinn Féin of some members should be viewed as a trend but that alone will not constitute the basis of a new political departure. As always, the future is with the young and they shall fashion any response to current circumstances but will, as always, do so under circumstances inherited from previous generations.

The Provisional IRA and its mass support played a huge part in smashing the Orange state and fittingly perhaps, these two great adversaries passed into history together. Ending the Orange state was a significant achievement but something that, unsurprisingly, fell short of a socialist republic. It is time to recognise this feat and move forward, and therein rests a challenge for Republicans and socialists.

Radical, anti-establishment Republicanism in Ireland has long drawn its support from among the more disadvantaged sections of society. This anger and alienation has usually led it to demand a fundamental change to the existing status quo, but, without a class analysis at its core, others have used this anger to satisfy their more limited goals. Partition matters, but the urgency of its elimination is less important than the ability we now possess – impossible during the era of the Orange state – to develop cross-sectarian working-class solidarities while putting differences on the national question to one side. With the overwhelming endorsement of the Good Friday Agreement having largely defused the national question at least for the current period, in order to survive, radical Republicanism in Ireland must emphasise the socialist as well as the independent nature of a republic. If this happens – and the potential is certainly there – Irish Republicanism will be undergoing a profound and important transformation. At that stage, a test will arise for socialists of other traditions who will be challenged to recognise what is taking place and to assist a development that would undoubtedly offer fresh hope to those seeking a fairer and better society, rid at last of the systemic social, economic and political inequalities that blight our society.

As always, the world is in the process of change. The point is how to influence what is happening.

Notes

PREFACE

1. Frantz Fanon, *The Wretched of the Earth*. London: Penguin, 2001), p. 66.

INTRODUCTION: FROM ORANGE STATE TO SECTARIAN STATE

1. Seamus Heaney, 'Requiem for the Croppies', *Door into the Dark*, London: Faber, 1967. Many years ago, Seamus Heaney expressed his discomfort at the way some in the Republican movement and elsewhere chastised him for what they took to be his very public retreat from an earlier explicit sympathy for those facing Orange repression. This followed another, related unease with the use of his work to elicit sympathetic association with those fighting the insurgency. Mindful of his sensibilities, we nevertheless find a poignancy in the lines we quote that gives some expression to our point of departure. 'Croppies' was a derogatory term originally used by the British during the United Irishmen's uprising of 1798 to delineate the insurgents. Throughout the nineteenth century, it became a general term of abuse for Catholics and typically within Orange circles.
2. The modern UVF (Ulster Volunteer Force), the self-proclaimed heirs to the tradition of Protestant paramilitarism, was not declared illegal until June 1966 when it was banned by Terence O'Neill after its units were linked to sectarian attacks, some of them, as in the case of Peter Ward, were fatal.
3. David Boulton, *The UVF, 1966–73: An Anatomy of Loyalist Rebellion*, Dublin: Gill and Macmillan, 1973, p. 21.
4. Robert Purdy, Politics in the Streets, 1990, pp. 244–52.
5. Graham Ellison and Jim Smyth's book, *The Crowned Harp*, (London: Pluto Press, 2000), has a good critical account of the role of the RUC and its history as the key repressive institution in Northern Ireland.
6. Purdy, *Politics in the Street*, p. 245.
7. To gerrymander is to divide (a territorial unit) into election districts to give one political party an electoral majority in a large number of districts, while concentrating the voting strength of the opposition in as few districts as possible.
8. There were, of course, occasional acts of lethal violence carried out by Unionist extremists, such as the murders by the Ulster Volunteer Force during 1966 in West Belfast of John Patrick Scullion (11 June), Peter Ward (26 June) and Matilda Gould (27 June).
9. Edward Carson was the leader of Irish Unionism and campaigned against Home Rule in the period before the First World War and is now an icon of Ulster Unionism. See Patrick Buckland, *Irish Unionism 1885–1923: A documentary history*, Belfast: HMSO, 1973.
10. Prorogation: to suspend, usually a parliament. Brian Faulkner, then prime minister of Northern Ireland, was summoned to London on 24 March 1972. Edward Heath, then British prime minister, informed Faulkner that security

policy would be transferred to Westminster. This was unacceptable to the Unionist-controlled Northern Ireland government and it prompted the British government to suspend the Northern Ireland parliament at Stormont and assume 'full and direct responsibility'. The Northern Ireland parliament met for the last time on 28 March 1972 and Brian Faulkner and his cabinet resigned, thus ending 50 years of Unionist rule of Northern Ireland, with Faulkner stating: 'We feel we, in our endeavour to provide just Government in Ulster, have been betrayed from London' <http://cain.ulst.ac.uk/events/abstract/72storm.htm>.

11. Peter Shirlow and Brendan Murtagh, *Belfast: Segregation, Violence and the City*, London: Pluto Press, 2006.

12. Sir James Craig, Unionist Party, then prime minister of Northern Ireland, 24 April 1934, reported in *Parliamentary Debates, Northern Ireland House of Commons*, Vol. XVI, Cols. 1091–95, Belfast: HMSO, 1934.

13. L. O'Dowd, M. Rolston and M. Tomlinson, Northern Ireland: Between Civil Rights and Civil War, London: CSE Books, 1980.

14. Ibid., p. 20.

15. Ibid., p. 21.

16. It must be also remembered that repression could also take the more obvious form in the shape of B' Special intimidation of Catholic communities.

17. Government of Northern Ireland, *Disturbances in Northern Ireland, Report of the Commission appointed by the Governor of Northern Ireland. Chairman: The Honourable Lord Cameron, D.S.C. Presented to Parliament by Command of His Excellency the Governor of Northern Ireland, September 1969*, Cmnd 532, Belfast: Her Majesty's Stationery Office, 1969 (hereinafter, The Cameron Report), Chapter 12 'The Causes of the Disorders', para. 138.

18. These statistics were compiled as a fact file by John Carron, Nationalist MP for Fermanagh (Northern Ireland parliament), in 1970, and presented to the then British Prime Minister James Callaghan. This fact file is lodged with the Linen Hall Library in Belfast as 'File P8140'.

19. Ibid, p. 2.

20. Campaign for Social Justice in Northern Ireland (CSJNI), 'Northern Ireland: The Plain Truth', Castlefields, Dungannon, Co. Tyrone, 15 June 1969, 2nd edn <http://cain.ulst.ac.uk/events/crights/pdfs/truth.pdf>.

21. Ibid., p. 12.

22. Government of Northern Ireland, *Higher Education in Northern Ireland. Report of the Committee appointed by the Minister of Finance*, Cmnd 480. Belfast: Her Majesty's Stationery Office (Public Record Office for Northern Ireland (PRONI). PRONI reference: ED/32/B/1/9/296) (hereinafter, Lockwood Report).

23. CSJNI, 'Northern Ireland: The Plain Truth', p. 15.

24. Seamus Heaney, 'The Ministry of Fear', *North*, London: Faber, 1975.

25. See Cameron Report, 1969.

26. Government of Northern Ireland, *Violence and Civil Disturbances in Northern Ireland in 1969. Report of Tribunal of Inquiry. Chairman: The Hon. Mr. Justice Scarman, Presented to Parliament by Command of His Excellency the Governor of Northern Ireland, April 1972*, Cmnd 566, Belfast: HMSO, 1972 (hereinafter, Scarman Report).

27. Ibid., para. 3.18.

28. Ibid., para 1.24.

29. Ibid., para. 2.4.

30. Ibid., para. 2.17.

31. Ibid., para. 3.8.
32 Shirlow and Murtagh, *Belfast: Segregation, Violence and the City.*
33. Ibid., p. 56.
34. Ibid., p. 26.
35. Ibid., p. 27.
36. Ibid., p. 56.
37. Ibid., p. 79.
38. Ibid., p. 171.

1 POLICE BATONS RESPOND TO DEMAND FOR CIVIL RIGHTS

1. Republican Clubs: in 1964, the Stormont government, using the Special Powers Act declared Sinn Féin illegal. To evade the ban, the party then organised under the name 'Republican Clubs', a name the Official Sinn Féin party in Northern Ireland continued to use into the early 1970s.
2. Austin Currie was a Nationalist Party member of the Stormont parliament.
3. *Disturbances in Northern Ireland Report of the Commission appointed by the Governor of Northern Ireland. Chairman: The Honourable Lord Cameron, D.S.C. Presented to Parliament by Command of His Excellency the Governor of Northern Ireland,* September 1969, Cmnd 532. Belfast: Her Majesty's Stationery Office, 1969.
4. RTÉ (Raidió Teilifís Éireann) is the Irish state broadcasting service.
5. For an example of the Orange Order asserting domination during the nineteenth century in the North of Ireland, see <http://www.irishtimes.com/newspaper/opinion/2009/0818/1224252768841.html> and Réamon Ó Muirí, 'Orangemen, Repealers and the killing of John Boyle in Armagh, 12 July 1845', *Seanchas Ard Mhacha,* Vol. 11, No. 2, 1985 (reprinted 2010).
6. Andrew Boyd, *Holy War in Belfast.* Tralee, Ireland: Anvil Books, 1969.
7. The Royal Irish Constabulary (RIC) was the precursor to the Royal Ulster Constabulary (RUC).
8. A Fenian was a member of the Irish Republican Brotherhood (IRB), especially those members residing in the United States. The word is sometimes used in Northern Ireland as a term of abuse for Catholics.
9. In May 1919, in the aftermath of the strike, over 100,000 took part in the Belfast May Day celebrations and when the Belfast municipal elections were held under proportional representation in January 1920, Labour put up 20 candidates in 60 seats. Thirteen of them were returned, including five strike leaders. Two of them even topped the poll, one of these in the Protestant working-class heartland of Shankill, trouncing the Edward Carson's Unionist Party-linked Ulster Unionist Labour Association (UULA): Nineteensixtyseven, *Forgotten History: The Belfast Engineering Strike 1919* <http://thegreatunrest.wordpress.com/2010/09/03/forgotten-history-the-belfast-engineering-strike-1919/>.
10. One important but often neglected point worth noticing here is that at the same time that they drove Catholic workers from the factories and shipyards, the Unionists also took the opportunity to clear out the left. There was a simultaneous purge of the so-called 'rotten Prods', that is, the Protestant trade union militants and socialists who refused to support the Unionist Party. According to Austen Morgan, historian of the Protestant working class, some 1,800 Protestant workers were expelled from their workplaces, consisting of 'almost the entire cadre of working class leaders in the industrial and political

wings of the labour movement': Austen Morgan, *Labour and Partition: The Belfast Working Class*, London: Pluto Press, 1991, pp. 261–2.

11. The Gaelic Athletic Association (GAA) was viewed with deep distaste by the Unionist authorities, in spite of the fact that the association was invariably supine on the issue of Partition. The following extract from the *Irish Times* of 23 August 1960 illustrates the length to which the Stormont government was prepared to go to curb what was deemed by it to be a Catholic sporting organisation: 'Feeling is running high in Nationalist quarters in Rathfriland, Co Down because police entered two houses in Newry Street and the Commons on Sunday and seized two black and red flags, which were being displayed in honour of the Down team playing in Croke Park, Dublin. Several of the players came from that district. Asked about the incidents, Rathfriland police stated that complaints were received from Unionist neighbours about the flags. There was a Black Preceptory parade in Rathfriland on Sunday.'

12. The stage play *Over the Bridge*, Sam Thompson's best-known work, deals with a sectarian dispute in the Belfast shipyard. Thompson offered the play to James Ellis, then director of the Ulster Group Theatre, early in 1958. Ellis accepted it, and rehearsals had already started for a production in April 1959 when the theatre's board of directors refused to produce the play. In a statement to the *Belfast Telegraph* in April 1959, the theatre directors said that the play was 'full of grossly vicious phrases and situations which would undoubtedly offend and affront every section of the public' and added 'It is the policy of the directors of the Ulster Group Theatre to keep political and religious controversies off our stage'; see <http://www.bbc.co.uk/blogs/artsextra/2010/01/>.

13. Liam S. Andrews, 'The Irish languages in the education system of Northern Ireland: Some political and cultural perspectives', in R.M.O. Pritchard (ed.), *Motivating the Majority: Modern languages in Northern Ireland*, Belfast and London: The University of Ulster in association with the Centre for Information on Language Teaching and Research (CILT), 1991, p. 83.

14. Feargal Eamonn Mac Ionnrachtaigh, 'Resisting and Regenerating through Language in the North of Ireland', paper delivered in Germany, 2008 <http://www.bunscoilmhicreachtain.com/feargal.pdf>.

15. Ibid., p. 23.

16. 'Operation Harvest' was the codename given by the IRA to its 1950–62 campaign; it is sometimes also referred to by IRA veterans of the period as 'the '56 Campaign'.

2   UNIONIST DETERMINATION TO DENY DEMOCRACY

1. In 1964, the Stormont government, using the Special Powers Act, declared Sinn Féin illegal. To evade the ban, the party then organised under the name 'Republican Clubs' (a name the Official Sinn Féin party in Northern Ireland continued to use into the early 1970s).

2. 'Operation Harvest', the codename given by the IRA to its 1950–62 campaign, is sometimes referred to by IRA veterans of the period as 'the '56 Campaign'.

3. Ed Moloney, *Paisley: From Demagogue to Democrat?*, Dublin: Poolbeg Press, 2008, illustrated edition.

4. Government of Northern Ireland, *Violence and Civil Disturbances in Northern Ireland in 1969. Report of Tribunal of Inquiry. Chairman: The Hon. Mr. Justice Scarman, Presented to Parliament by Command of His Excellency the Governor*

of Northern Ireland, April 1972, Cmnd 566, Belfast: HMSO, 1972 (hereinafter, Scarman Report).

5. Andrew Boyd, *Holy War in Belfast*, Tralee, Ireland: Anvil Books, 1969.

6. 'The attack was organised locally by representatives of the Orange Order and the Special Constabulary, in close collaboration with some members, at least, of the Royal Ulster Constabulary. It may well be that local branches of the clandestine organisation known as the Ulster Volunteer Force were involved. But the overlap of personnel between these organisations renders such distinctions of purely academic significance. The police force on duty, as a whole, knew of the place and approximate magnitude of the attack. Specifically, or by clear indication, the members of the force learned that they were not expected to resist or arrest attackers. Those responsible for organising protection led the march to a trap': Bowes Egan and Vincent McCormack, *Burntollet*, London: Lars Publishers, 1969.

7. *Disturbances in Northern Ireland Report of the Commission appointed by the Governor of Northern Ireland. Chairman: The Honourable Lord Cameron, D.S.C. Presented to Parliament by Command of His Excellency the Governor of Northern Ireland, September 1969*. Cmnd 532. Belfast: Her Majesty's Stationery Office, 1969.

8. Eamonn McCann, *War and an Irish Town*, London: Pluto Press, 1993, 3rd edn.

9. On Monday, 14 July 1969, Francis McCloskey (aged 67), a Catholic civilian, died one day after being hit on the head with a baton by an officer of the Royal Ulster Constabulary (RUC) during street disturbances in Dungiven, Co. Derry. On Thursday, 17 July 1969, Samuel Devenny (42) died as a result of injuries he received when he was severely beaten by Royal Ulster Constabulary (RUC) officers using batons. The attack took place in Devenny's home in William Street, Bogside, Derry, on 19 April 1969.

10. Scarman Report, paras 2.2–2.7.

3 THE VIOLENT STORMS OF AUGUST '69

1. With 99 of its residents killed in the conflict, Ardoyne was to become one of the areas with the highest level of fatalities. Of those who died, 50 were killed by Loyalist death squads, 2 by the RUC, 12 by the British Army, 11 by the IRA, 3 by the INLA, 1 by the Official IRA, 2 by unknown assassins and 18 Provisional IRA volunteers died on active service. See Ardoyne Commemoration Project, *Ardoyne, the untold truth*, Ardoyne: Beyond The Pale Press, 2002.

2. Michael Farrell, *Northern Ireland: the Orange State*, London: Pluto Press, 1976, p. 263.

3. 'The attacks by loyalist mobs, by the paramilitary B Specials and the RUC on the nationalist areas of west, north and east Belfast were a replay of similar pogroms that had been a feature of life in Belfast for over 100 years': Gerry Adams MP and MLA for West Belfast, in an introduction for Gerry Collins' photographic portfolio 'Bombay Street, taken from the ashes', Red Barn Gallery, Belfast, 2009 <www.rbgbelfast.com>.

4. 'Between July 1920 and July 1922, 453 people had been killed in Belfast, 37 members of the Crown forces and 416 civilians: 257 Catholics, 157 Protestants and two of unknown religion. Of the city's 93,000 Catholics, a quarter of its population, nearly 11,000 had been put out of their jobs and 23,000 driven from their homes. Over 500 Catholic-owned shops and businesses had been

burned, looted and wrecked. Outside Belfast, at least 106 people had died, 45 Crown forces and 61 civilians; 46 Catholics and 15 Protestants. The Catholic population had been beaten into submission': Farrell, *Northern Ireland, the Orange State*, p. 62.

5. Reports of bloodshed in Belfast during the 1930s:

> 15 July 1935 … Five dead and 35 wounded in Belfast. Catholic districts again invaded. Police use machine guns. Dastardly shooting of Catholic girl.
>
> 17 July … Brutal treatment of Catholics. New areas attacked by mobs. Catholic houses marked with crosses.
>
> 19 July … Heart-rending scenes. Hundreds of Catholic refugees. Catholics ordered to clear out. 24-hours to leave or homes wrecked.
>
> 22 July … New phase of Belfast pogrom. Catholic girl workers attacked. Two more deaths in Belfast.
>
> 24 July … Belfast Orange mobs active: *Derry Journal*, cited in Eamonn McCann, *War and an Irish Town*, London: Pluto Press, 1993, pp. 255–6.

6. *Northern Ireland. Text of a Communiqué and Declaration issued after a meeting held at 10 Downing Street on 19 August 1969. Presented to Parliament by the Prime Minister by Command of Her Majesty*, Cmnd 4154, London: Her Majesty's Stationery Office, 1969.

4   WIDESPREAD CONFLICT LOOMS

1. Government of Northern Ireland, *Text of a Communiqué issued on 29 August 1969 at the conclusion of the visit of the Secretary of State for the Home Department to Northern Ireland. Presented to Parliament by the Home Secretary, by Command of Her Majesty, August 1969*, Cmnd 4158, London: Her Majesty's Stationery Office, 1969, para 8.1 <http://cain.ulst.ac.uk/hmso/bni290869.htm>.

2. Duncan Philip Connors, 'Government intervention and the decline of British shipbuilding 1964–1970. The role of negotiation and compromise between the Harland & Wolff shipyard, Belfast and government institutions in determining programs of industrial modernization', paper delivered to the Economic and Business History Society, Providence, Rhode Island, 25 April 2003 <www.unige.ch/ses/istec/EBHA2007/papers/Connors.pdf>.

3. According to an article in the *Sunday Times* by Marc Horne, Field Marshal Montgomery stated in his memoirs that during the Second World War: 'I was told to prepare plans for the seizure of Cork and Queenstown in southern Ireland so the harbours could be used as naval bases': Marc Horne, 'Churchill had plan to invade "Nazi" Ireland', *Sunday Times*, 21 March 2010 <http://www.timesonline.co.uk/tol/news/uk/scotland/article7069684.ece>.

4. See 'Heated memos over Cold War data' <http://news.bbc.co.uk/go/pr/fr/-/2/hi/uk_news/northern_ireland/8537025.stm>.

5. Peter Brooke said Britain had no 'selfish strategic or economic interest' in Northern Ireland and would accept unification, if the people wished it: 'It is not the aspiration to a sovereign, united Ireland against which we set our face, but its violent expression', 9 November 1990 <http://news.bbc.co.uk/2/hi/uk_news/northern_ireland/4072261.stm>.

6. Paul Bew, 'The blind leading the blind. London's response to the 1969 crisis', *History Ireland*, Vol. 17, No. 4, August 2009, p. 49.

7. Government of Northern Ireland, *Violence and Civil Disturbances in Northern Ireland in 1969 Report of Tribunal of Inquiry. Chairman: The Hon. Mr. Justice Scarman. Presented to Parliament by Command of His Excellency the Governor of Northern Ireland April, 1972*. Cmnd 566. Belfast: Her Majesty's Stationery Office, 1972 (hereinafter, Scarman Report), Paragraph 2.5.

8. Ibid., para. 2.7.

9. Ed Moloney, *Paisley: From Demagogue to Democrat?* Dublin: Poolbeg Press, 2008, illustrated edn.

10. Scarman Report, para. 1.13.

11. Government of Northern Ireland, *Report of the Advisory Committee on Police in Northern Ireland, Chairman: Baron Hunt, C.B.E., D.S.O., Presented to Parliament by Command of His Excellency the Governor of Northern Ireland, October 1969*, Cmnd 535, Belfast: Her Majesty's Stationery Office, 1969.

12. Croppy: the name 'Croppy' derives from the 1790s as a reference to people with closely cropped hair, a fashion which was associated with anti-aristocrat French revolutionaries of the period. Those with their hair cropped were automatically suspected of sympathies with the Society of United Irishmen. 'Croppies Lie Down' is the title of a Protestant Loyalist folksong dating from 1798.

6 TRAINING PEOPLE FOR INSURRECTION?

1. Mr Harold Wilson, writing to Campaign for Social Justice in September 1964: the Campaign for Social Justice in Northern Ireland, Castlefields, Dungannon, 15 June 1969 <http://cain.ulst.ac.uk/othelem/chron/ch69.htm>

2. Ibid.

7 ATTEMPTING TO QUELL THE INSURGENCY BY BLOODSHED AND BLANDISHMENT

1. Nell McCafferty, *Nell: A Disorderly Woman*. Dublin: Penguin Ireland, 2005, p. 265.

2. Coogan, Tim Pat, *The Troubles: Ireland's ordeal 1966–1996 and the Search for Peace*, London: Hutchinson, 1995, p. 126.

3. On Friday, 12 March 1971, thousands of Belfast shipyard workers took part in a march demanding the introduction of internment for members of the Irish Republican Army (IRA). Belfast shipyard workers were exclusively Unionist and the Stormont regime viewed them as a crucial support base.

4. 'Army "warned against internment"…' <http://news.bbc.co.uk/2/hi/uk_news/northern_ireland/1737078.stm>.

5. 'Internment: methods of interrogation …' <http://news.bbc.co.uk/2/hi/programmes/uk_confidential/1731567.stm>.

6. Community Relations Commission Research Unit (CROP),'FLIGHT, A Report on Population Movement in Belfast during August, 1971', 1971 <cain.ulst.ac.uk/issues/housing/docs/flight.htm>.

7. See, for example, a note by Lord Saville in his report into events of Bloody Sunday 1972 in Derry, when he described the atmosphere in Northern Ireland's second largest city:

   'The situation in Londonderry in January 1972 was serious. By this stage the Nationalist community had largely turned against the soldiers, many believing that the Army, as well as the RUC, were agents of an oppressive regime. Parts of the city to the west of the Foyle lay in ruins, as the result of the activities of the IRA and of rioting young men (some members of the IRA or its junior wing, the Fianna) known to soldiers and some others as the "Derry Young Hooligans". A large part of the Nationalist area of the city was a "no go" area, which was dominated by the IRA, where ordinary policing could not be conducted and where even the Army ventured only by using large numbers of soldiers': *Report of the Bloody Sunday Inquiry, Chairman: The Rt Hon. The Lord Saville of Newdigate, The Hon. William Hoyt QC, The Hon. John Toohey AC*, 2010, Vol. I, Ch. 2, para. 2.6 <www.bloody-sunday-inquiry.org>.

8. Bloody Sunday in Derry. Thirteen men were killed on the day with a fourteenth dying some time later.
9. *Report of the Bloody Sunday Inquiry*.
10. Ibid., Vol. I, Ch. 3, para. 3.79.
11. McCafferty, *Nell: A Disorderly Woman*.
12. Broadcast made by Prime Minister Harold Wilson, 25 May 1974.
13. Robert Fisk, in the preface to his book *The Point of No Return: The Strike Which Broke the British in Ulster*, London: André Deutsch, 1975.

8   IRISH REPUBLICANISM AND CLASS

1. Karl Marx, *The Eighteenth Brumaire of Louis Bonaparte*, Chapter 1, first issue of *Die Revolution*, 1852, New York. See also Karl Marx and Joseph Engels, *Selected Works in One Volume*, Moscow: Progress Publishers, with London: Laurence & Wishart, 1968, reprint 1980: *The Eighteenth Brumaire of Louis Bonaparte*, Chapter 1, p. 96.
2. 'We therefore declare that unable to endure the curse of the monarchical [*sic*] government, we aim at founding a Republic based on universal suffrage which shall secure all the intrinsic value of their labour. The soil of Ireland at present in the possession of an oligarchy belongs to the Irish people, and to us it must be restored. We declare also, in favour of absolute liberty of conscience and the complete separation of Church and State': on 5 March 1867, the eve of the Fenian uprising in Ireland, the leaders of the Irish Republican Brotherhood (IRB or Fenians) delivered a communiqué to *The Times* in London; full text at <http://www.eirigi.org/pdfs/irish_politics/1867_Fenian_Proclamation.pdf>.
3. The Democratic Programme was a declaration of economic and social principles adopted by the First Dáil at its first meeting on 21 January 1919.
4. In December 1918, Sinn Féin won 73 of the 105 Irish seats in the Westminster general election, virtually wiping out the previously dominant Irish Party. In January 1919, those TDs who were not in jail or on the run gathered in the Mansion House in Dublin to set up their own sovereign parliament, and to declare a republic.
5. Michael O'Riordan, *Connolly Column*, Dublin: New Books, 1979, p. 160.
6. The Army Comrades Association (ACA), later named the National Guard and better known by the nickname 'The Blueshirts', was an ultra-right-wing political organisation in the 1930s, active under the leadership of Eoin O'Duffy. They were later to merge into the newly formed Fine Gael party.

7. A basic survey of the make-up of two H-Block wings during the Blanket protest illustrates this fact. Of the 40 prisoners that made up the constant membership of one wing (that of the author), none had a third-level qualification and only five could be described as having worked in clerical employment. The most common occupation was construction worker, several had worked in the bar/hotel trade, a few had worked in factories and many had found irregular employment in a variety of jobs while most had experienced terms of unemployment. Many, of course, were so young that they never had entered the labour market while others had been full-time IRA personnel since leaving school. Among the 40 considered here, there were approximately five (INLA) Irish National Liberation Army personnel but their occupations or backgrounds did not differ from the Provisional IRA and hence do not distort the sample.

The second wing surveyed by a former occupant, recorded a remarkably similar profile of the IRA prisoners. He recalled, 'The average age was around 21 in 1978 and it increased by a year from then on for each year the protest endured. The economic backgrounds of the protesting prisoners were at the lower end of the scale however measured. No one on the wing worked in a profession. One older man had been a self-employed builder. A small minority had served some time as apprentices. In one case one had been an apprentice tiler while another had served some time as an electrician. Most were building or agricultural labourers. Quite a few were permanently unemployed. Some had found work as doormen in clubs. They all, with the exception of one, hailed from working-class areas. Two at least had grammar school education. The vast bulk was secondary intermediate. In a small minority of cases there was no formal education.'

9   THE POLITICAL AND MILITARY STRATEGY OF THE PROVISIONAL IRA

1. The 2002 Census recorded the Northern Ireland's Catholic population as 43.76 per cent. See 'Fascination of religion head count' <http://news.bbc.co.uk/2/hi/uk_news/northern_ireland/2590023.stm>.
2. Raidió Teileifís Éireann (RTÉ) is the national broadcasting agency in the Republic of Ireland.
3. In 1977, for example, a statement by some RTÉ journalists included the following:

    'The ultra cautious atmosphere which Section 31 has fostered in the news room and in programme selection has meant that enquiries into controversial issues have not been encouraged. Establishment views, on the other hand, are aired at length often without analysis or counterpoint. There is now a general anxiety about tackling stories which might embarrass the government on issues of security': quoted in Niall Meehan and Jean Horgan, 'Survey on attitudes of Dublin population to Section 31 of the Broadcasting Act', Dublin: National Institute for Higher Education, January 1987 <http://www.cain.ulst.ac.uk/othelem/media/meehan/meehanhorgan070187.pdf>.

4. Nell McCafferty, *Nell: A Disorderly Woman*, Dublin: Penguin Ireland, 2005, p. 373.
5. France suffered a huge military defeat at the hands of the Vietnamese resistance in 1952 at the critical battle of Dien Bien Phu in North-west Vietnam.

6. The term 'Éire Nua' (New Ireland) indicated a policy advocating a federal solution based on the four ancient provinces of Ireland. All provinces would have an administration subject to a central and national government. In the case of Ulster, the province would be based on the older nine-county version rather than the six-county version now adopted by Unionists. This would have meant that the Ulster regional parliament would have a 'Protestant' majority, albeit answerable to an Irish national parliament.

7. Possibly the best example of this occurred in Paris which, after the defeat of the1870 Commune, was extensively redesigned by George-Eugene Haussmann on the orders of Napoleon III, so that insurgents would have difficulty capturing or holding the city.

8. Sinn Féin had won 76 seats in the 1918 general election to the British House of Commons but had decided not to attend and instead convened a parliament in Dublin (Dáil Éireann), which declared itself to be the government of an independent republic in Ireland.

9. On Friday, 31 July 1970, 19-year-old Daniel O'Hagan, a Catholic civilian, was shot dead by the British Army for allegedly throwing a Molotov cocktail during a riot in the New Lodge Road area of Belfast.

10. D. McKittrick, S. Kelters, B. Feeney and C. Thornton (eds), *Lost Lives*: London: Trafalgar Square, 1999), first published Edinburgh: Mainstream Press, 1999. *Lost Lives* states that 293 Provisional IRA members died in the Troubles, and approximately 105 of these were due to premature explosions: p. 1479.

11. 'Sparrow warfare is a popular method of fighting created by the Communist-led anti-Japanese guerrilla units and militia behind the enemy lines. It was called sparrow warfare because, first, it was used diffusely, like the flight of sparrows in the sky; and because, second, it was used flexibly by guerrillas or militiamen, operating in threes or fives, appearing and disappearing unexpectedly and wounding, killing, depleting and wearing out the enemy forces', from Lin Biao, *Long Live the Victory of People's War!*, Peking: Foreign Languages Press, 1965.

12. In County Tyrone, for example, the name Devlin is so common that in certain parts of that county, to distinguish one family from another of the same name, the old custom of applying a patronymic is often still used.

10   THE WAR IN ENGLAND

1. The Troops Out Movement was an organisation created by elements within the British left with the objective of forcing a British military withdrawal from Ireland.

2. 'But it is worth remembering that for people living in Britain in the 1960s, '70s and '80s, particularly those without family or cultural ties to Ireland, making the leap from vague disquiet about the British Army in Ireland, to committed activism to get it out was no easy thing. So much militated against it. Irish history was not taught in schools, even as part of the history of the British Empire. There was social disapproval, apathy and, perhaps most crucially, lack of information. When Ireland was not being studiously ignored, it was being misrepresented': from the introduction to the Troops Out Movement website <http://www.troopsoutmovement.com/index.htm>.

3. On Sunday, 27 August 1978, approximately 10,000 people took part in a civil rights march from Coalisland to Dungannon, Co. Tyrone, to commemorate the first civil rights march ten years earlier and to call for political status for

Republican prisoners in the H-Blocks: CAIN (Conflict Archive on the Internet) website <http://cain.ulst.ac.uk/othelem/chron/ch78.htm>.

4. The IRB (Irish Republican Brotherhood) or Fenian movement was an insurrectionary Republican organisation founded in 1857, often referred to as the Fenians and historically viewed as the predecessor of the IRA.

5. On 8 March 1973, the Provisional IRA conducted one of its operations in Britain, planting four car bombs in London. Two bombs exploded, killing one person and injuring 265 others. Ten members of the IRA team were arrested leaving the country.

11 BRITAIN'S RESPONSE

1. Ian Cobain, 'Inside Castlereagh: "We got confessions by torture"', *Guardian*, 11 October 2010 <http://www.guardian.co.uk/uk/2010/oct/11/inside-castlereagh-confessions-torture>.

2. Peter Taylor, 'Reporting Northern Ireland', *Index on Censorship*, Vol. 7, No. 6, 1978 <http://cain.ulst.ac.uk/othelem/media/docs/freespeech1.htm#murray>.

3. Father Raymond Murray, 'Censorship and the North of Ireland' <http://cain. ulst.ac.uk/othelem/media/docs/freespeech1.htm#murray>.

4. Frank Kitson, *Low Intensity Operations ... Subversion, Insurgency, Peace-Keeping*, London: Faber and Faber, 1971.

5. Kitson, in the classic *Low Intensity Operations*, stressed the need for the British military in Ireland to 'dictate how others saw the essence of the conflict'.

6. Ibid., p. 93.

7. See 'Dublin paid expenses to prominent SDLP figures', *Belfast Telegraph*, 30 December 2009 <http://www.belfasttelegraph.co.uk/breaking-news/uk-ireland/government-paid-expenses-to-sdlp-14616079.html?r=RSS>.

8. 'Deep state' is a phrase used to describe the type of state-sponsored activities that have been used in Latin America and elsewhere to crush political opposition by unattributable methods. More recently, sections of the Turkish establishment have been accused of operating such a system <http://www.bbc.co.uk/2/hi/europe/7225889.stm>.

9. Diplock courts were named after the English law lord Kenneth Diplock who recommended the system.

10. Britain has a record of torturing opponents while denying that it does so. Recent revelations about MI5 involvement in torturing suspected members of al-Qaeda has resulted in the UK government paying compensation to 16 men who were detained by US forces at Guantanamo Bay. See <http://news.bbc.co.uk/2/hi/uk_news/8538884.stm> and <http://www.bbc.co.uk/news/uk-11769509>.

11. The UDR was the Ulster Defence Regiment, a largely Protestant/Unionist, locally recruited, part-time regiment of the British Army.

12. The RIR is the Royal Irish Regiment, a locally recruited, full-time regiment of the British Army that replaced the UDR in 1994.

12 REVIEWING STRATEGY IN THE MID-1970s

1. 'Ulsterisation' was a term adopted from the Vietnam conflict: when the US attempted to lessen its manpower contribution to the war by placing more

combat responsibility on Vietnamese recruits, the US Army called this process 'Vietnamisation'.

2. Brigadier Frank Kitson of the British Army had written several books on counter-insurgency tactics, for example, *Low Intensity Operations ... Subversion, Insurgency, Peace-Keeping* (London: Faber and Faber, 1971). Many Republicans believed that Kitson's writings on the subject had inspired Loyalists to form death squads designed to terrorise the IRA's civilian support base, that is, the Catholic working class.

3. In May 1987, the IRA lost an eight-man Active Service Unit as it attempted to demolish an unmanned RUC station in the Co. Armagh village of Loughgall. On 6 March 1988, British soldiers shot dead three members of the IRA in Gibraltar.

4. From the mid-17970s onward, IRA officers gave lectures to their men on anti-interrogation techniques based on an instruction manual known within the organisation as 'the Green Book'.

13   THE GRADUAL ADOPTION OF PARLIAMENTARIANISM

1. 'Talking to the Taliban', *Telegraph*, 28 June 2010 <http://www.telegraph.co.uk/comment/telegraph-view/7859644/Talking-to-the-Taliban.html>; Richard Norton-Taylor, 'Britain and US prepared to open talks with the Taliban', *Guardian*, 28 July 2009 <http://www.guardian.co.uk/world/2009/jul/27/britain-us-talks-taliban-afghanistan>.

2. James Harkin, 'Middleman in the Middle East', *Financial Times*, 3 January 2009 <http://www.ft.com/cms/s/0/3d753b44-d938-11dd-ab5f-000077b07658.html#axzz1E86aUzH0>.

3. Thirteen men died on Bloody Sunday in Derry and a fourteenth man later died from wounds received at the hands of the British Army.

14   OPTIONS AND OPPORTUNITIES

1. Karl Marx, *The Eighteenth Brumaire of Louis Bonaparte*, Chapter 1, first issue of *Die Revolution*, 1852, New York. See also Karl Marx and Joseph Engels, *Selected Works in One Volume*, Moscow: Progress Publishers, with London: Laurence & Wishart, 1968, reprint 1980: *The Eighteenth Brumaire of Louis Bonaparte*, Chapter 6.

2. *Ard fheis*: Feis (Irish Gaelic) usually translates as 'festival' and *ard fheis* as a large or national 'festival', but in this context means an annual convention.

3. Abstentionism was a policy adhered to by Sinn Féin, that was a refusal to take seats in any assembly that recognised Partition either *de jure* or *de facto*, that is, Stormont, Leinster House, or Westminster.

4. Ed Moloney, *A Secret History of the IRA*, London: Allen Lane, The Penguin Press, 2002, pp. 244–5.

15   THE ROAD LESS TRAVELLED ... THE LEFT ALTERNATIVE

1. The Workers Party won seven seats in the 1989 general election in the Republic; see Hanley Brian and Millar Scott, *Lost Revolution. The story of the Official IRA and the Workers Party*, Dublin: Penguin Ireland, 2009.

16   PARLIAMENTARY SINN FÉIN, 'SURRENDER AND RE-GRANT'

1. The policy of 'Surrender and re-grant' was one adopted by Tudor England to subvert the Gaelic system that existed in much of pre-Tudor Ireland. English policy was not to attempt total genocide – that would have required more manpower than was considered safe to risk in Ireland – but to persuade the rebellious clan chieftains to surrender to the Crown, promise to abide by English ways and laws, and in return for compliance, they would be allowed to remain nominally in control of their bailiwicks. See Brian Inglis, *The Story of Ireland*, London: Faber and Faber Ltd, 1956, p. 49.
2. The Fureys are an Irish folk group composed of members of the Travelling community.
3. Ed Moloney, *A Secret History of the IRA*, London: Allen Lane, Penguin Press, 2002, pp. 574–8.
4. See, for example, the BBC report from 26 November 2002, when in the aftermath of convictions arising out of an attempted IRA gun-running operation, both Unionist parties called for Sinn Féin's exclusion <http://news.bbc.co.uk/2/hi/uk_news/northern_ireland/2515541.stm>.
5. Inglis, *The Story of Ireland*, p. 111.

17   FROM ARMALITES TO POPULIST CONFORMITY

1. Dr Sydney Elliott, senior lecturer in politics at Queen's University, Belfast, explained the d'Hondt system: 'The basic idea is that a party's vote total is divided by a certain figure, which increases as it wins more seats. As the divisor becomes bigger, the party's total in succeeding rounds gets smaller, allowing parties with lower initial totals to win seats': <http://news.bbc.co.uk/2/hi/uk_news/northern_ireland/91150.stm>.
2. John Bruton, 'North needs new politics that transcends divisions', *Irish Times*, 3 February 2010; John Bruton is a former Taoiseach and former EU ambassador to Washington <http://www.irishtimes.com/newspaper/opinion/2010/0203/1224263658103.html>.
3. 'Internal party documents actually reveal a cynical attitude to the PFI question when MLAs and other public representatives were instructed … to support them (i.e. S/F ministers introducing PFI) with coordinated statements that are stronger in their opposition to PFI and which emphasise the degree to which the Minister is bound and restricted by the Executive in their choice of funding public projects': Colm Breathnach, 'The crisis of Irish Republicanism', *After the Troubles, Republicanism, Socialism and Partition*, Dublin: Irish Socialist Network, 2005, p. 13. See also <www.irishsocialist.net>.
4. Ibid., p. 16.

18   GENERAL ELECTION UPSET IN THE SOUTH

1. At Stormont, 108 members had a total salary for 2008–09 of £5,217,631.25 and a handsome allowance of over £70,000 per member per year <http://www.niassembly.gov.uk/members/expenses/salaries0809.htm>.

19   THE END OF A JOURNEY

1. An Act of Union between Britain and Ireland came into effect on 1 January 1801, which meant that the old Irish parliament was abolished and Ireland was governed directly from London throughout the nineteenth century.
2. For a breakdown of election results in Northern Ireland over the past decades, see <http://www.ark.ac.uk/elections/>.

20   A NEW REPUBLIC AND A RELEVANT REPUBLICANISM

1. Karl Marx and Frederick Engels, *Collected Works*, Volume 3, London: Lawrence and Wishart, 1975, pp. 133–45.
2. See Fintan O'Toole, *Ship of Fools: How Stupidity and Corruption Killed the Celtic Tiger*, London: Faber & Faber, 2009.
3. Ireland's Central Statistics Office recorded a 13.4 per cent level of unemployment (281,700 persons unemployed) in March 2010.
4. For facts about disadvantage in the Republic of Ireland, see Central Statistics Office Ireland, *Survey on Income and Living Conditions (SILC) in Ireland 2009*, 25 November 2010 <http://www.cso.ie/newsevents/pressrelease_silc2009.htm>.

   - Ireland has one of the highest rates of poverty among developed countries, ranking third highest in the 2005 United Nations Human Development Index.
   - Approximately 23.9 per cent of all children in Ireland in 2003 were 'at risk of poverty' – the official EU definition of income poverty.
   - In 2003, 242,000 children were living in households where the income was less than 60 per cent of national median income.
   - Some 18 per cent of children leave school early, 15 per cent leave school without a Leaving Certificate (high school diploma) and 3 per cent leave with no qualification at all.
   - The unemployment rate among children who leave school early averages almost 21.9 per cent, compared with an overall unemployment rate of 4.4 per cent.

   For facts about disadvantage in Northern Ireland, see Northern Ireland Statistics and Research Agency (NISRA), *Northern Ireland Multiple Deprivation Measure 2010*, May 2010: <http://www.nisra.gov.uk/deprivation/archive/Update-of2005Measures/NIMDM_2010_Report_Large_Print.pdf>.

   - One-third of the children in Northern Ireland live in poverty.
   - Children are four times more likely to die before age 20 and five times more likely to die in accidents.
   - Children are three-and-a-half times more likely to develop a limited, long-term illness; and are committing suicide at a rate three times the norm.

Index

Compiled by Sue Carlton

Page numbers in **bold** refer to photographs. Page numbers followed by n refer to the end notes.